PRIESTLY FICTIONS

PRIESTLY FICTIONS

Popular Irish Novelists
of the Early 20th Century

**Patrick A. Sheehan
Joseph Guinam
Gerald O'Donovan**

by

CATHERINE CANDY

First published 1995 by
WOLFHOUND PRESS Ltd
68 Mountjoy Square
Dublin 1

and Wolfhound Press (UK)
18 Coleswood Rd
Harpenden
Herts AL5 1EQ

Wolfhound Press receives financial assistance from the Arts Council/ An Chomhairle Ealaíon, Dublin.

British Library Cataloguing in Publication Data
A catalogue record for this book is available from the British Library.

ISBN 0 86327 334 3

Typesetting: Wolfhound Press
Cover photograph: Print by David H. Davison, Pierterse — Davison International Ltd, Dublin. Courtesy of E.E. O'Donnell, S.J. From the Father Francis Browne SJ Collection.
Cover design: Joe Gervin
Printed in the Republic of Ireland by Colour Books, Dublin.

TABLE OF CONTENTS

Acknowledgements 6

Introduction 7

SECTION 1: THE WRITERS

Chapter 1: Canon Sheehan 21

Chapter 2: Canon Guinan 45

Chapter 3: Gerald O'Donovan 54

SECTION 2: IRELAND — National Identity, Religion, Land 66

Chapter 4: Sheehan's Ireland 67

Chapter 5: Guinan's Ireland 94

Chapter 6: O'Donovan's Ireland 114

SECTION 3: THE RECEPTION

Chapter 7: Sheehan 129

Chapter 8: Guinan 155

Chapter 9: O'Donovan 162

Closing Comments 171

Appendix I 178

Appendix II 181

End notes 184

Sources 202

Acknowledgements

I wish to acknowledge the generous financial assistance from the Lawrence and Elizabeth O'Shaughnessy Irish Research Fund, administered by the Irish American Cultural Institute, St. Paul, Minnesota, USA, which enabled me to revise this study for publication. I am grateful also to Professor Aidan Clarke of the T.W. Moody Research Trust, Trinity College and to the Maynooth Scholastic Trust for funding research in England; and to Loyola University, Chicago for a small grant towards publication.

Thanks are due to the staffs of the following institutions: The National Library of Ireland; National Archives, Dublin; the Longman archives, University of Reading; Royal Irish Academy; Eason and Co. Ltd; the library at Loyola University, Chicago; and particularly the library of St Patrick's College, Maynooth. I owe a great debt to the research of John F. Ryan, the author of 'Gerald O'Donovan, priest, writer, intellectual: forgotten leader of the Irish Revival' (M.A. thesis, University College Galway, 1983).

For insights into the publishing world and the reading tastes of those before my time, my thanks are owed to Kevin Etchingham, Dr Liam Brophy, Canon John Corkery and all those who answered queries about what they, their parents and their grandparents read. My sincere thanks to Mary Pat O'Connor for her encouragement; to Ted Karamanski and Eileen McMahon for valuable support and advice and for assistance with research. Thanks are due to Lawrence McCaffrey for his help in Chicago. I am exceptionally indebted in many ways both to my supervisor Professor R.V. Comerford, and to Msgr Patrick J. Corish. Their dedication, open-mindedness and inspiring personal qualities are largely responsible for the writing of this. My only regret is that I have been unable to follow up on all of their suggestions for further research. My largest debt is to my parents, and to all the members of the Candy and Kelly families for their remarkable support: to them the book is dedicated.

Introduction

This volume comprises three case studies of priests who wrote Irish popular fiction, Canon P.A. Sheehan, Canon Joseph Guinan and Gerald O'Donovan. All three were closely involved in the Irish Catholic intellectual culture of the late nineteenth and early twentieth century. Although these three figures were very much individuals, they were all deliberately trying to upgrade the image of the Irishman, and to redefine 'Ireland'. Joseph Guinan, Canon Sheehan and Gerald O'Donovan were amongst those who intended their literary efforts to improve Ireland directly. Individually, there is the often confused intellectual in Sheehan, a forthright, ambitious and radical O'Donovan, and the very humane and less questioning Guinan. Comparing them with each other is necessarily close to comparing some of the nerves of Irish society in the period. All were priests, though O'Donovan left the priesthood at thirty-three years. All shared a sympathy, concern and preoccupation with Ireland. They worried about its future, were anxious to interpret and explain its past and were less than happy with current conditions.

Until 1847 Maynooth staff were forbidden by canon law to publish.[1] Such was the perseverance of the distrust of non-sacred printed matter that all three of these writers were regarded as deviating from clerical norms by writing at all, and particularly by writing fiction. Even though Sheehan and Guinan were deliberately writing in an effort to counteract what they saw as the poisonous influence of modern literature on the pure, innocent, native mind, they drew upon themselves the suspicion, amusement and opprobrium of their clerical brethren from the mere fact of putting pen to paper. That they were priests is an added complication and an added bonus because, working in parishes, they were alert in so many ways to the 'ordinary' conditions of Irish life in a way that many other writers of the time were not. The fact that they were priests meant that they were closely knit into the community at large, but being priests they were also slightly isolated from it.

The work of these three novelists was first published between 1895 and 1928. They were interesting and relatively new in that they were writing mainly, though not exclusively, to Irish Catholics, and not directly for the English and Anglo-Irish market as had been characteristic of so much of the Irish writing business until the last quarter of the nineteenth century.

The nine works of fiction penned by Patrick Augustine Sheehan (1852-

1913) may be divided into two categories: those that are particularly
clerical works, and those of more general Irish interest. The first group
includes the extremely popular *My New Curate* (1900), *Luke Delmege*
(1901), *A Spoiled Priest and other Stories* (1905) and *The Blindness of Dr
Gray* (1909). The second includes *Glenanaar* (1905) — a fastmoving tale
which traces the lives of the descendants of an informer of the 'Doneraile
conspiracy' trial of 1829. It is a very curious novel full of latent contra-
dictions between what Sheehan says and what he shows.

Lisheen, or the Test of Spirits (1907) is modelled on Tolstoi's *Resur-
rection*. Wishful thinking on Sheehan's part, it tells the story of an altruistic
young man of the Irish landlord class who undertakes to live as a labourer
with the peasants of Kerry. It allows much scope for reflections on the
'national character', as it is defined against Englishness. *The Intellectuals:
an experiment in Irish Club Life* (1911) must be included in a study of
Sheehan's fiction as it comprises a series of debates amongst an educated
professional class on various matters relating to Irish identity. It was
intended 'to show that there are really no invincible antagonisms amongst
the people who make up the commonwealth of Ireland'.[2] *Miriam Lucas*
(1912), another strange and dark novel, is an attempt to forewarn of the
problems which Sheehan's version of socialism would cause in his version
of Catholic Ireland. *The Graves at Kilmorna* (1915) is an interesting
follow-up to *Miriam Lucas*. Published posthumously, it is an indictment
of the tactics of the Irish Parliamentary Party and a prescription for the
revival of Sheehan's vision of the noble idealism of the Fenian movement.

Gerald O'Donovan (1871-1942), a useful counterpoint to the other two
has left us six novels, four of which are directly concerned with (if not
autobiographical accounts of) his Irish experiences. The first of these, the
notorious *Father Ralph* (1913) deals with the crisis of a young priest who
feels he cannot accept the terms of the papal encyclical on modernism and
subsequently leaves the priesthood. It provides a very telling picture of the
attitudes which underpinned some hidden areas of Irish life.

His next novel, *Waiting* (1914), continues by recounting the pains of a
young couple of mixed religion caused both by the papal decree *Ne Temere*
of 1908 and by the prejudices running alive in Irish country life. It is also
a statement of O'Donovan's revulsion against the ways of the clergy in
local politics and economics. 1920 saw the publication of *Conquest*, a
valuable commentary on events from the early 1890s to 1919. It presents,
again in a series of debate-like conversations, the many and various

attitudes to the Irish question. It is useful in its portrayal of the fractured nature of thinking on national identity and nationalism. This was followed by *Vocations* (1921) a most daring novel concerning 'the splendours and terrors of life behind the veil', the relations of priests and nuns, and the danger of confusing a religious vocation with a career.[3]

Joseph Guinan (1863-1932) wrote eight works detailing the experiences of Irish rural life. Most of these treat of the intimate relations between priest and people, interlaced with scenes and tales from the point of view of a sincere, if simple country curate. The works include *Scenes and Sketches in an Irish Parish*; or *Priests and People in Doon* (1903); the phenomenally popular *The Soggarth Aroon* (1905); *The Moore's of Glynn* (1907); *The Island Parish* (1908); *Donal Kenny* (1910); *The Curate of Kilcloon* (1913), and *Annamore, or The Tenant at Will* (1924) and *Patriots* (1928). They are precious accounts of Ireland as seen from the point of view of a fairly typical parish priest. Because they met with enormous popular success, and in the same period as the works of Sheehan and O'Donovan, they provide another important dimension to the popular image of Ireland.

A closer look is needed at those who had a real influence on their contemporaries rather than at those who gained posthumous success or the admiration of worldwide scholarship. The popular response to a novelist is often a very significant indication of the fancies and preoccupations of a culture. If, as Claude Cockburn claims, the novel is a mirror of the mind the popular novel is usually a very flattering mirror.[4] Neither are we, by reading fiction, as some would see it, 'eavesdropping upon an actual, and unedited passage of dead life'. The worlds of fiction can never be either actual or unedited.[5] Innocence plays no part in fiction. It is its very culpability which made it vital then and which now gives it its value as an incubator of fashionable opinions and images.

Before an overall survey of the complexity of Catholic intellectual life can be achieved, it is necessary that individual studies be made of the Catholic novelists. Each writer had his own axe to grind. Each had a distinctive personal vision of what 'Catholic Ireland' *ought to be*. Naturally many of these visions were at odds with each other. It is the combined vigour of these Catholic individuals to change the image of the Irish Catholic which is my subject.

R.V. Comerford's study of Charles J. Kickham's phenomenally popular novel *Knocknagow* (1873) suggested new areas for investigation in

Irish Catholic intellectual and cultural history. Comerford shows how in *Knocknagow*, Kickham attempted to tone down the stereotypical image of the riotous Irishman and highlighted instead the quieter, sensible, respectable sides of Irish life. Comerford concludes that Kickham both expressed and nurtured much of the basic mentality of the modern Irish nationalist community.[6] He calls for an examination of that profuse and lively (if largely undistinguished) tradition of Catholic-nationalist literature which flourished from the 1850s onwards.

John Wilson Foster in an attempt to broaden the received contours of the 'Irish Literary Revival', recently classified Irish writers of the period into three categories: those selfconsciously writing for a British audience; those writers of broad appeal whose fiction was set unselfconsciously in Ireland; and a handful of what he terms 'proper' writers who wrote out a need for self-realisation, in order to illuminate the universal in the particular (here he includes George Moore, Joyce, and Brinsley McNamara).[7] Another category is that group of writers whose work was largely directed to the Catholic Irish, and with particular attention to the needs of the Irish abroad.

Foster rightly argues that many of the writers of the time simply wanted to resuscitate 'elder Irish values and culture' in order to transform the reality of Ireland, while others tried to satisfy the need for a vigorous realist fiction in Ireland. There is in the work of the three writers considered in this book a curious refusal to admit to the reality of Ireland, side by side with urgent pleas for its transformation.

Amongst Foster's many useful observations, he identifies an 'emerging coalition' of those 'Anglo-Irish renegades' (who recruited themselves to the ranks of 'native Ireland'), with Catholic writers and intellectuals who together formulated a definition of Irish culture and nationality. This study opens further the question of 'coalition' or 'competition' between Anglo-Irish and Catholic Irish in the struggle to define Irish culture and nationality. Foster makes the point that 'the nation-building and culture-binding that were accomplished should be balanced by the damage that they may have inflicted in the domains of human happiness, cultural self-respect, and political stability'.[8] It is anti-individualism which irks Foster, and he holds the revival period largely responsible for the victory of cultural nationalism over individualism.

One might question the togetherness of this 'coalition' in the effort to define Irish culture and nationality. Even if there was such a superficial coalition, the more lasting and deep rooted influences on the national self-image emerged from that most definitely Catholic camp whose members, as Foster puts it, were writing 'in conscious reaction against the Irish literary revival'.[9]

The relationship of this Catholic ideology to the Anglo-Irish revival has not been sufficiently teased out. It is an extremely complex problem. Oliver MacDonagh constructs a useful framework in his *States of Mind* showing how Catholics took over and Catholicized the celebration of 'the native culture' from the Anglo-Irish, who had first revived interest in it.[10] D.P. Moran's *Leader* of 1904 noted with glee the replacement of the Anglo-Irish note with that of the Gaelic note, though he saw and hoped for a purely Gaelic literature in the future.[11] MacDonagh shows well the ambiguities, ambivalences and overlapping in ideology of the individuals involved in these ideological movements: Anglo-Irish revival; Gaelic revival; Catholic revival. However, the popular Catholic-nationalist values which were transported in this literature, and by other means, were reinforced around the turn of the century and prominently carved into the Irish Free State. These were not the attitudes of Yeats, Synge, Joyce or O'Casey. The ideals of the likes of Guinan, Sheehan and their fans became the fixed, mainstream values of 'the silent middle' of Irish society in post-revolutionary Ireland. One cannot hold these individual writers, or either of them, responsible for the transmission of a complex of values, but they are distinctive in baldly defining their purposes and in being popularly read. How they defined Ireland, what they identified as her problems, and how they each proposed that these problems be solved is the subject of the middle section of this study.

Literature in the period had, (and was seen to have perhaps more than it did), a curious role to play in the debate about nationality. Literature in English, as it was then known, was viewed with suspicion as a plot to 'denationalize' as well as with promise as a weapon for 'renationalization'. Owing to the paranoia in the minds of leaders and educators of Irish society about 'dangerous books' and 'light and licentious reading' which was allegedly available at book stalls and railway stations, a new literary crusade developed. This was the first time that Irish Catholics began to capitalize on their capacity to define Ireland in print. These authors reflected some of the popular Catholic moods of the times. In 1912 a Limerick priest, Thomas Murphy, published *The Literary Crusade* blaming literature for instances of insanity, suicide and crime. He was perplexed to be told by a newsagent that sales of 'foreign' magazines, newspapers and fiction were highest after Sunday mass.[12] The ageing cultural nationalist, Charles Gavan Duffy, 'made enquiries' and was 'assured' that

> the books chiefly read by the young in Ireland are detective or other sensational stories from England and America and vile translations from the French of vile originals.[13]

W.B. Yeats' co-operation with Duffy, in their attempt to bring out a new library of Irish fiction to be published in London by T. Fisher Unwin, was also prompted by his panic about denationalization.[14] Duffy asked for the support of the priests, but they would fight their own battle. This literature which was required to stimulate, purify and nationalize (in particular the new breed of owner-occupier farmers) would have to conform to what was best for its leaders in the eyes of priests and intellectuals. Priests were only too well aware of the new and growing social stratum of people who had come up a little in the world, signifying a shift in the centre of power, from the Protestant landlord to the Catholic flock. That most of them could read was a source both of terror and of solace to the priest.

Joseph Guinan was a leader in the campaign to establish an innocent wholesome national Catholic literature, calling frequently for 'a single-minded effort to counter the insidious evil of bad literature, whether foreign or native'.[15] In this regard, he approved of such respectable harmlessness as was available in Kickham's *Knocknagow*, and the publications of the Catholic Truth Society of Ireland, but feeling that there was not enough of this type of literature to stock the parish lending libraries, he decided to write some of his own. He felt he was filling a lacuna in Irish literature, as his opening paragraph in a 1911 article of the *Catholic Bulletin* attests:

> The intimate and endearing relations that exist between the priest and his flock in Ireland, constitute a peculiar phase of our national life the real significance of which few Anglo-Irish writers, whether in poetry, drama, or fiction have rightly understood. Some have missed it entirely for the all sufficient reason that they knew nothing about it, while others, ignorantly informed and maliciously inclined, have made such a travesty of it as would in any other country but forgiving Ireland ensure them well merited castigation. Even those who have honestly attempted to expound this tempting feature of Irish life have not infrequently failed utterly through being alien to the peasantry in creed, nationality or social station. Indeed, its true

inwardness and sacred can only be known as a sort of esoteric knowledge, from which the non-Catholic writer is hopelessly shut out, and which the Catholic *litterateur* who is ignorant of country life in Ireland can scarcely appreciate. Hence the need of an author-ised and sympathetic interpreter of the tenderest and most fascinating aspect of the inner or parochial life of Catholic Ireland — a *terra incognita* to very, very many.[16]

Catholic writers of popular fiction wished also to rescue the image of the Irishman from the caricatures of the earlier Victorian press. Through the nineteenth century the fictional Irishman had been examined, misrep-resented, laughed at, and transformed into a curiosity exhibit.[17] Guinan, also, is hurt by the established image of the Irish in the Anglo-Irish fictional tradition and even by the one peasant voice of nineteenth century Ireland, William Carleton:

> The mirth-provoking Mickey Frees, Handy Andys, and Paddy-go-Easys of Lever, Lover, and Carleton are not so commonly to be encountered among us as those gallery-loving humorists would lead strangers to imagine.[18]

> The spurious Anglo-Irish literature, foisted on the public by clever, unscrupulous writers, should and must be repudiated by a nation Catholic and proud of it.[19]

G. O'Brien points out that by 1850 the end of the caricatured fictional Irishman was in sight owing to the development of realism and psychol-ogy: 'The Irishman at long last began to receive a literature worthy of him, a literature conceived for his sake'.[20] However, it was still, from the point of view of the Catholic peasants and farmers, being written largely by foreigners. Though their pen-portraits may have become more sympa-thetic they were still writing in terms of explaining 'the Irish'; acting as their interpreters. The interpreted meanwhile needed something, as Cork-ery put it, 'to focus the mind of his own people' in order to give security to that national consciousness which he described as 'a quaking sod'.[21]

The massive changes in land ownership from Protestant to Catholic, the subsequent adaptation in the structure of society and the feedback from children abroad, was giving the rural farming Catholic community a sense of itself as distinct and important in a wider world. There is a sure, but now buried sense in which many Catholics urgently demanded and ex-pected a literature for themselves, to accompany and publicize their new values and sense of identity.

Taking a literary look backward from the point of view of the writers under review here, there was a clear split between the voice of the Protestant ascendancy and that of the majority of the Catholic population. From the end of the 18th century the writers of the first background included a long roll call of names from Edgeworth to Lever, while good writing of the latter side was represented only by Carleton, the Banims, Griffin and Kickham. Far from tapering off, the tradition of Anglo-Irish writing was very much alive, but now, however, it was to be purposely challenged by the Catholic community. Contemporaries of Sheehan, Guinan and O'Donovan included Joseph Campbell, Ethna Carberry, Nora Hopper, Seamus MacManus, Alice Milligan, Seamas O'Sullivan, Rosa Mulholland, and Katherine Tynan. A.P. Graves and George Birmingham of Protestant backgrounds, drew volumes of kindly, amusing pictures of Ireland.

The self-assertiveness of the Catholic community was both encouraged and catered for by new confessional and national journals. As early as 1873 Ireland was consecrated to the Sacred Heart and the periodical *Catholic Ireland* (soon to be renamed the *Irish Monthly*) was launched. In 1877 the *Messenger of the Sacred Heart* began publication, gaining a circulation of 47,000 by 1894 and 73,000 by 1904, already combining cultural with religious nationalism.[22] Amongst the 'aims and hopes' of the *Irish Rosary* established in 1897 was the counteraction of the 'weeklies, monthlies, quarterlies that meet the eye at booksellers, railway stations and street kiosks'; while it concluded that the multitude of readers 'is simply beyond counting'. In an unusually realistic finishing note comes the admission to having 'not the faintest hope of any change in our time; our business is to see what good, if any, can be drawn from it'.[23]

The Catholic Truth Society of Ireland, established in 1899, along the lines of the German *Katholiekentag* was intended specifically as another counter influence. By promoting the work of very Catholic writers they hoped to corner this new market and promote Catholic values and 'a sense of nationality'. That it had difficulties getting off the ground is not as surprising as the efficiency and enthusiasm with which the clergy set it up.[24]

The confessional nature of Irish nationalism has only recently come into focus. For those who lived through the period it was naturally more blurred. E.J. Cahill writes in the *Irish Ecclesiastical Record* of 1930 that a catholic social movement was practically impossible up to very recent times. The land struggle, the fight for educational freedom, the national contest, the work of church building and religious organisation engaged the energies of priest and people.[25]

On the contrary, while it may not have enjoyed quite the same institutional status as its counterparts on the continent, Cahill is describing a very real social movement. For underlying and co-ordinating these campaigns was indeed a firm and steady movement of Catholic self-assertion, with the forays into, and expression of concern about literature another string in the same bow. This idea and ideal of a Catholic state had its origins in the early nineteenth century, but in the last quarter of the century its fulfilment became a more realistic proposition.[26]

It is difficult to estimate the power of the novel. How significant a role literature in general, and fiction in particular played in the formation of culture in late nineteenth and early twentieth century Ireland is far from clear. How did it connect into the wider network of Irish life? It was forced to compete after all in the shaping of attitudes, with newspapers, reviews, platform speeches, handed down values, a tenacious folklore and the more social and lively world of the theatre.

Literacy statistics suggest a dramatic rise from 33% in 1851 to 84% in 1911. Yet even by 1911 only one child in 17 continued beyond primary school.[27] It is beyond dispute that many read no literature at all. Mary Casteleyn notes as one of the main features of the literary movement the fact that from 1902 to 1914, the newly established rural libraries fell rapidly into disuse.[28] It is more difficult to identify the reading diets of those who did read. An article in the *Leader* of 1904 is informative:

> They buy *The Story of Ireland* and *Speeches from the Dock* when they can get them conveniently. They buy the cheaper publications of the Gaelic League. But, on the whole, they have not got into the habit of writing all the way to Dublin for books and paying the postage thereon, or of walking miles to the chilly country towns for them.[29]

Although Sheehan, Guinan and O'Donovan may have been unusual amongst the clergy at large, and amongst the Catholic community in general, in harbouring worries about the security of the 'Irish Catholic race', their work is evidence of the fairly sharp turn around in social reference and of the efficacy with which some Catholics learnt to play with the upper hand. While in some respects it is surprising that these men had worries, in other respects it is more surprising that they formed only a small minority. The growing general prosperity, literacy and geographic mobility, as well as being reason for celebration, was a threat to the status quo of priest and people.

The tension between the traditional and the modern informs almost all of the writing and thinking of this period. It is not surprising that it should appear in the fiction if it was not the central reason for the fiction in the first place. There were tensions also of course within the complex of the clergy. The Maynooth Union of secular priests originated from a paper read in the college by Walter MacDonald in 1896.[30] The union amounted to an annual one-day meeting of Maynooth priests and sprang from an impulse of self-questioning. It indicates that amongst the overwhelming majority of the clergy who were more than satisfied with the conditions of Irish Catholicism and the priesthood, there were a few priests querying the directions of the Irish church. This ginger group felt that Irish society was on the brink of powerful changes and suspected that their flock would be only too ready to greet them. These, however, were soon overwhelmed by those who simply preferred to spend the day of reunion at the *alma mater* eating, drinking and being social. Gerald O'Donovan was an especially enthusiastic supporter of the union, delivering three addresses in its early years. Many others, however, were quite calm, complacent, and confident that in general things would continue to tick over for the next hundred years as they had for the last fifty. 'Nothing short of a spiritual earthquake would make them even question their belief in themselves' quipped a frustrated O'Donovan.[31]

In 1908 Paul Dubois greeted with a sigh of relief the appearance of a new and modernizing breed of cleric: the 'O'Growney's, O'Hickeys and Lethebys' (the latter being the progressive younger priest in Sheehan's *My New Curate*) who were energetically engaged in starting co-operatives, hosiery factories and promoting temperance and the Irish language. These new curates, owing to the over crowding of the clergy in Ireland, often had spent their first ordained years on the English mission. Having served in English cities, catering both to English Catholics and to the Irish in England, they returned with zeal to implant what they thought was the best of English culture, while at the same time thanking God that Ireland was poor, rural, backward and innocent. However, their spell away, while strengthening their national sentiment, induced a respect and envy of English punctuality, thrift and hygiene. The ambivalence of the returning clergy on these issues is a consistent motif through this group of novels. This was not the first era in which this particular problem became apparent; the ambivalence between attitudes to supposed 'Irish' virtues and necessary English habits is also characteristic of much of the literature from the 1820s and 1830s, but it is interesting to catch sight of the clerical comparison of the two cultures, as they were coming evermore closely together.

With clerical numbers almost trebling in the second half of the nine-teenth century despite a falling lay population, and with the experiences of the changes in land ownership, continuing emigration and the triumph of disestablishment in 1869, this period allowed the clergy a breathing space to take stock of their role in their fast changing Ireland. It also allowed room for outside critical review.[32] The reality of the influence of the clergy is evident in the frequency with which they were asked to enrol in national movements from the new Irish library to the Gaelic League, to Horace Plunkett's co-operative scheme. 'The clergy', however, had res-ervations about joining any organisation over which they did not wield control.[33]

An almost nervous sense of waiting characterised this era throughout Europe, and while it may not have been so general in Ireland, there was a certain anxiety in some quarters about how the cards might be reshuffled;

> And if we, the Irish priests, do not leap to the front and lead — well, we shall not find ourselves seated on the box when the triumphant car of the Irish renaissance drives into Ireland.[34]

The most frightful feature of the modern to Irish priests and to tradi-tionalists was the spread of socialism. Again, literature was the chief suspect for the spread of the virus. It was more often than not the priests themselves, having seen or heard of anti-clericalism and socialism com-bine on the continent, raised the debate at home in advance in order to prevent it gaining a foothold:

> Principles distinctly socialistic in their character are being taught amongst our people, not now by many or with wide success, but quite sufficiently to call loudly for that prevention which is better than cure.[35]

The clergy railed more against the hopelessness, stupidity and violence of the socialist cause than they did against its principles. Because socialism was not supposed to be cheerful it was feared that it would blight 'those social traits that make an Irishman such a charming companion'.[36] Though the clergy wished for a greater sense of 'manliness and self-respect' in Irish society, they feared the breeding of a secular monster.

The works of Sheehan, Guinan and O'Donovan reflect a certain curi-osity about the role of the clergy in this period, brought on by their growing profile in Irish life. The independence of attitude associated with the celebrated clergy of the early and mid nineteenth century, in Banim's song of the 'Soggarth Aroon', was being replaced now by, as John A. Murphy puts it, the 'dominance of the new gombeen ethic of respectability and propriety'.[37]

George Birmingham saw reasons for this in the isolation of their seminary life (as opposed to the more socially integrated university training of their Protestant brethren); in the fact that they were 'denied free intercourse with men on terms of equality'; and in the lack of a freely critical Irish literature to hold them in check.

> The 'insistence by poets and men of letters' that we shall be solemn in our diatribes against the shadowy influence of priestly power, solemn in our sentimentalising over the virtues of some soggarth aroon... only a few years ago it was possible for Mr. Alfred Graves to write a cheerful song about a priest. Who would dare do so now? And before Mr. Graves' time things were even worse, more pro-fanely light-hearted — who can forget the rollicking priests of Lever's novels?[38]

The decline of landlordism concentrated further the local respect for the priest in the rural community. This more than anything else accounts for the prominence of the clerical in popular fiction. The question at the heart of the contemporary criticism of the clergy was whether the clergy wished to replace the Protestant ascendancy with a clerical ascendancy. But because the clergy had made such a sensible, quiet job of assuming social control, a real anticlerical movement was avoided.

While M.J.F. McCarthy contrasted the pomp of the priesthood with the poverty of the people, F.H. O'Donnell campaigned against clerical ma-nipulation of local government and economy. The titles of many of McCarthy's works summarize their contents: *Five years in Ireland* (Lon-don, 1901); *Priests and people in Ireland* (Dublin, 1902); *Rome in Ireland* (London, 1904); *Gallowglass, or, life in the land of the priests* (London, 1904); *Irish land and Irish liberty: a study of the new lords of the Irish soil* (London, 1911). O'Donnell, F.H., *Paraguay on Shannon: The price of a political priesthood* (Dublin, 1908). W.P. Ryan gave voice to disgrun-tled opinion on clerical control of the schools. His *Pope's Green Island* was reviewed by Francis Sheehy Skeffington as 'too mellow'.[39] After the earlier assaults, Plunkett's refusal to exonerate the clergy from blame for the lack of 'moral courage' in the national character, seems rather gentle.[40] George Russell blamed the clergy for stifling the imagination of the Celt because 'its genius was pigeonholed' by Roman Catholic theology.[41]

The lack of a widespread anti-clerical movement was noted by Paul

Dubois in 1908. At least he found it confined to a small group of intellectuals who 'naively admired the worst anti-clericals of France', some politicians who had occasional quarrels with the clergy, and the Fenian hard core, but here he distinguishes between the politics of the clergy and the clergy themselves.[42] Walter MacDonald also noted the overwhelming support of the great body of clergy and laity for clerical dominance.[43]

The air of sensationalism and voyeurism, with which our anticlerical writing is often misleadingly associated, may stem from this prim self image cultivated in Victorian times by the Irish priests. If there was no coherent, anti-clerical opinion there was certainly a market for angled criticism of the clergy. A contributor to the *Leader* in 1904 wrote:

> Intellectual life is still rather 'slow' in Ireland, most of us talk little about a book, unless it happens to be an attack on the Catholic church. Then we abuse its fortune, instead of writing or buying a better book.[44]

The earlier nineteenth century 'robust criticism' of the earlier robust cleric was replaced by 'private grumblings'.[45] The phenomenal run-away successes of books like those of M.J.F. McCarthy and Frank Hugh O'Donnell does not indicate a pent-up anti-clericalism as much as an intense curiosity about clerical life, and the need to take stock of peculiarly Irish social phenomena. They reveal a society simply trying to make sense of its clerical and Catholic saturated self. It provided opportunity for the silent critics to enjoy gripes at the expense of a clergy with whom overall they were reasonably satisfied.

The arch-modernizer, and well respected Horace Plunkett brought the debate to the surface with his *Ireland in the New Century*, prompting the clergy quickly to re-explain themselves. It is significant that unlike Plunkett's book, Fr Michael O'Riordan's 510 page reply, the hard-hitting *Catholicity and Progress* went to several editions in 1905 and 1906 despite the high prices being charged for it.[46]

The very real way in which certain members of the clergy felt themselves to be targeted from at least two sides was explained by Fr J. Fullerton writing in 1920:

> This is the world which tells us it is our duty to lead the van in every movement which presumably makes for social progress, and then blames us for bossing and bullying if we try to follow the dictates of our conscience and do our best. As long as I pay my taxes I claim my right to a voice in the affairs of the state.[47]

It was amid these questions, challenges and complacencies, that the work of Sheehan, Guinan, and O'Donovan emerged. The first section of this book explores the lives of the three writers. Why they wrote at all is one of the main questions under consideration here. The middle section compares their images (or identifies the absences of images) of many features of Irish life. Each writer's sense of nationality and nationalism is sketched first, followed by the attitudes in their novels to the state of Irish Catholicism, the role of the clergy, and perspectives on Protestantism. Included also are socio-economic issues: discrimination between classes; the significance of land and perceptions of the conditions of the economy. The shabby features of their portraits of the Irish completes this section.

The final section assesses the popular appeal of the novels. Their immediate impact on the reading public may be estimated from contemporary press references, the number and speed of editions issued, correspondence with publishers and occasionally, sales records. As a general rule of thumb, however, it can be taken that at least one thousand copies were published per edition. The endurance of the popularity of each novel is necessarily a far more sketchy affair. Apart from reprintings, it is exceedingly difficult to calculate the fondness of the reading public for old books, passed around second-hand as they often are. The paucity of bookshop and publishing records is here a major problem. Although the number of copies published is of course no indication that they were sold, it is all too frequently the only guide. However, the stir which they created in the press and the reception of each novel, alongside popular memories, combine to piece together some idea of the impact which they had on society. This is not an attempt to provide a complete bibliography or checklist of any of the writers, but rather a sampling of the reactions which their work provoked.

Section One: The Writers

1: Canon Sheehan *(1852-1913)*

Canon Patrick Augustine Sheehan was born on St Patrick's day in 1852 in New Street (now O'Brien Street), Mallow, Co. Cork. His parents had moved to Mallow from the Cloughlucal district a few miles north of the town 'during the period when small tenant farmers were being forced by economic circumstances and landlords' pressure to give up'.[1] His mother, Joanne Regan, was of a family widely connected in Mourne Abbey and other parts of North Cork.[2] His father, Patrick Sheehan owned a small business.

Patrick was the third eldest of a family of five. Hanna and Margaret, his two older sisters, entered the Order of Mercy at Mallow and died young from tuberculosis. Denis Bernard was later to become customs officer with the civil service in Cork. John, the youngest, died at only five years. In the summer of 1863, when Patrick Sheehan was just 11 years old, his father died. This blow was followed, in the February of 1864, by the death of his mother. The guardianship of the young family was entrusted to Father John McCarthy, then parish priest of Mallow. After the sale of the house and business, they were placed under the care of a lady, a trusted friend of their parents. Their parents, well respected locally, were keen to have their children educated.

It is hardly surprising to learn that Sheehan was shy, dreamy, and much fond of reading though he also enjoyed cricket, handball and rambling through the fields.[3] He makes little reference to his father in his writing but attributes to his mother his enthusiasm for faith and fatherland. When the girls were old enough they were sent to the Loreto Convent in Fermoy; Denis attended the Christian Brothers' school in Mallow while Patrick was set aside for St. Colman's junior diocesan seminary, also in Fermoy. Here he developed a fondness for classical studies. While not outstandingly precocious, he was usually among the first in his class in all subjects. At the end of Summer term 1868, as well as being a prefect he held first place in Geometry, Algebra, History and English composition, second place in Christian Doctrine, third in Latin and fifth in French.[4]

While still at Mallow he came into contact with some local 'fenians'. He subsequently reminisced at length about these heroes of his youth.[5]

Amongst them were ballad singers, for whom he acted as a look-out on street corners. He delighted in such ballads as 'When on Ramillies field' and 'The battle-eve of the brigade'. Another local rebel 'used gather us boys into a corner of that old market-house, and pour floods of hot rebellion into our eager minds'.[6] Their 'fierce, unswerving and unselfish love for Ireland' impressed him indelibly and was to provide material for his later writing. While at St Colman's he followed anxiously the news and rumours associated with the Fenian rising of 1867.[7] It is obvious that during these early years he absorbed many of the circulating stories and sentiments around him.[8] Probably owing to his orphanhood, he paid special attention to adult figures who were out for the common good.

> And in higher circles of society, there was that grand priest, the typical *soggart* of the past, Justin McCarthy, mighty in stature, and great of heart, the hero of two tithe wars, the foe of felonious landlordism, who revenged an eviction in his parish by putting a price of one shilling per head on every fox's head that was brought to his hall door.[9]

Patrick Sheehan entered Maynooth in Autumn 1869. Having done well on his entrance examinations, he was exempted from the preliminary course in Humanities, and joined at once the Logic class. An unsettled atmosphere pervaded the college as it tried to reorganise itself in these first years after disestablishment of the Church of Ireland and concomitant withdrawal of the Maynooth grant. Finding Logic dry, and with his weak grasp of Latin, cumbersome, he turned to more literary pursuits. He later reminisced about this period;

> Far back in the 'sixties, literature had to be studied surreptitiously, and under the uncongenial but very effective shadow of Perrone or Receveur [authors of theological textbooks]. It was a serious thing to be detected in such clandestine studies, and I dare say our superiors were quite right in insisting that we should rigidly adhere to the system of pure Scolasticism, which was a college tradition.[10]

He was most impressed by a young priest, Fr. Wilson,[11] who took over the teaching of *Belles Lettres* in the absence of the usual lecturer and who 'opened up to our wondering eyes the vast treasures of European, and particularly, of English literature'. Thus was Sheehan introduced to the unofficial curriculum which, changing with each generation, was to remain a feature of intellectual life in Maynooth for the better part of another century. In 1871, he wrote for Wilson a dissertation on 'Schools of English Poetry'.[12] When asked one night during Lent for a recitation, Sheehan promptly rendered Speranza's 'The year of revolutions', one of the several poems he had memorised from the *Nation*. Though he recognised his naivety 'in selecting such a fierce, revolutionary ode, in a house which was at that time distinctly conservative, if not anti-national'[13] he was glad to note that at that very time the young priest lecturer, Fr Wilson, was writing similar material for the Dublin *Nation* under a *nom-de-plume*. Wilson's career, Sheehan evasively tells us, was 'tragical; one other instance of genius misplaced, and therefore, hurled to prompt and inevitable ruin'.[14]

Fr Matthew Russell S.J., Sheehan's friend and literary patron wrote in January 1902:

> It seems a puzzle to most men who knew him in after days ... how a youth of such exceptional ability was able to escape distinction during his Maynooth course so completely that, since he has become famous, many who were his contemporaries at college have been slow to believe that he was ever a student at Maynooth.[15]

Much of his leisure time was passed in the college libraries. The characters in his novels of Geoffrey Austin and Luke Delmege suggest authorial experience of an early restlessness, depth and introspection. In 1872, three years after entering Maynooth, he became ill. He had been frequently upset by periods of ill-health. Now he was obliged to remain at home for almost a year. While he was at Maynooth, his sister Margaret, then directress of a convent national school, died. As he neared the end of his studies his early guardian Fr John McCarthy was appointed Bishop of Cloyne. Sheehan was ordained on 18 April 1875.

Sheehan spent the first three years after his ordination on the mission in England, the diocese of Cloyne being sufficiently manned at the time. His first appointment was in the cathedral of the diocese of Plymouth, Devonshire, under Dr William Vaughan (brother of the famous Cardinal of Westminster). It is told how Dr Vaughan used to initiate after-dinner discussions on Ireland's political claims so as to cause Fr Sheehan to defend his country and his race. Once when the bishop instanced certain Irish atrocities, an English member of the chapter, Canon Graham, came to the Irish priest's assistance by reading from the daily paper a horrifying case of British wife-beating, and thus turned the tables on his bishop.[16] It is difficult to discern if Sheehan rose to the bait, but that the discussions continued would seem to suggest that he did. When Fr Hobson the rector in Exeter fell ill Sheehan was sent to take charge of his mission and remained there as administrator for the last two years of his period in

England. Here he followed a hectic schedule, constantly visiting homes, convents and schools and meeting with various parochial organisations. As preaching of a high quality was expected in England particularly in those doubt-filled, questioning years the young priest was under the constant pressure of delivering well argued, impressive sermons. While in Exeter he became actively involved in several associations established for humanitarian and social purposes. These activities brought him into contact with many Protestants so that he developed some sympathy and toleration for their attitudes and values. Later, when writing, he often drew on this period as a complement to his Irish parochial experience.

Once while visiting Dartmoor prison he recognised Michael Davitt by the empty right sleeve of the prison tunic. While Heuser notes he was not allowed to speak with Davitt, there is no evidence that he tried.[17] In fact, Davitt had the impression that the usual Catholic chaplain avoided him as fenian while in both Millbank and Dartmoor prison.[18] However the incident was later to be written into *The Graves at Kilmorna*. While there is no evidence that the character of Luke Delmege is a thorough self-portrait, the many incidents in the novel of that name which parallel Sheehan's personal experiences suggest it is more of an autobiography than later Sheehan fans would allow. The haughty, ambitious self-consciousness of the early Luke Delmege are drawn with too much insight and care to pass for the warning to young priests on the England mission which some critics were content to take them for. Luke is reprimanded by his bishop for his fiery, intellectual sermons and asked to rely more closely on strictly Catholic teaching. Like Luke's, Sheehan's years in Exeter served to overhaul and readjust many of his prejudices and opinions. Luke was grieved to discover he was being sent home to Ireland. From 1877 to 1881 Sheehan served as a curate in his native town of Mallow. Perhaps it was simply felt that familiar surroundings would be easier on his health or, as Boyle notes, that here, 'he would be amongst the associations of his youth, and this, in itself, would be a check on the Quixotic zeal with which his work in England may have inspired him'.[19]

Neither was Fr Letheby altogether a figment of Sheehan's imagination, judging by the figure he cut as a young priest in Mallow. It was during these years that his lifelong concerns began to surface. He lamented the backwardness of education in Ireland and worried that it would not provide protection against the dangers of the future. Much of his time was spent on instructing the young in the reason behind their faith. In 1880 he established a literary and debating society in Mallow. By means of lectures and the distribution of good books he sought to raise the consciousness of his flock. His inaugural address, explains rather militantly his ideals:

> Catholics should take a pleasure in studying those subjects that have had such an attraction for the greatest minds. And to take a utilitarian view of the matter, we must remember that we are by compulsion a migratory race, that it is not given to all to die in sight of the fair hills of holy Ireland; but that hundreds and thousands are compelled to go amongst the stranger, and to be subjected to the critical glance of the freethinkers, who identify every Irishman with Rome and Catholicity. Is it not well that we would show them that our religion is not a superstition, and that our love for it is not founded on ignorance; that if we have been denied the blessings of education for seven centuries, we had amongst us the greatest civilizing agent of the world — the Catholic Church, that she supplied what our rulers denied, and that at any moment we are prepared to enter the lists even against trained controversialists, and to take our stand on the eternal principles of truth and justice to prove the teaching of the Church to be in all things consistent with the eternal verities of God?[20]

In 1881 Sheehan was appointed curate at Cobh. Here he was confronted daily with the sight of the emigrant ships and often spoke to the emigrants. Again he worried that they and their faith would be corrupted by contact with foreign influences. It was during these years that he began writing articles for the *Irish Ecclesiastical Record*. The importance of religious instruction in Irish schools formed the subject of his first article in the *Irish Ecclestiastical Record*. [21] 'If religious instruction', he declared, 'be practically eliminated from our public schools, by not being raised to a level of importance with secular learning, we shall not remain a high-principled race nor become a cultured one.' He proceeded to discuss the inadequacies of the 1878 Intermediate Education Act. These ideas were later repackaged in fictional form, and the article was also transferred to the London *Tablet*. This essay was soon followed by 'A visit to a Dublin art gallery'[22] where he urges that Christianity should re-enter art. It was probably a response to Pateresque ideas. In 'The effects of emigration on the Irish church'[23] of October 1882 he rather brazenly argues that 'in the last thirty years the Catholic community spent four million pounds on ecclesiastical architecture alone (a figure not wildly inaccurate judging by the findings of recent scholarship).[24] 'What', he continues, 'would the Irish church have been if the towns, now half-deserted and impoverished, were filled with Catholic populations, full of Celtic faith and generosity?' He was alarmed to record that the Irish population in America ought to be *at least* 20,000,000 whereas in reality the total number of professing Catholics varied between seven and ten million, a great many of these being German. Rather optimistically he suggested that the church decoration trade could do a lot to inspire home industry and so stem emigration.

These articles attracted little attention but no doubt gave the young priest confidence in his voice. He wrote many short and simple stories during his time in Cobh, most of them unconcerned with Irish problems. Some were later published in *A Spoiled Priest and other Stories* (1905) and were reprinted by the Catholic Truth Society of Ireland amongst their penny publications.

In 1888, seven years after he arrived in Cobh and at thirty six, Patrick Sheehan's health broke. Mrs Sophie O'Brien tells us that he had an 'utter breakdown' always having suffered greatly from depression and want of sleep.[25] He spent some time with a Fr Keller, an old friend, improved a little and returned to Mallow again as a curate. The Mallow parish priest, Canon Wigmore (former president of St Colman's College) had Fr Sheehan and his brother Denis regularly to dine with him where he entertained them with amusing anecdotes which he later delighted in claiming as the originals of *My New Curate*.[26]

Back in Mallow he relaxed a little, spent much time talking with the local people, observing their habits and listening to their stories. It was during this period also that he began to realise that the place and power of the essay was being superseded by the novel. He saw how Dickens had succeeded in highlighting the miseries of the English poor and how George Eliot had created a wider moral world from the activities of a small English village. He began writing *Geoffrey Austin* in Mallow. In 1895 when the neighbouring parish of Doneraile became vacant, Dr Browne, the new bishop of Cloyne, appointed him parish priest. Browne, 'had recommended it to him as an out-of-the-way place offering abundant opportunity to a priest of literary habits to indulge his bent while serving the simple peasantry in the capacity of pastor.'[27] As for Sheehan's response, chapter two of *My New Curate* is helpful:

> I was a dreamer, and the dream of my life, when shut up in musty towns, where the atmosphere was redolent of drink, and you heard nothing but scandal, and saw nothing but sin — the dream of my life was a home by the sea, with its purity and freedom, and its infinite

expanse, telling me of God.[28]

Doneraile, notwithstanding its inland location, proved very conducive to Sheehan's literary activities, but how did he feel as he pushed pen towards paper? Like most fledgling writers venturing into print he felt insecure. But his fears were compounded by his self-consciousness as a priest writer. The tradition of Irish priestly fiction writers was hardly reassuring. John Boyce, a Donegal priest, who served in America from 1845 until his death in 1864, published under the pseudonym of 'Paul Peppergrass' three novels, *Shandy Maguire, The Spaewife* and *Mary Lee, or, The Yankee in Ireland.* Richard Baptist O'Brien, (1809-1885) dean of Limerick, wrote three novels. Dr George Crolly, Archbishop of Armagh and Primate of Ireland, wrote at least one story 'Mary Anne O'Halloran' and Dr Matthew Kelly, an erudite antiquarian began writing 'The life and labours of a Catholic curate' in Duffy's *Irish Catholic Magazine* but it was a short lived affair.[29]

There were other scattered examples, but the overall total was so small that Sheehan rightly felt himself to be a pioneer, venturing where angels feared to tread. The general paranoia of the clergy about the power of literature seems to have overawed them. While they launched appeals for a counter-offensive they were prepared only to supervise the operations of the laity.[30] They were not, in the main, already overworked. Many of them found time to involve themselves in various extra-pastoral activities and organisations. As one insider wrote:

> We hear a great deal, and are likely to hear a great deal more, of the necessity of the average priest of having a hobby — something he can turn to when time hangs heavy on his hands. It would be altogether unnecessary here to emphasise the truth of that necessity.[31]

Sheehan knew he would have to come to terms with his pioneering stance as a priest writer and brace himself for the inevitable scrutiny and possible ridicule from his co-religionists. His dilemma was expressed by the older priest Fr Dan, addressing Fr Letheby in *My New Curate*:

> There are whole fields of literature yet untrodden by us, but where heretics and others are reaping rich harvests. Yet, who would dare to make the attempt? Don't you know that the ablest professors in your own time in Maynooth never ventured into print? They dreaded the chance shots from behind the hedge from the barrels of those masked bandits, called 'critics'.[32]

A later Sheehan character referred to 'that dread or shyness of print

which seems to be the *damnosa hereditas* of the Irish priesthood'.[33] More
was involved than the recurring Christian unease about the frivolousness
of fiction and the vanity of literature for its own sake. Sheehan's fellow
ministers, with a few notable exceptions, had an aversion to committing
themselves to print, even on doctrinal and pastoral matters. This was
enshrined in the assumptions of a collective clerical ethos which the
intellectual Sheehan never understood:

> But what are the opinions of the hundreds of Irish priests who never
> speak in the press or on platform? And what is the meaning of the
> attitude of silent watchfulness which they assume?[34]

There is in Sheehan's commonplace book however a poem, dated 1873
(two years before his ordination) and headed, 'On the occasion of a
declaration by the priests of Cloyne that they make a stand on Home Rule':

> They've been passive long enough — Till the Orange fades from
> Derry and the shadow from the Boyne
>
> Let the words be carried outwards by the farthest lands they reach:
> 'After Christ, their country's freedom do the Irish Prelates preach!'[35]

Sheehan's attitude to fiction reveals a sense of excitement and novelty:

> 'Truth is stranger than fiction'. No! My dear friend, for all fiction is
> truth — truth torn up by the roots from bleeding human hearts, and
> carefully bound with fillets of words to be placed there in its vases
> of green and gold on your reading-desk, on your breakfast table.
> Horrid? So it is.
>
> Irreverent? Well, a little. But you, my dear friend, and the rest of
> humanity will have little else.[36]

Sheehan worried himself about the future of humanity in general and
Irish humanity in particular. Many of his later characters, projections of
the writer, are burdened by deep, constant and insoluble puzzles. Excited
by the intellectual world which he discovered in his wide, energetic
reading, he felt impelled to bring it to the people:

> The desire to form even one link in the electric chain that stretches
> down through the ages, magnetising generation after generation with
> thoughts that thrill and words that burn — this, so far from being
> ignoble, may assume the sacredness of a vocation and an apos-
> tleship.[37]

The purpose of fiction, Sheehan held, was primarily to popularise
philosophy and inculcate moral standards. M.P. Linehan, a biographer and
devotee of his, attributes to him the credit of responding to the challenge

of the 'uncatholic' literary revival:

> Was the Irish revival ... to have the same effect on the philosophical outlook of Ireland as had the medieval renaissance of the fifteenth century on that of Europe?[38]

Though R.D. Blackmore's *Lorna Doone* (1869) was his favourite modern novel, Jean Paul Richter (1763-1825) a German Lutheran pastor, was the writer whom he most wished to emulate for his 'humour, gentleness, strength and sublimity'.[39] Richter's influence on Sheehan is obvious. His *Levana* for example, published in 1807, is a treatise on education, the aim of which is 'the elevation of the human soul above the limitation of its age'. Tennyson, he later wrote, influenced his sentiment but Carlyle made a deeper and more lasting impression.[40] However, 'it took many years and some suffering to see that ... this too was vanity'.[41] Goethe interested him despite his 'covert atheism and pagan voluptuousness'.[42] Sheehan liked to see himself as a self-educated Arnoldian missionary popularising 'the best that is thought in the world'.

> Let us try the effect of Christian idealism; and let us try the experiment at home. The literary instinct has died out in Ireland since '48. Our colleges and universities are dumb. The act of conversation is as dead as the act of embalming. And a certain unspeakable vulgarity has taken the place of all the grace and courtesy, all the dignity and elegance of the last century.[43]

Having been impressed, through his reading in German literature and philosophy, by the German educational system and holding strong critical views on the Irish system, with which he acquainted himself at first hand, it is no surprise that his first novel, *Geoffrey Austin: Student* (1895) was a hard-hitting critique of the lack of proper religious instruction in Irish schools. It was based on Gayfield (Mayfield in the book), a secondary school near Dublin which he passed only once on his way from England.[44] However, his brother Denis spent a while studying there and it was from him that Sheehan learned the details of its educational system. As a novel *Geoffrey Austin* is marred by its shallow character portrayal, loose plot and all too obvious didacticism. Initially it had a very limited sale, staying on the shelves for months.[45] That Sheehan had not exaggerated the detective powers of the clerical critics was evidenced by their prompt response. 'Mayfield was found to have its prototype in half a dozen Irish colleges, and some of my *dramatis personae* were supposed to be easily recognised in certain well-known professors'.[45]

Geoffrey Austin was published under a *nom de plume*. While some Catholic reviewers expressed appreciation of its literary merits they showed their resentment at its vigorous condemnation of the Irish Catholic educational system. They queried why what had operated 'from time immemorial' should only now be subject to adverse comment and then by an unknown, (and very possibly lay) critic.[47] It was largely ignored in Britain, recommended by *The Catholic World* in New York and translated into German (1898) though mainly because it struck a chord in the debate on German educational policies. Later it was translated into French also. Barely three years later *The Triumph of Failure* was published. Fr Matthew Russell, editor of the *Irish Monthly* and steady supporter of many literary aspirants constantly encouraged him and guided him particularly in the direction of American Catholic magazines like *The Messenger of the Sacred Heart,* the *Catholic Word* and *Ave Maria.*[48] It was to be through these channels, rather than through Irish ones, that Sheehan's merits were recognised. Russell read through the manuscript of *The Triumph of Failure* in 1898 and offered detailed suggestions. *The Triumph of Failure* was written as a sequel to *Geoffrey Austin*. It is more surely written and continues the story of Geoffrey's battle with the world. He wrote a preface for it, to head off the condemnation which *Geoffrey Austin* had attracted, but in the event it was excluded from the volume. Defending its unrealism he insisted that a writer of fiction must aim at being an 'architect and framer of personalities, which may not exist just now'.[49] The second book treats of Geoffrey's intellectual pride versus the solace of religion. Life eventually beats him down so that he finds peace at last as a monk. Set in Dublin, it can be seen as a deliberate attempt to break away from the Catholic rural peasant tradition of the earlier nineteenth century and reflects the growing interest in town life. Sheehan was later bravely to remark that he put more effort into this, his second novel, than into any other.[50]

He cannot have been but discouraged by its almost non-reception. He had great difficulty in finding a publisher for it. Not until after the success of *My New Curate* was *The Triumph of Failure* acknowledged and published by Burns and Oates of London (1899), American publishers having earlier refused it. Herman J. Heuser, professor of Theology in the seminary of St. Charles at Overbrook, Pennsylvania, and editor of the *American Ecclesiastical Review* had read Sheehan's *Geoffrey Austin* and praised it in his journal. In March of 1898 Heuser wrote to Sheehan suggesting he write 'sketches of character and priestly life, written in a mingled vein of humor and serious thought':

> Where they happen to point out any weak phrases it should be done
> in a way which could not possibly wound, though it might suggest
> correction. If you do not find such writing to your taste, could you
> suggest to us someone who possesses the talent to portray men, and
> describe their doings in the parish, in the home of the priest, the church,
> etc, in company with his brother priests etc.

And Sheehan eagerly replied:

> In reference to your suggestion that I should write a series of papers
> on clerical life, it is rather a curious coincidence that I had already
> in my portfolio ten chapters on clerical life in Ireland, which I had
> purposed to develop into a volume. They were intended, however,
> for popular reading: and my thought was to introduce my own ideas,
> suggestions, etc, under the sugar coating of a story. I venture to send
> you these chapters. It is quite possible they will not meeet your views,
> in which case I would thank you to return them.[51]

The serialisation of *My New Curate* in *The American Ecclestiastical
Review* of 1898 and 1899 brought American acclaim and publication in
book form. *My New Curate: a story gathered from the stray leaves of an
old diary*, explores lightheartedly the relations between an old parish
priest, Fr Dan, and his new and young curate, Fr Letheby. It was the work
for which Sheehan was, and still is, most popularly acclaimed. It succeeds
in balancing youthful enthusiasm against knowing cynicism and in the
process reveals much of Sheehan's shrewd analysis of the Irish religious
scene. Set in rural Ireland, its success prompted from him a spate of similar
'clerical' stories.

Shortly after the success of *My New Curate*, Sheehan reflected on his
position in a letter to Heuser:

> For the years I was writing for the *Irish Ecclesiastical Record* I never
> received one word of encouragement. You and my dear friend, Fr.
> Russell, are the only priests that have ever said a kindly word of my
> work hitherto. Now I am on the full swing of the tide; and my last
> book has made me a thousand friends. But it was weary work; only
> that I felt that I was working for our Lord and He would reward me.
> And He has a thousandfold. But venturing into the field of Catholic
> literature is a greater risk than many are aware of: and many a writer
> can say, as Dr Barry says, *aquae inundaverunt animam meam.*[52]

In the same letter he delights about letters of praise received from priests
in America and France and gripes that 'No magazine at this side of the

Atlantic would have published *My New Curate*. They are all old-fashioned and conservative,' but thinks that it has 'caused some searching here in Ireland.' *My New Curate* had been published anonymously at first. When it first became successful as a book Sheehan claimed it, and once his name appeared his two earlier novels acquired value. Even *George Austin* leaped into a new edition. An illustrated edition of *My New Curate* was published by the Art and Book Company of London in 1899 and in Boston by Marlier in 1900. It had an immense circulation and was translated into a dozen languages. *My New Curate* was not published in Ireland until 1928, by an arrangement with the bishop of Cloyne, to whom Sheehan had bequeathed all the income from his books.

This novel proved to be his most popular because it broke new ground. It refreshed the image of the priest both for the priest and laity and it gave the laity an inside view of the way they were thought of by an Irish priest. Hitherto the priest had been depicted rather than explored. As Sean O'Faolain observes, you either had a jovial, hunting, hearty priest, or a rigorous unbending ascetic.[53] That a changing society was trying to make sense of an unchanging priesthood is suspected by George Birmingham, an observant outsider:

> Poets and novelists insist on our thinking of priests as saints and devils. Politicians, apostles of 'causes' and reformers of every kind insist on trying to rope priests into their enclosures, but the human priest survives.[54]

Sheehan does not consciously try to 'humanise' the priest but by placing varying clerical personalities in familiar and unfamiliar situations he does succeed in showing the richness and diversity of clerical life. Part of the charm of the individual priests in Sheehan derives from Sheehan's own dilemma as a priest writer. He must always remember to be responsible. At best he should be a missionary writer, at worst he should supply harmless amusement. The creative urge in him prompted some of the less saintly features of some of his characters and this is what gives his writing credibility and interest. It also accounts for both his popularity and his unpopularity. By displaying features of clerical minds he inevitably draws on both the secular and the spiritual. As each of his main characters is an extension of his self, they form an intriguing drama between priest and man. It is remarkable, as Peter Connolly noted, that this attitude, fruitful for Irish writing, is quite unknown to contemporary fiction about the priest in other countries. He concludes that this insistent underlining of the tension between priest and man 'bears witness to something genuine and deeply rooted in the consciousness of contemporary Ireland, a consciousness which so often comes to a point in the priest.'[55]

Sheehan watched carefully the reception of his works. Before *My New Curate* was published in book form, there was a sizeable order for the *American Ecclesiastical Review* from Ireland, which goes to show the efficiency of Irish-American relations. In a letter again to Heuser he writes 'The bishop is taking round with him the May number and reading it at the visitation dinners here in Cloyne'.[67] In 1904 when *My New Curate* became known in Rome, Propaganda recommended him to Pope Leo XIII for the honourary degree of Doctor of Divinity, which was immediately conferred upon him, in recognition of the services rendered by his writing.

His next novel, the notorious *Luke Delmege*, was published by Longmans in 1901. According to the author, its central idea was 'the doctrine of vicarious atonement'. It tells the story of a priest's spiritual and psychological adventures from ordination, through work in England to his experiences in a homely, Irish parish. Incidentally the author criticises the educational equipment of the Irish priesthood and the inadequacies of old time methods. The weary, soul-searching Luke Delmege must be Sheehan's closest self-portrait. Perhaps it is because of this and because it is padded with abundant philosophy that it gives the impression of the author's absence of control — 'It is withal, a solemn history; and many, perhaps, will find in it deeper meanings than we have been able to interpret or convey'.[68]

> Why should a cloud ever have rested on that sacred brow? Why are the great and holy dishonoured in life; only honoured in death? Why are men so cruel and vindictive towards each other? What is the dread secret of man's inhumanity to man?
>
> Poor Luke! he can never leave these turbulent questions alone.[69]

Although it enjoyed general popularity, it was received in clerical circles with hostility. The most cutting blow came again from Monsignor Hogan of Maynooth, then editor of the *Irish Ecclesiastical Record*. His first point of criticism was directed at the consistently 'unIrish' names of Sheehan's characters.

> Perhaps Fr. Sheehan knows best what his public likes. He may have taken his Irish readers at their own estimate, knowing the weakness of so many amongst them for the style and title of people whom they regard as their betters. But then we should not quite expect that a seer and a prophet would allow himself to be influenced by the vitiated taste of the

public. Is it not his mission to educate and reform? ... Fr. Sheehan, no doubt wrote for English and American readers, as well as for the people of Ireland. He is the very last person, we are quite sure, to whom the intention could be imputed of holding up his own countrymen to the ridicule of foreigners; and yet we can scarcely deny that some things at least in his book, whether he wished it or not, are calculated to leave the impression that he has done so on the mind.[70]

According to Hogan, Sheehan's contrast of learning and piety is to the detriment of the former and is thus opposed to the teaching of the best spiritual guides. He concludes that though it is a book full of 'stilted nonsense', it is also 'a clever, an instructive and a good one'. This onslaught, coming through the pages of the quasi-official organ of the church and of Maynooth, almost ended his writing career. Sheehan avoided writing a predominantly clerical novel again until 1909. During those eight years he had seven other works published. Referring in a letter to Heuser to an article he had contributed to the *American Ecclesiastical Review* in 1902, Sheehan writes:

I expect there will be diversity of opinion about it as about my other work; but in view of the hostility that has been raised against me in clerical circles on this side, on account of *Luke Delmege*, I would urge upon you the advisability of keeping its authorship a secret. Attempts may be made to discover the writer; but I am aware that many would be glad to quote it as another example of my desire to lampoon and discredit the Irish priesthood. Although the verdict of the world is the other way, we must yield a little to insane prejudices; and I had determined not to touch on this delicate clerical question any more, nay even to rest altogether from literary work, and devote all my time to my parish and people, but you will see the necessity of maintaining the anonymity of the article intact.[71]

Sheehan's early reputation, held especially by his clerical brethren, as an erudite pedant who affected learning which he could not possibly possess (having experienced the same educational system as themselves) was revised by the appearance in 1903 of *Under the Cedars and the Stars*. Here we have a composite of the author's notes on a wide range of subjects, including religion, philosophy, art, literature and science. They revealed a mind immersed in the great questions of life and satisfied many that there was some depth to his thinking. It did not, of course, achieve the same popular heights as the novels but it bolstered his reputation and confidence. The respect which it encountered is evident from a comment in the *Irish*

Monthly — 'for it is a book quite out of the common run and such as London or New York do not expect to be sent to them by Dublin'.[72] Without the continuous support of Fr Russell and Fr Heuser, it is doubtful that Sheehan would have continued to publish novels, though he might have continued writing them. Evidence of respect from another quarter came in 1903 when the parish priest of Doneraile was made a Canon of the Cloyne Diocesan chapter. The official church had come to terms with Sheehan's literary role, but that did not make him any less exceptional among his fellow diocesan priests.

His next literary attempt was a play — *Lost Angel of a Ruined Paradise*, about girls leaving school. Though published by Longmans it was never staged. Russell discouraged future attempts in the same direction and that ended his playwriting career.[73] Meanwhile his *Glenanaar* was being carried, not this time in the *American Ecclesiastical Review* but in the *Dolphin* and with great success. Published as a book in 1905, it is as with *My New Curate* lightly written, fast moving and entertaining. It owes its inspiration to Sheehan's discovery in the house of Mr P.H. Barry of an old file of the *Southern Reporter* containing the trials for the Doneraile conspiracy of 1829 and O'Connell's colourful defence of the prisoners.[74] Sheehan went to Cork and obtained permission to examine the old court records of the famous trial. He had the book completed in six weeks.[75] Everywhere it was received warmly but especially in Ireland.

In 1904 he made the first of two trips to the German Rhineland. He must have been excited at touring the country which had produced many of his favourite philosophers and writers. Here he admired the piety of German Catholics and received warm adulation from the many German readers of his works.

A Spoiled Priest and Other Stories (1905) and *Early Essays and Lectures* (1906) were then published. They had been written much earlier and required little work to prepare them for publication. He offered the essays rather pompously as a 'record of certain phases of thoughts or problems of great moment during a literary novitiate extending over many years'.[76] They included his thinking on Emerson and on the writings of St Augustine, but for the most part they have little to say to the modern reader.

1907 saw the publication of *Lisheen, or The Test of Spirits*. It was his most socially concerned novel. The influence of Victorian English critics is evident here as he attempts to apply their vision to Irish circumstances. Earlier in *My New Curate* he had revealed his awareness of the complexity of attitudes within Irish life as Fr Letheby is warned:

> You have, as yet, no idea of how many ways, all different and
> mutually antagonistic, there are, of looking at things in Ireland ....
> There are a hundred mirrors concentrated on the same subject, and
> each catches its own shape and odour from passion and interest.[77]

Sheehan lived through and watched closely some widesweeping
changes in Irish life. The Local Government Act in 1898, followed by the
Wyndham Land Act of 1903 all seemed to point to a new independence
and comfort for his once oppressed Catholic flock. His later novels
therefore are much more concerned with the quality of Irish life, with
nationality and with his reservations about how well the new Ireland would
adapt to these changes, some of which were already accomplished and
more of which were already on the horizon. *Lisheen* was Sheehan's
equivalent of Tolstoi's *The Power of Darkness* (the comparison was his
own) where, he tells us 'the author clearly wants to prove that, deep down
beneath the stagnant surface of peasant life in Russia, there are hidden
springs of nobility, that only need a strong hand to spread abroad and
sweeten all the land'.[78] Here Sheehan reveals clearly his confidence in an
idyllic, feudal society as an alternative to the anarchy of democracy. From
this point on alas his novels assume a mildly eerie, exotic complexion. The
introduction of such lurid elements as Indian magic and ghosts in ruined
castles was probably intended as a brightening effect but all too often tends
to obstruct awkwardly on the main plot.

Lisheen was also a popular success. The response from Hogan of the
Irish Ecclesiastical Record was as sharp as ever as he reduced the novel
to a compilation of influences:

> Substitute Maxwell for Nekludoff, (of Tolstoi) and you have the
> skeleton of the novel ... Hamberton, in like manner, can be traced to
> George Eliot or Mrs. Humphrey Ward: and people somewhat like
> Outram are to be met with in Haggard and Kipling. Finally, the
> major's oaths and expletives are more reminiscent of Charles Lever
> than of present-day realities ... but it is so much better than anyone
> else can do at the present day in the same line, that it may be disposed
> of with almost unqualified praise.[79]

Parerga, a companion volume to *Under the Cedars and the Stars* was
published in 1908 along with another volume of short stories called simply
Canon Sheehan's Short Stories, a reasonably sure indication of the cur-
rency of his name. The fact that he always had several works in progress
at any time is shown in his tendency to overspill his ideas of one into

another, and in his all too tidy and fantastic manner of sewing up plots when he decided he had made his point in that particular work.

The Blindness of Dr Gray appeared in 1909. The closely detailed character study of the aging parish priest and his image and self image in the community is the chief merit of this novel. Having a very episodic structure, there are perhaps too many lives here woven too closely together. The orphaned niece of Dr Gray arrives from America much to his consternation but eventually succeeds in softening the hard edges of this stern character. The idea was possibly prompted by the visits to the writer's house in Doneraile of a young school girl whom he entertained with stories by the fireside.[80]

The Sunetoi published in 1911 as *The Intellectuals: An Experiment in Club Life* consists of a series of reports of an imaginary discussion society. The individuals involved include a university professor, a bank manager and his wife, a Catholic curate, a young engineer, 'a young lady B.A. of the Royal University of Ireland', a poet and a doctor and wife. It is a brave effort on Sheehan's part to show that 'thought, opinion and judgment is in each individual nothing but the subjective impression of objective facts'.[81] Despite their consistent clashes of opinion, the book is dull and the characters unrealistic. It was published serially in the *Irish Rosary* but as it proved unpopular it was soon terminated. Sheehan told Russell of his letter from the editor, Fr Coleman, who thought its continuation would put his magazine in jeopardy. In a slightly hurt tone he wrote:' I confess I saw all this; and that it was with much reluctance and only at his repeated solicitations I placed the manuscript in his hands'.[82]

However, it was reprinted twice in 1911 and again in 1919 and 1921. *The Queen's Fillet*, Sheehan's historical romance of the French Revolution, was published in the same year. His aim here was to prove his two favourite theories — that injustice begets injustice and that fear has been the cause of the world's greatest crimes. It is hardly surprising then that a novel like *Miriam Lucas* should follow in 1912. Because socialism was causing some concern also in America, Heuser had since 1904 been pressing Sheehan for a story on the subject. Sheehan's lukewarm response reveals his confusion, his possible openmindedness and his intellectual isolation from current affairs.

> I have been thinking much about your socialist novel; but it is a good deal outside my sphere of thought. What should be the underlying principle? Do atheism and socialism go together? How are we to keep the golden mean between labour and capital? What of christian

socialism? These are a few of the questions that keep cropping up
when I allow myself to think of the matter .... Books are no guide.
One or two facts about socialists would guide me better.[83]

In another letter of the same period he wrote to Heuser:

When I wrote 'The Monks of Trabolgan' [later part of *A Spoiled
Priest and other stories*], some years ago, I had in view a large work
on the monastic life as you have suggested. But I found I was
anticipated by Huysmans; so I left it a mere sketch, I am now
labouring at the *Labour and Capital* novel, but am making no
headway. The agony of the thing does not strike us; and all my
sympathies are with the labouring classes.[84]

The work for the *American Ecclesiastical Review* was eventually given
to one Richard A. Maher. It was another eight years before *Miriam Lucas*
appeared. It is a strange novel. Many of the characters never come to life
owing to Sheehan's unfamiliarity with city life in Ireland. The publicity
in the press accorded Fr O'Kane's Lenten lectures in Gardiner Street
church, attacking socialism, and Connolly's consequent pamphlet in defence, *Labour, Nationality and Religion* possibly triggered a guilt complex
in Sheehan, so that his novel, of class and religious prejudices in action,
evolved. Speaking of the novel, he claimed it was the completion of the
trilogy for which *My New Curate* and *Luke Delmege* were the first parts:

It is an idea of forecasting a perfect civilization founded purely on
religious lines. You will notice the refrain running through *Luke
Delmege*: we must create our own civilization. I am anxious to
formalise such a civilization founded on simplicity, and self-surren-
der: and as often as possible to all our modern ideas of progress. You
will perceive that Luke's failure sprang from his want of touch with
his supernatural element.[85]

The *Irish Ecclesiastical Record* welcomed it as a weapon against
'Godless realistic fiction' which could join forces with Fr. Benson's *None
Other Gods* and the work of Rene Bazin in France, but recognised the
'heavy and elaborate background' as a defect.[86]

The Graves at Kilmorna, published in 1915 two years after his death,
was written out of a sense of nostalgia for the idealism of the fenian
movement which he recalled from his very early years in Mallow. Although during the writing of it, Sheehan was constantly interrupted by
bouts of ill health, the intensity of his feeling for the subject give it power
and cohesion. It is essentially a pathetic contrast between the fenian leaders
and what Sheehan saw as the slippery politics of the Irish parliamentary

party. It is a valuable interpretation of the nature of 19th and 20th century nationalism as Sheehan compares also the popular nationalism of the two eras. He blinds himself to many of the undesirable conclusions which the comparisons suggest in his determination to place his fenians as idols before the 1912 generation:

> They did not love their motherland because she gave them a scrap of her bogs, or fields, or mountains, or because they could sell her interests at a brigand's valuation; but because she was Ireland, and she had wrongs to be avenged and sorrows to be redressed.[87]

It is difficult to pinpoint Sheehan's political sympathies. They were complex and confused. It is clear that in theory he wished the connection broken with England but in fact he worried that Home Rule might be a disaster for Ireland: 'We are in the throes of expectation about the Home Rule Bill. It will be the best for England; the worst for Ireland since the Act of Union'.[88] Yet he feared and hated the image of English civilisation as industrialized and low thinking and wanted nothing of it for Ireland, but beyond that he had no image of how an independent Ireland might be governed. Neither had he any faith in democracy and least of all in socialism. In *The Graves at Kilmorna* he gave voice to disdain for the 'elephantine hooves of democracy' which since the French Revolution 'have been trampling out all the beauty and sweetness of life'.[89] He could never come to terms with any form of government based on popular rule, as this would inevitably induce a vulgar ignorant society.

It is curious that *The Graves at Kilmorna* was hardly noticed when first issued in 1915. It was not until after the 1916 rebellion that it drew the attention of many as a work of prophecy and began to sell. Later Sheehan fans delight in denting Yeats' stature as the ideologue of the period by claiming it was *Kilmorna* which 'sent out those men the English shot'. It is more probable that Pearse and Sheehan both, were simply and separately complying with their myth-filled consciences which dictated a revulsion against a modern Ireland in a modern world.

In an article for the *Irish Monthly* of 1899 later published as a pamphlet for the Catholic Truth Society of Ireland, *Our Personal and Social Responsibilities* Sheehan anticipates the fury of the Catholic Association (formed in 1903). Sheehan adopts a most paranoid tone and reveals a deep seated fear of Freemasons, Presbyterians and Jews. In a later pamphlet of the Catholic Truth Society, *How Character is Formed*, he enlists in the campaign for temperance, urges a more responsible attitude to the celtic use of language — 'The responsibility of words has never dawned on us' and feels obliged to call for mutual toleration in religious differences.[90]

Sheehan wrote also a plethora of religious or devotional works. *Mariae Corona* is probably his best work of this type. His volume of poems *Cithera Mea*, published in 1900 in Boston was justly neglected. He also managed to find time to write hymns, one of which 'O Sacred Heart' became popular, at least in Doneraile.[91] His sermons were collected by his good friend Fr Michael Phelan and published in 1920. Some of his most revealing essays in autobiography and literary matters, *The Literary Life and Other Essays,* edited by Edward McLysaght, were also published in 1921.

It is hardly surprising that he never became a great novelist. His priestly conscience cramped him but his personality also tethered him. Owing to his lack of confidence in himself he often resorted to culling the works of others. The care with which he kept his commonplace book suggests it was a cherished possession. He did have a certain giddy sense of vanity, but it was curbed by fear of strong criticism, and an intensely shy disposition. *Glenanaar,* the novel which he dashed off in six weeks, is his most entertaining, realistic and well-structured work. Happily here, he threw off his missionary collar in his passion for the tale. His literary achievement never amounted to more than consistent indication of potential. Only the occasional lapses in his missionary zeal permit glimpses of an artist. Perhaps he simply wrote too quickly and suffered for the want of sound, constructive criticism. He was, in a sense, spoilt by Heuser of the *American Ecclesiastical Review* who was satisfied with any mediocre copy which would amuse the American clergy. Fr Matthew Russell of the *Irish Monthly* was more discriminating. His confidants would seem to have included only his brother Denis and Fr Daniel Keller, P.P. of Youghal and later Dean and Vicar General. Most accounts testify to his general shyness and particularly on the subject of his writing and his politics. The responsibility attached to his writing frightened him and he worried greatly about misinterpretation.

In a rare interview for the student magazine *St Stephens* he refers to his hasty readership:

> I have a feeling that my works but half interpret my thoughts: and I know that my meaning is but faintly grasped. And then there is the danger that people will not read a book as a whole, or with a view to understanding the author's own point of view .... What I fear is that my writings may be read by the ignorant and perhaps perverted to evil purposes .... I think I should have given up writing long ago,

if I could. But I cannot. I do not know why I write, except that I am positively impelled to do so.[92]

In the same interview he admitted to his 'unconscious plagiarism' and his decision to give up reading altogether while writing. *The Queen's Fillet*, it was noticed, takes its plot from Talleyrand's memoirs. Yet the author had no recollection of ever having read Talleyrand.[93]

Sir Francis Burnand, editor of *Punch* and of *Who's Who* described him rather equivocally as 'one of the best read men of the day' and reported that Tolstoi hailed him as 'the greatest living novelist',[94] while Oliver Wendell Holmes, U.S. supreme court judge, read all his novels, visited the writer, and kept up a remarkably consistent correspondence with him. Sheehan also pasted newspaper clippings of Holmes' published verse into his commonplace book. Fr Matthew Russell encouragingly wrote to Sheehan that Joel Chandler Harris, author of *Uncle Remus* listed his favourite reading as Newman, A. Kempis and Sheehan: 'There is the company you keep'.[95] G.K. Chesterton admired him as he admired J.M. Barrie. In July 1909 Canon Sheehan received a telegram from the archdeacon of the diocese of Lismore, New South Wales to tell him that he had been nominated as one of the candidates for the see left vacant by the death of Dr Jeremiah Doyle. The Australian press was already busily describing Sheehan as a churchman of worldwide fame. Urgently he pleaded with Cardinal Logue of Armagh via Fr Keller to frustrate any possible appointment, on the grounds of ill health. To a certain extent this may have been his real reason, but it is more likely that he felt he had neither the personality or the capacity to administrate at that level. It is doubtful too whether he would have wanted to leave the country which so preoccupied him and Doneraile in particular, where he had time to indulge his writing and reflection. He remained in Doneraile much to the pride of his parishioners.

Apart from two trips to Germany and occasional trips to Cork and Dublin he led a very quiet life. It may have been his lonely, monotonous life which drove him to write in such volume — 'No matter how close the ties of affection may be, the priest moves through his people, amongst them but not of them.[96] Sheehan felt his greatest want to be intercourse with other stimulating minds. The Abbey Theatre interested him greatly but he regretted the negative attitude of some of its members towards Christianity. He felt Synge had attempted a compromise with paganism, and Yeats, while being 'an unquestionable poet', lacked a genuine faith in life. In T.C. Murray, whose *Birthright* had just been produced, he was very interested. He also allegedly wished to meet Daniel Corkery, the animating figure of the Literary Revival in Cork but 'modesty bred of restricted environment kept them apart'.[97] Neither did the youthful Corkery bring it upon himself to make Sheehan's acquaintance. In Kenneth McGowan's brief sketch of Sheehan, we are told that owing much to his enjoyment of friends more learned than himself, he cultivated numerous friendships amongst the Jesuits, Capuchins and Dominicans. This is borne out by their many fulsome tributes to him later. Yet, McGowan adds, that though Fr Vincent McNabb was 'a close friend' of Sheehan's, he considered it 'a great honour' to be invited to visit.[98]

Though later biographers are at pains to point out that his literary work never interfered with his pastoral activity in Doneraile, it would appear that his involvement was usually in a passive, supervisory capacity. He did promote, however, many practical improvements in the town. The electric light was introduced from a plant at the local mill, the water supply was extended and a bridge was built. The local community elevated him to heroic status when, during one night, he smelt smoke from the burning flour mill and warned the occupants of the nearby convent and other houses. He may have been instrumental in inducing Lady Castletown to build the town hall with stage, greenrooms, reading rooms and billiard room, as he was on friendly terms with her husband. No doubt, the town hall provided a venue for the St Vincent de Paul Society which he also established.[99]

A hint appears, in McGowan's biography, of tension between the priest and his flock when we are assured that the priest 'would not tolerate anything whether words or actions which tended to demean him in any way. There was no compromise for any offender who invariably suffered at least a severe reprimand'.[100] Perhaps the affected nonchalance of 'Dr Gray', born of his misunderstanding in the parish, was inspired by the pain of experience.

Sheehan contributed much from his own pocket to the renovation of the church and schools and donated a handsome sum to the refurbishment of his earlier college of St. Columba's, and handed over the entire proceeds of one of his works to found a cot in the children's hospital of Temple Street, Dublin, though he had no other relations with the institution.[101]

In 1905 he ceded all his valuable literary work to the Bishop of Cloyne for the support of the sick and aged priests of the diocese.[102] In 1910, suffering with severe pain he consulted Sir Charles Ball in Dublin and was told that his illness was fatal. He was advised to desist from his writing and strenuous duties. Two years later his condition grew very serious and he was removed to the South Infirmary in Cork. His correspondence during this time however was remarkably cheerful and even humorous. After five months and much pleading, he was eventually allowed return home to Doneraile, where he insisted on resuming some of his parochial duties. He died on Rosary Sunday, 5 October 1913, three years after he first fell ill. During this time he had published *The Intellectuals, The Queen's Fillet* and was almost certainly writing *The Graves at Kilmorna*. According to the death certificate, the cause of death was cancer of the pelvis, a condition which had been diagnosed in 1911. Shortly before he died, he burnt his memoirs, saying to his brother Denis, 'These may do harm to someone else'. He had earlier sent them to Russell, with a note specifying that they were not at any time intended for print, and though he feared Russell would not find them 'too entertaining' he added 'there are a few interesting episodes here and there'.[103] Apart from *Tristram Lloyd*, an unfinished and unremarkable novel later completed by Rev Michael Gaffney (1928), it is believed that there were other unfinished writings left when Sheehan died. These, however, were withheld from publication, by the express desire of the writer made known to his executors and close friends.[104]

His funeral by all accounts was huge. 'Lords, members of parliament, farmers, labourers, professional men and artisans', with the entire town of Doneraile mourned at his grave.[105] Nearly every house in the town had a draped portrait of the deceased canon hanging over the door, the portrait chiefly in use being that given as a supplement with the *Cork Free Press* a year earlier.[106] He was buried in the churchyard of Doneraile, according to his wish, so that the school children would say a prayer on their way to the school building. A plain Celtic cross marks his grave with an inscription of his own choosing —

Where dwelst thou Rabbi?

And Jesus said 'Come and See'.

He died relatively poor. After deduction of one hundred pounds for masses for the repose of his soul, the remainder was to be divided between the St Vincent de Paul societies of Doneraile and Mallow. His extensive library, which largely comprised the works of nineteenth century philosophers and theologians, was sold, and the proceeds devoted to the poor of Doneraile and Shanballymore.[107] His obituaries filled the pages of the *Cork Free Press* and the *Cork Examiner* for days afterward with tributes from many including his few close clerical friends, Doneraile GAA, the All-For-Ireland League and Urban Council.[108] His benign bishop contributed a panegyric in which he insisted for the benefit of those who may have harboured other suspicions that 'Canon Sheehan was a priest first and last'.[109] Plans were soon afoot to erect a monument in his honour. There was argument as to whether it ought to be placed in Mallow or in Doneraile. It was twelve years before the life size bronze statue of the Canon standing with pen and notebook in hand was eventually unveiled in the Doneraile courtyard. The statue by F. Doyle Jones of London was unveiled by the most Rev Dr Browne, Bishop of Cloyne. An old friend Rev Michael Whelan S.J. delivered an oration to thousands. He described him as 'a man of masterly self possession whose higher faculties held in complete subjection the baser impulses of our nature'.[110]

2: Canon Joseph Guinan *(1863-1932)*

Material relating to the early life and family of Canon Joseph Guinan is scarce indeed. He was born at Millbrook House, Cloghan, County Offaly in 1863. Judging at least by the fairly uniform background of all his fictional priests, Guinan enjoyed a comfortable existence during his early years:

> Father John's parents were of the respectable and fairly comfortable class of tenant farmers, a class to which most of the parochial clergy in Ireland belong, and one too, which for moral rectitude and God-fearing, simple-minded conduct and living have no equals, probably, or few compeers on the face of the broad Earth.[1]

In the second, highly autobiographical (and most successful) novel, *The Soggarth Aroon*, he indicates that his father had a servant boy 'who married our buxom servant girl'.[2] At any rate, it seems that his parents were intent on educating the young Guinan as best they could. Though it is claimed in *A History of Ardagh*[3] that Guinan's earliest teacher was Thomas MacDonagh who figured in the 1916 rising, it is asserted in the *Journal of the Ardagh and Clonmacnoise Antiquarian Society* that the credit was due to a Mr Timothy Gardiner 'one of nature's gentlemen and scholars'.[4] Though the writer of the latter would probably have been better acquainted with Guinan than that of the first, owing to Guinan's connections with the journal, it is always possible that both men may have contributed to his education.

Another point of conflict between the two is in his choice of seminary college. While the journal would have him travelling to St Mary's in Dundalk,[5] the more patriotic local history places him in St Mel's, Longford, where he later spent a short while teaching.[6] In 1881 he entered Maynooth. 'Here', the writer of his obituary notice tells us, 'as at every large college, the talented but shy and reserved student passes unobserved'.[7] Though never as shy as Sheehan, he was equally adept at hiding his interest in literature. After being ordained in 1888, he spent his first five years like Sheehan 'on the mission' in England. He began his writing career with a series of articles 'Amongst the Liverpool Irish'.[8] Called home in 1893, he joined the staff of St Mel's College until 'failing health' compelled him to leave. It is recollected in the *History of Ardagh* that Guinan was 'a gentle, sympathetic professor — with a voice like an angel and with methods differing *toto coelo* from all his colleagues'. He taught English, happily, and Mathematics, and on Saturdays 'gave beautiful lectures on Christian doctrine'. He returned to Legan (near Lenamore) after one year in Rathcline, Lanesborough.[9] From 1900 to 1908 he was to be found serving as curate in St Mary's parish, Athlone from where he was moved to a curacy in the parish of Wheery and Tisaran near Ferbane. Two years later he was made parish priest of Bornacoola at the age of forty seven. His predecessor here, Father Michael O'Flynn, had erected the curate's residence at Clonturk. Guinan further improved the comfort and no doubt the status of the parish and of himself by providing a fine parish priest's residence, this time at Bornacoola.[10] It was a small parish of 10,180 acres near Dromod, with a population of 1,700, 1,650 of these being Catholic. Here he remained until 1920 when he was transferred to Ardagh parish and dignified with the title of Canon.

In 1927 while in Ardagh, he purchased 'the Court' for use as a school of domestic economy to be controlled by the Sisters of Mercy. It was originally the home of the Fetherston family. He was also instrumental in securing a portion of land for the use of the parish priest in Ardagh. In 1921 he helped found the Ardagh and Clonmacnoise Antiquarian society, served it as secretary for some time, and edited their journal which began in 1926. One member regretted that 'with characteristic modesty he left all the space for others'. When it became apparent however that the 1932 volume called for additional matter, 'with a martyr's fervour he set himself, during the last months of his life, under the shadow of death, to prepare an article on "Ardagh in the 16th century"'.[11]

On the occasion of his death the *Catholic Herald* noted that Guinan had a deep interest in Irish archaeological research.[12] This, however, is scarcely reflected in his writing, though he did express an interest in the old tales and customs of the older peasantry. The *Longford Leader* remembers him especially for unveiling the monument to 'the '98 men' at Ballinamuck in 1928.[13] On the 5th of January 1932 he died at St Brigid's, Ardagh. Though his funeral was allegedly 'huge' there is no evidence that it was any more 'huge' than that of most parish priests.[14] In frail health for most of his life, he was remembered for his 'sunny cheerfulness and quiet sense of humour'.[15] In *The Soggarth Aroon* Guinan gives some indication of his motivations to write. The Soggarth Aroon remembers 'Killanure':

> The quiet, restful, dreamy little valley was calculated to make one with an imagination, a poet, an enthusiast, a visionary — and I fancy I have a dash of all three in me .... I had long entertained a much-be-hugged conceit that I could and would, some time before I died, write

something — ay, and get it printed, too. The loneliness of my life, my romantic mountain home, the tranquil solicitude and grateful peace of everything around me, all seemed to incline and woo me towards a life of literary leisure, combined with the simple routine of pastoral duties[16] [he is careful to add].

He continues justifying his indulgence by relating how he was disgusted (probably in his Liverpool years) by the 'Briarean London press' and decided that instead of 'everlastingly denouncing it, ... he could do something better'. He would try 'by writing for the popular magazines, to provide a wholesome literary pabulum for the populace'.[17] In this he anticipated the work of the Catholic Truth Society. His articles, 'Amongst the Liverpool Irish' had some difficulty finding their way into print if one judges by his repeated references to the disappointment of fledgling writers receiving rejection slips from 'matter of fact' publishers.[18]

He copes with the sceptical notions of his clerical colleagues in a remarkably independent spirit:

In passing I might mention that about this time I happened to confide, in my simplicity, these dreams and literary aspirations to a neighbouring curate, a man of predominantly horsey tastes. After regarding me for a long time with mingled surprise and amusement — not unmixed with pity, I fancied — he seriously advised me to put aside the notion as a temptation, declaring that I would be almost certain to make a laughing stock of myself by going into print. 'Don't be an —,' he said with friendly familiarity; and he used a certain well-known short three lettered word that crystallized his ideas on the subject. But I would see out my Darling notwithstanding.

.... When the typomaniacal spirit that impels mortals to inflict their lubucrations on an inoffensive public once takes possession of a man, he is with difficulty driven out; and, even if he is expelled, he will frequently return, bringing with him seven other scribbling, romancing spirits worse than himself.[19]

His 'attack of *cacoethes scribendi*', he tells, replaced 'a horse-fancying craze' which was no doubt induced by his watchful colleague, and of which he later has some reasonably amusing stories to tell.[20] His nephew, still living in Cloghan in 1987, remembers how the priest 'clipped' his horse in the style fashionable at the time. The priest-author's remarkable honesty provides a more truthful picture of his dilemma than any biographer could deduce:

During the time I had the horsey fever I scarcely gave a thought to the literary projects which at one time so preoccupied my mind; or, if I did, it was only to dismiss them as visionary and ridiculous in the extreme. The natural fear of ridicule had prevented me from taking counsel with anyone on the subject of my literary ambition: and, now that I believed the scales had fallen from my eyes, and that I saw my egregious folly, I was glad I had held my peace on the subject. In truth at this period of mental lethargy, so much afraid was I that my absurd pretensions to authorship might be discovered that I burned the rough sketch of a novel of Irish life, on which I had expended much time and thought. I felt half inclined too, to consign my series of sketches to the flames, and thus rid myself of the temptation to get them printed. I confess it cost me no small effort to overcome, as I afterwards did, the haunting dread I felt of some day being unmercifully quizzed over my literary dreams, and made a laughing stock of for the whole diocese. But the paternal instinct prevailed, and I respited these darling children of my brain, which I had lived to see arrayed in all the glory of print. At any rate I sent my typescript to a well-known American magazine [*Ave Maria*] and I think that day is amongst the happiest of my life when I got a reply saying my contributions were accepted, and that I would receive payment on a liberal scale for anything more I might write in the same stream.[21]

Guinan could not have been unaware of Canon Sheehan's successes though he chose not to mention them. Perhaps it was that fiction 'about Ireland' had earned itself such a bad reputation amongst Catholics, the clergy in particular being most sensitive to the stage Irishisms of the Victorian press, that 'the novel', as an institution, was instantly repulsive. An uncertain naivety is apparent however as he reflected on his early aspirations: 'Thus, I hoped to do some good by my pen, as well as turn an honest penny thereby — ay, and perhaps, leave behind me a name, too, that would not altogether die'.[22]

In an 1910 article for the *Irish Monthly* he shamelessly reveals his egotism: 'I rejoiced to think that, from my obscure corner of the globe, I could send words through this medium to the utmost bounds of the earth'.[23]

The purpose of the article, however, was to encourage Catholic writers, and, as at this time Guinan had a reputation as the author of the winning *Soggarth Aroon*, he could therefore cast modesty aside in offering himself as an inspiring advertisement for the rewards of writing Catholic fiction.

It is my fondly cherished hope that, through dead, I shall yet live on
to preach through my books the gospel I felt called on to deliver;

that, even in my grave I shall still continue my mission, and more effectively than in life, mayhap, for is it not a notorious fact in literature, that the dead writer only begins to live when he is a long time departed hence?[24]

Yet, he leaves one with the suspicion that while he was using literature to spread the gospel he was perhaps subconsciously also using 'his mission' to satisfy personal ambitions. Counter to that, however, runs another more realistic comment on his literary scruple;

But I am proud to think ... that the smiles I may unconsciously provoke, will not be purchased at the expense of bringing even the faintest blush of shame to the cheek of tender innocence. Nay more, I have the splendid effrontery and magnificent egotism to ask, how many Irish novelists of yesterday, or to-day, can say the same? But in very truth I am no novelist — only a posing, reminiscent, solilo-quizing, dreaming Irish country curate with an unfortunate penchant for preaching at people betimes.[25]

The idyllic *Scenes and Sketches in an Irish Parish; or Priest and People in Doon* (1903) (hereafter referred to as *Doon*) was followed in 1905 by his bestseller *The Soggarth Aroon*. This novel is his most cautious. It steers away from social and political comment. It made its first appearance in *Ave Maria*, the American Catholic magazine, telling the experiences of a curate who 'possessed and exercised quasi-parochial authority under the nominal suzerainty of the parish priest'.[26] *The Island Parish* (1908) and *The Curate of Kilcloon* (1913) are similar. The reviewer of the latter in Stephen Brown's *Ireland in Fiction* (1921) puts it plainly: 'the story has the same qualities as the author's former books and in fact differs little from them'.[27]

The Moores of Glynn (1907) and *Donal Kenny* (1910) have slightly less of the 'priest and people' theme. The first is an interesting and bigoted tale of the fortunes of a Catholic family who supplant a Protestant farm;

There was great rejoicing, therefore, in all the countryside over the weeding out of 'a bad ereb', and the uprooting of an old 'nest of Protestants' of a bad type, such as the Black family always were.[28]

Donal Kenny is unusual for its acknowledgement of the alcoholic father of the priest and the misery he causes his family. Guinan published no novels between 1913 and 1924, possibly owing to the demands on his time as parish priest, but he did lend himself with enthusiasm to the campaign for Catholic literature.

From the preface of his first book, *Doon* his mission was to rescue the stage Irishman:

> In a country where even still the peasant is 'badly housed, badly fed, badly clothed, and badly paid for his labour' [the Devon Commission] he must necessarily be a gloomily serious individual enough.[29]

> See the poor peasant absorbed in prayer in the mountain chapel on a Sunday, or at the nightly Rosary in the blessed sanctuary of his humble cabin, and he is no longer the same individual you saw at the fair or the merry-making, but a transfigured being, soaring on the wings of faith into serene heights of ecstatic happiness, which the sordid materialist knows nothing of.[30]

He echoes Sheehan's denunciation of 'George Mooreism', pointing to Crashaw, Patmore, Francis Thompson and Aubrey de Vere as proper models for 'the newest type of Anglo-Irish writer now in the making':

> It is far preferable to that of a foreign junta in our midst or would-be founders of a new school of aesthetics — cynical dramatist and Art critics chiefly — who utterly misunderstand and misinterpret the true inwardness of Irish life.[31]

The priests are to be the standard bearers in Guinan's war of image though he is careful not to rule out fierce members of the laity:

> We need the services of the freelance *litterateur* who is not dependent on the pen for a livelihood, the Catholic enthusiast, or fanatic, if you will, who seeks neither fame nor *Kudos* in single-minded effort to counter the insidious evil of bad literature, whether foreign or native.[32]

While in the *Irish Monthly* of 1917 and in the CTSI pamphlet *Months and Days* he refers respectfully to his flock as 'the Irish people', in the *Catholic Book Bulletin* he feels safe in calling them 'peasantry'.

> As the peasantry for obvious reasons, seldom find a voice amongst themselves capable of expressing adequately their real sentiments towards their idolized *sagart a ruin*, I am emboldened to try and interpret them. I some times think that Irish priests are to blame for allowing the scoffer and the philistine to invade and occupy a field that is theirs by right.[33]

In his article 'The Apostolate of the Press' for the *Irish Monthly* (1910) he instructs its reader (having assured them that they are 'Catholics of culture and literary tastes') to feed any 'young aspirants of literary fame' on the great Catholic journalists 'from Veuillot to Lucas and from Boyle O'Reilly to Bulfin'.[34]

He paints in *Doon* (1903) an idyllic picture of the reading habits of three local children. The oldest was absorbed in *Knocknagow* which he had borrowed from the parish lending library, while the younger two 'with their heads close together, and their arms entwined round one another's waists, were reading the same book — one of the little publications of the Catholic Truth Society of Ireland'.[35] By 1911 he had become more aware or more depressed:

> Instead of wool-rolling for the spindle the modern Irish colleen spends her evening wool-gathering with gallivanting heroes in the realms of fiction.[36]

He calls for a Catholic *Tit-Bits* and Irish *Tablet* and *America*. On a note of pessimism he appeals for more support for the monthly Catholic family magazines such as *The Catholic Bulletin,* the *Irish Rosary* and the *Irish Monthly* since 'they are fighting the cause of pure, clean literature against desperate odds'. By 1917 he is realistic enough to admit defeat in the face of the 'Kinema Screen', but expects, 'it will probably pass some day, like every other craze'.[37]

It is no surprise that it was an American Catholic magazine *Ave Maria* which first published his material. *Doon* was published in 1903 by M.H. Gill and Benziger brothers of New York, Cincinnati and Chicago, publishers also of many of the works of Canon Sheehan. In its preface he advertises its appeal to the 'sea divided Gael' and especially 'those who were themselves actors in such scenes as we attempt to delineate'.[38] Interestingly, he hopes that *Doon* may 'help to revive the holy and sacred, yet maybe fading spells of home' amongst Irish Americans. *The Soggarth Aroon* was carried serially in *Ave Maria* also before being published in book form. His books did find a large readership in both Ireland and America.

His interest in the land question is reflected in his frequent treatment of it in his fiction but his interest hardly progressed to any activity. The 'Soggarth Aroon' became president of the local branch of the [United Irish] league in order 'to exercise a wholesome restraining influence on possibly very injudicious, or even dangerous and mischievous courses of political action in the parish'.[39] Like Sheehan he had some patriotic feeling but was not quite sure of his political views beyond that. The priest of *Annamore or, the Tenant at will* (hereafter *Annamore*) accounts for his caution:

> Ever since I came to this parish as pastor I managed — without sacrifice of principle or patriotism, I hope — to stand well with the landlords who own property in it. In the interests of my people I considered it the wisest and most prudent policy. You see, I made some bad mistakes in my young curate days, when, I must admit, I

was a bit of a Fenian at heart. Since then I have never been an ardent politician. The truth is, the Keogh scandal taught me a lesson I have never forgotten. Since then I have been cautious and suspicious of public men, to an undue extent, perhaps .... I dread the consequence to religion and morality which these irresponsible men in the west [U.I.L.] are engaged in preaching .... It has ever been the fate and the experience of our unfortunate country, during the seven-hundred years' war, that the law must be broken in order to be redressed ....[40]

In a lecture 'The Famine Years' delivered at St. Joseph's Temperance Hall, Longford, on 12 November, 1907 (while he was parish priest of Bornacoola) and published by the CTSI in 1908, he declares he would go one further than John Mitchel, O'Meagher Condon (author of *The Irish in America*), Lister's *Glory and Shame of England*, and Smith O'Brien, in loading the blame for the Irish Famine on England's shoulders:

> 'Black Forty-Seven' was the outcome of the union, which Lecky characterized as 'a crime of the deepest turpitude', and which Byron spoke of as the 'union of the shark with its prey'. Dr Johnson once said England would unite with us only to rob us. They did worse than that, they starved us.[41]

Annamore, one of his later works appeared in 1924, published in London by Burns, Oates and Washbourne Ltd. (publishers to the Holy See). It is an amusing, observant account of the struggle to stay on the land in the 1870s and 1880s, with a happy ending.

In 1928 Guinan published *The Patriots* with the American publishers Benziger Brothers (printers to the Holy Apostolic See). The novel was modelled on the exploits of Longford hero, Sean Mac Eoin, the legendary 'Blacksmith of Ballinalea' who fought in the War of Independence and took the Treaty side in the Civil War with his close friend Michael Collins. Guinan was emphatic in his support for the Treaty side in the Civil War while loudly condemning the irregulars. In his foreward to *The Patriots* Guinan described the contents as a sketch of:

> the various phases in the process of evolution by which the literary Gaelic movement, under the inspiration of Sinn Fein, broke away from the policy of the old Irish party and dramatically resulted in the rising of 1916, which was apparently a dismal failure . . . The brutality of the Black and Tan regime and the heroism, pity and pathos associated with the memorable stand of the IRA supply the more stirring incidents introduced. In this connection, the charge of exaggeration need scarcely be feared, since the reality of the horrors of that period simply beggars

description and renders invention unnessary. All the same the author deprecates perpetuating a bitter feeling in view of the good effects for Ireland which resulted from the costly and inglorious British failure.[42]

The Patriots was never published in Ireland or Britain. One possible reason for this may have been that Guinan's surprisingly frank and open treatment of national politics through the period of the War of Independence and Civil War would surely have caused a little embarrassment amongst the moderate majority of priests.

In *The Patriots* Guinan wrily addresses the isssue of the cultural service of the priest writer when he has the Parish Priest encourage the younger curate to use his writing gift as a corrective to the 'degeneracy' which marked other forms of contemporary Irish writing:

> 'Ireland will have her literary Mecca as distinctive as that of England's. But, we must not allow a degenerate class of professional writers to control it, licentious sceptics, whose books are doing a vast amount of harm amongst our educated young men and women.'
>
> 'Eloquently expressed, as usual, Father Darragh. I think you yourself should seriously consider the possibilities for good of that mighty instrument, the pen.'
>
> This was such an unexpected compliment that the curate of Druminara shrank into silence.[43]

Guinan, having appointed his bishop Rev. James J. McNamee, executor, willed to him all his literary rights. He directed also that the cost of a plain monument in his memory be taken out of his estate (which totalled £411-13s-8d). He bequeathed £50 to the Reverend Mother of St. Brigid's convent, Ardagh, and the rest after funeral expenses, was to be used for masses for the repose of his soul. At a public auction, his household goods, jewels, books, horses, and instruments of husbandry, fetched £405.

3: Gerald O'Donovan (1871-1942)

Gerald O'Donovan was born Jeremiah O'Donovan in Kilkeel, Co. Down in 1871. Because his father was employed as a superintendent of public works, the family were required to move home rather frequently. This they did, moving first to Galway, then to Cork, and finally to Sligo. This experience, unusual to most Irish children growing up, may have served to sharpen the perceptions of the young O'Donovans of the unevenness of Irish life. While allowing for exaggeration in his highly autobiographical *Father Ralph*, his mother would yet seem to have been a devotedly pious woman who tailored her eldest son for the priesthood. Though it was her wish to have her son join the Carmelite order, Jeremiah eventually entered Maynooth in 1889, for Killala diocese. Clerical students in Maynooth with a similar background to his formed a small minority: most came from farming backgrounds. Like the other two writers, O'Donovan failed to attract any notice for his academic work, probably because he was more interested in extra-curricular reading. Books he ordered in his Third Divinity year had to be returned by order of the Administrative Council.[1]

After three years studying in Maynooth he left the service of Killala Diocese to join a religious order. Two years later (1894) he re-entered Maynooth, this time for Clonfert Diocese. These changes in direction suggest a restlessness or discontent in his young character. In June 1895, O'Donovan was ordained a priest for Clonfert. His first appointment was as curate for Kilmalonoge and Lickmolassy near Portumna. In 1890 he was moved to Loughrea as curate. Apart from a short time spent on the staff of St Joseph's College, Esker, Athenry he spent the rest of his priesthood in Loughrea. Loughrea at that time was fast decaying. With a population of only 3,000 people, there was much squalor and poverty. This was possibly aggravated by and certainly attributed anyway to the absenteeism of the local landlord, the Marquis of Clanricarde.

In the same year as O'Donovan's appointment to Loughrea, Dr Healy, coadjutor since 1884, was made Bishop of Clonfert. O'Donovan flourished under Healy and soon distinguished himself in the diocese as a man who was not merely brimming with new and lively ideas but who was able and determined to put them into practice. It was he who persuaded Bishop Healy to employ Irish artists on the new cathedral then being built at Loughrea. He hired Professor William Scott, Sarah Purser, Jack Yeats and John Hughes, whose artistic experiences in Loughrea were fictionalised by George Moore. It was O'Donovan also who later brought John McCormack, then just a schoolboy, from Sligo to sing in the new cathedral choir. In 1901, he brought to Loughrea the Irish National Theatre Company. Though they played to packed houses there they were not invited to perform in any of the other provincial towns.

As was the case with Sheehan, O'Donovan first began writing for the *Irish Ecclesiastical Record*. After two articles on better convents and workhouse reform he turned to 'The Celtic Revival of Today'.[2] O'Donovan, also, believed that the deanglicisation of Ireland, by the revival of the Celtic, was an urgent need. He conceded that the Irish language was not necessary to express 'Celtic' thought, and moreover felt it would probably impede its transmission abroad. On this point he received an angry reply from *An Claidheamh Solais*.[3] In 1901 he joined the National Literary Society. In order to clear up any confusion as to what precisely 'Celtic' literature was, he declared it to be a literature based on faith and spirituality.[4]

When the *Irish Homestead* introduced in 1899 a 'Village Literary Competition' asking readers to list one hundred 'suitable' books, Professor W.P. Coyne of University College, Dublin won first prize, but the Rev. J. O'Donovan C.C., came second. However, he had trouble in getting his list accepted as a basis for the village library scheme at the annual conference of Co-operative Societies in 1899. As many delegates were in favour of books of technical instruction only, O'Donovan withdrew his list.[5] However, he later contributed an article accompanying the *Irish Homestead*'s revised list. In it he pressed for the inclusion of O'Grady's *Bardic History,* the Cuchulain sagas and *Ireland's Ancient Schools and Scholars.*[6] One anonymous correspondent, while allowing that works of this type would raise consciousness of nationality, feared that it would 'encourage narrowness'.[7] Eventually, in 1904, the Rural Literary Association of Ireland was founded. O'Donovan served on its first committee with Stephen Gwynn, T.W. Lyster, T.W. Rolleston, Hugh Law M.P., P.J. Boland and George Russell.[8]

In February 1899 Horace Plunkett wrote in his diary:

> Reverend Jeremiah O'Donovan C.C., a young cultured gentlemanly priest who is supposed to have influence on his bishop (Dr. Healy) joined the organization [Irish Agricultural Organisation Society]. He also writes for the Eccles [sic] Record which the priesthood consult and I wanted him to study our movement in hopes he will educate the clergy about it.[9]

O'Donovan saw the real economic problem of rural Ireland lay in the

failure of the new landowners to make the most of their opportunities. The
majority of them had contented themselves with their old 'laissez-faire'
methods and had 'gone steadily down the road to ruin'.[10] He pointed out to
those of William O'Brien's fold that 'the national idea must be underpinned
by social and economic improvement, as otherwise the idea would be realised
in a depopulated island'.[11] He was critical of the work of the Congested
Districts Board, contrasting the experimental schemes set up by the Board
with those of the IAOS and concluded that those of the Board were 'pitch-
forked' in by outsiders, whereas the IAOS involved the people themselves in
the schemes, and to much better effect.[12] Rather daringly he urged for the
organisation of village banks in order to usurp the role of the gombeenmen.
His social ideals are outlined clearly in the *Irish Home*stead of 1899:

> It is the bringing together of all classes, high and low, rich and poor,
> educated and uneducated, on terms of equality, for the common
> good. It is a levelling up and a levelling down. It is the raising of the
> poor and uneducated, and it is the bringing down of these from the
> exclusive position of isolation they hitherto occupied in Ireland.[13]

Galway's proportion of the membership of the cooperative movement
was attributed by R.A. Anderson, general secretary of the IAOS, to the
organisational ability of P.J. Hannon who lived in Loughrea.[14] No doubt
it was he who encouraged O'Donovan. At the 1901 Annual Conference
of the IAOS O'Donovan found himself elected as one of the Connacht
representatives to the Executive Committee, and he was re-elected every
year until 1908. O'Donovan consistently opposed Plunkett on the question
of whether the movement should accept government funding, approving
of state funding for education only.[15]

As a member of Co. Galway Technical Instruction Committee he
secured the services of a teacher to instruct local tradesmen and equipped
the rooms in the local barracks to serve as a nightschool for handicrafts
and general education.[16] When the traders of Loughrea voiced their
opposition to these activities, Plunkett decided the IAOS should try only
to improve the agricultural system. Anderson and Mounteagle of the IAOS
took a more aggressive line. O'Donovan was willing to follow Plunkett's
cautious policy but he still held that industrialisation should not wait for
the settlement of the land question. He realised there was a problem in
finding capital, but pointed, with a familiar finger, to natural resources
such as the Killaloe falls and their energy-giving potential.

He secured some rooms from the Mercy Convent in Loughrea to

establish 'St Raphael's Home Industries Society', in 1900. This one specialised in the making of lace but there were fifteen other similar schemes started throughout the country in the same year. It was established on a co-operative basis with the workers owning some of the shares.[17] A few comments from the *Irish Weekly Independent and Nation* reveal an impassioned idealist:

> I have a sort of undefined dream of a happy rural Ireland brought about by the co-operative movement. Religious and political differences must be excluded from social life. The Irish tongue, which is above and outside politics, must be restored. Reading-rooms and social centres must be established, not, however so as to interfere with home recreation. The 'Ceilidh', with its accompanying innocent dances, must be revived. When this era arrives, the amusements of today in country districts — drinking and bad reading, petty gambling and ribald talk — will cease.[18]

He had a prescription even for women. Though his attitude to the role of women is hardly liberal, he was unusual in raising the matter at all. He laments the inactivity of women in general in the language revival, but this he felt was because they were trained to be ladies — to be accomplished rather than to be accomplishing.[19] At the 1904 annual meeting of the Maynooth Union he placed the blame for the inadequate training of women in domestic affairs on the clergy. As a priest, O'Donovan felt obliged to speak out on this subject, because if a layman said anything he was bracketed with the notorious Michael J.F. McCarthy.[20] He also urged the introduction of district nurses into rural Ireland and served on an organising council to that end.[21]

1902 saw him on a lecturing tour in the USA. He promoted Irish art, literature and industry, an enterprise which proved compatible with a collection for the Loughrea Cathedral fund. The following year he was sent back again, this time with an IAOS delegation which included Fr Tom Finlay and R.A. Anderson. Their functions were poorly attended and they collected a meagre £1,500. They had their hands full it seems trying to dissipate the commonly-held notion that the co-operative movement was simply a diversion to distract people from national independence.[22] This notion of course was not by any means peculiar to Irish America, but it is another irony of the nationalism of Irish Americans that the conditions which exiled them were not the conditions which they wanted altered.

O'Donovan described Plunkett as a 'Sir Galahad in politics' but admired him as a sound and practical economist. He recognized that

Plunkett's caution engendered distrust in those who could only focus on
Home Rule but he called attention to the supporting role of economics to
politics, and appealed for the recognition which Plunkett's work deserved.[23] Plunkett repaid the tribute in his *Ireland in the New Century* of
1904. He is consoled by the pioneering work of priests like Fr Finlay, Fr
Hegarty of Erris and O'Donovan 'in the teeth of innumerable (and unman-
ageable) obstacles'.[24] He noted in his diary:

> Father O'Donovan came out to the barn. We had a 'tate a tate'
> evening and he told me his sorrows. He sees Irish character as I do
> and admits all I say about the Roman Catholic clergy in my book.
> His position is very bad. He has no sympathy with the clergy.[25]

Though it was not O'Donovan who started up a branch of the Gaelic
League in Loughrea it was he who ended up running it. Alongside this he
established in 1900 a total abstinence society to whom he read Joyce's
History of Ireland.

Amongst the more colourful activities of the League were concerts, a
play by Alice Milligan, a St Patrick's night *tableau* and the inauguration
of an annual commemorative *feis* at Killeneen between Loughrea and
Gort, the burial place of Raftery — 'the last genuine Gaelic poet'. It began
rather modestly in 1901 but the 1902 event attracted thousands and was
chaired by Douglas Hyde.[26] He tried to keep the branch non-sectarian and
non-political though rebel songs were sung.

O'Donovan joined in the chorus of revivalists who blamed the national
schools for producing 'a curious race who deep down in their hearts, had
a spirit of patriotism, but who in their daily acts were antagonistic to
everything Irish ... a thoughtless, illiterate, idealess, useless product of the
schools of Ireland of the last century'.[27] This lecture, delivered at the
Rotunda in November 1901, 'Our Duty to the Language Movement', was
reinforced by 'An O'Growney Memorial Lecture' the following year in
Dublin. Here he warned of the frailty of the initial success of the Gaelic
League. He divided the nation into anti-Irishmen, those who had a love
for Ireland but were apathetic to her language, and those who saw her
language movement as sentimental nonsense.[28] He could not accept that
politics was the sum of the nation's ideas. The lecture, though ignored by
the *Irish Times* won coverage in the *Leader, Freeman's Journal* and
Independent. In 1903 he was elected to the *Coiste Gnotha* of the Gaelic
League, a position which he held for two years. He was not re-elected in
1905 or 1906 though he went forward.[29]

His real belief in his ideas was proven by his willingness to read two extremely critical and progressive papers at the Maynooth Union of 1900. In 'Priests and Industrial Development in Ireland' he declared that the priest must necessarily involve himself in politics but only on a moral basis, not he stressed, on a political one.[30] Yet in a private letter to John Redmond in 1902, seeking introductions for his American tour, he praised Redmond's leadership of the Irish Parliamentary Party.[31] This would seem to suggest his approval of the trend of the clergy at large to leave politics, ostensibly, at least, to the laity.[32] He compared the reluctance of the general clergy to become involved in the parish co-op schemes in Ireland with the enthusiasm of their brethren on the continent and remarked on the natural advantage which the Irish priest inherited as a focus for the affections of the people.[33] In a characteristically practical fashion he urged clerical school managers to adapt schools to technical instruction. He called for the introduction of an economics course to seminaries in the same way that some Louvain students were trained in agriculture. Interestingly he told how his ideal priest would be formed of a combination of Fathers Letheby and Dan, of Sheehan's recently published *My New Curate*. The priest should be both a man of faith and a man of action but to be of any use he must have a more exact knowledge of industrial methods. In 'Priests as Nation Builders' he echoes Sheehan in urging the clergy to use the church's capital to employ Irish designers, artists and materials, rather than importing them.[34]

O'Donovan applauded the establishment of the Catholic Association in 1902. Suspiciously greeted by the bishops owing to the responsibility it placed on the laity, its appeal for a higher profile of Catholics in the businesses and industries of the towns, met with O'Donovan's approval. He was unusual amongst the clergy of the period for his equal concern for both urban and rural regeneration, and possibly unique in his desire for lay involvement in the internal organisation of the church.[35]

'The Churches and the Child' published first in the *Independent Review* of 1905 and republished the same year in *Littles Loving Age* and *Eclectic Magazine* is his most firm pronouncement on the educational system.[36] He disapproved of episcopal control over school managers and appealed for the introduction of local Boards of Management. While he objected to the American church schools because they had promoted sectarianism, were frequently staffed by 'bad teachers' and were too expensive he supported the separation of church and state as in Germany and France. It is a concern which reappears later in his novels with no less anger.

In September 1904 O'Donovan left both Loughrea and the priesthood. For 'Father Ralph' it is the papal encyclical condemning modernism *Pascendi Dominici Gregis* (1907) which finally drives him to leave in despair. In O'Donovan's case the clash of personalities had more to do with it. His bishop Dr Healy had treated O'Donovan with flexibility and sense. When he was translated to the diocese of Tuam in 1902, Dr Thomas O'Dea succeeded to Clonfert. Many of his progressive friends had hopes that O'Donovan would be the next bishop and he was actually the favoured candidate of the priests of the diocese. What really happened has never been clear,[37] but O'Donovan sounds a note of soreness on the procedure of episcopal appointments in *Waiting* when Fr Mahon admits his jealousy at having lost the appointment. Though the incident here hardly matches O'Donovan's own experience, it is interesting that he raises the issue at all;

> The greatest mistake of his [Fr Mahon's] life was fighting with the old bishop, Dr Murray. It made him popular with some of the Parish Priests and got him their votes at the election for bishop on the old man's death; but it gave him a bad name with the bishops of the province, who ignored the priests' votes, passed him over, and secured the appointment of Hannigan. He frowned at the memory of this, but, in a moment he laughed his harsh cackle and said aloud, 'Pooh, pooh, a man must be sensible'.[38]

Young as he was at 31 he had proven his capability, though in the quarters that mattered this was a decided disadvantage in view of his activism. The Vatican passed him over in favour of Dr O'Dea. Now O'Donovan found himself, though promoted to administrator, working for a man put in over his head. Matters were further exacerbated when O'Dea chose to live in Loughrea, rather than in Ballinasloe as Healy had. Very quickly relations between the two became difficult. They reached a crisis after O'Donovan's return from his IAOS expedition to America. His last baptism was in August 1904, and shortly after he left the priesthood: by December the new administrator was in office.

He went first to Dublin, and then to London, taking with him letters of introduction to various publishers from George Moore. How wise a policy this was is arguable in view of Moore's tempestuous relations with his publishers. Moore and O'Donovan had met on five or six occasions between 1887 and 1891. Writing to his brother Colonel Maurice Moore, in 1901, George described O'Donovan as 'one of the cleverest men in Ireland'.[39]

At this time he began to sign himself Gerald O'Donovan. From London, where he supported himself on the fringes of the publishing world, he tried to keep up his interest in the Gaelic League and IAOS. He was not re-elected to the *Coiste Gnótha* but he did represent Ireland at the first meeting of the Joint Board of the Co-operative Organisation with R.A. Anderson and Col. Everard. A conference of the Irish, English and Scottish organisations, it was held in Edinburgh in September 1908.[40] Soon after he resigned from the IAOS. He made the acquaintance of members of the London Society of the Irish Literary Society. He had been introduced to Yeats by George Russell of the IAOS. In the spring of 1910 he was appointed subwarden of Toynbee Hall, a Christian socialist educational institution in the east end of London.[41] In October 1910 he married Beryl Verschoyle. They met while both were the guests of Hugh Law, M.P., of Marble Hill, Co. Donegal. Her father, Colonel of the Duke of Cornwall's Light Infantry Regiment, was the eldest son of an English upper middle class family. Her mother was of the Church of Ireland. In the years to come, his wife's family was to provide much support for O'Donovan and his family. Three children were born, a son Dermot now (1986) living in Jersey, Bridget (deceased) and Mary who died tragically young.

In July 1911, O'Donovan left Toynbee Hall as his wife was beginning to find it too stressful. In 1911 he started writing *Father Ralph*. His mind was alive with ideas now. His writing provided a means for him of making sense of his unusual and painful experiences. Little is known of his parents' reaction to his departure from the priesthood, but the mother of Ralph disowned him. While some speculators in the novel decide he must have had an alcoholic problem others are convinced that he had 'perverted to Protestantism'. O'Donovan here is visibly trying to catch up on his recent experiences to define himself.

During the writing of the novel, he contributed three short sketches to the *Saturday Review*. The first 'An Irish Station' considers the plight of another broken-hearted country priest.[42] 'An Irish Marriage' deals with the crude economics of Irish marriage,[43] while 'An Irish Peasant' is a pathetic story of an old farmer who gives his land to his son to enable him to marry and is finally driven to the poorhouse by his daughter-in-law.[44]

Father Ralph appeared first in April 1913 and enjoyed six more printings by November 1914. 7,000 copies were printed in all.[45] It caused quite a sensation. Beryl recalls her delight at the daily pile of reviews and the 'flow' of introductions which 'gush' for every successful author. She recalls one review entitled 'Slime from an Irish Gutter' which amused him and which he liked to keep in his pocket.[46] Noting that the book had been banned by the Public Library of Belfast, on the proposal of a committee member, he assumed that a priest was responsible. He hoped that a few more of them would take action, presumably in order to boost sales.[47] They were now living at Northneps Cottage, near Cromer on the Norfolk Coast. He tells of Moore having wished to stay with them at Cromer and of his having discouraged it, as it would interfere with work on his own book.[48]

In 1913 Sidney Webb of the *New Statesman* wrote Horace Plunkett in search of 'brilliant well informed articles on Irish life'. He asked specially for 'AE', Rolleston, Hone and George Birmingham.[49] AE and Plunkett agreed that O'Donovan could cover the areas of the Roman Catholic Church and Education.[50] He did not, possibly because he was busy. In April 1914, *Waiting* appeared. It is a perceptively named book. It deals with the pain caused to a liberally-minded Irish nationalist who was married to a protestant, by the *Ne Temere* decree of 1907. The Vatican now ruled that all children of mixed marriages were to be brought up as Catholics, as distinct from the earlier custom where sons followed their father's religion and daughters their mother's.

In October 1916 he wrote to Beryl of his plans for a further book.[51] This would detail, 'as practically as these things can be done', his ideal vision of Ireland. He would represent conditions for which he hoped, but scarcely expected. In 1915 he had been granted a commission as first lieutenant in the service corps. Appointed to the depot of the Humber garrison at Hull, he was detailed to cater for the troops at the nearby village of Hornsea and had the job of organising houses and barracks for their accommodation. He was horrified to discover the exploitation in which the landlords engaged, particularly as they tried to profit from the war effort. He managed to reduce the cost of billeting troops locally from 4.5d to .33d.[52] Some time in late 1915 or early 1916 he was invalided out of the army.[53] In March 1916 he was employed by the ministry of munitions. He later satirized the petty officialdom and internal squabbling of the ministry in *How They Did It* (1920). During 1917 he worked with Collins publishers as a reader when Collins established a London office at Pall Mall. Geoffrey Collins's wife, Faith, had enthused about *Father Ralph* and understood that hundreds in the west end of London were reading it.[54] While with Collins, he published Mrs Humphry Ward, Henry James, Richard de Galliere and Francis Brett Young, among others. He intimated, interestingly, that he would not ask his contemporary Ulster novelist, Shan Bullock, for a book.[55]

In June 1918 he was appointed head of the Italian propaganda section of the Department of Foreign Affairs, where his wife's family connections were of use to him. But his character was too impassioned for the subtlety and compromise of diplomacy. Because he supported the independence of the subject nationalities of Austria and Hungary, he ruffled the feathers of Baron Sonnino, Italian foreign minister, who did not. This was compounded by his earlier reputation, so that his appointment was taken as an insult to the Roman Catholic Church in Italy. O'Donovan was apportioned some of the blame for the unpopularity of Sonnino. Though his shortlived diplomatic career was not a success it is more surprising that it was so quiet. It was during this period that he first met Rose Macaulay. They shared an interest in writing and enjoyed each other's wit. She became his secretary in Italy and fell in love with him.[56] Rose was an independent woman who was not anxious to marry.

Returning to London the O'Donovans met with hard times. He found well paid work hard to come by, though they continued to mix in a literary circle which included Dorothy Lamb (cousin of Rupert Brooke), Walter de la Mare, Dominic Spring-Rice (a journalist at the *Morning Post*), Mary Agnes Hamilton (later a Labour M.P.), Arnold Bennett, Yeats, Aldous Huxley, Edith Sitwell and Storm Jameson (who described the group as 'an urbane backwater of the literary establishment').[57]

In 1920 *Conquest* was published. All his life his imagination was preoccupied by the problems of Ireland. He is saddened by the position of Ireland down to 1919 and the grief caused by the narrowness of politics.

> Would love, the solvent, ever do for them what it had done for her and her husband?[58]

In a letter to Beryl he described the 1916 rising as 'a tragic comedy' but that the foolish rebels were 'otherwise a good sort' and that Birrell was the most absurd figure in a generally ridiculous government.[59] Norryes O'Conor of the *Boston Evening Transcript* and later author of *Literary Backgrounds of the Irish Free State* (1924), described *Conquest* as a potential '*Uncle Tom's Cabin*' and brought to his readers' attention the impression created by O'Donovan: that though complicated by religion, the Irish problem was not fundamentally a religious issue.[60] O'Donovan exerted enormous influence over Rose Macaulay and her literary work. In 1920, *Potterism*, her satire on the popular press, became a best seller both in Britain and the USA. As work was scarce in London the O'Donovans moved to Italy for a short while again. During these years he published *How They Did It* (1920), *Vocations* (1921) and *The Holy Tree* (1922).

In *Vocations* he assembles many of his strong criticisms of the convent system in Ireland. He describes the convent schools where girls are taught embroidery and piano but are given no practical or technical instruction, and are earmarked from a very young age for a 'vocation' by devoted mothers and not given a chance to experience the world. Earlier in an article entitled 'Dishonouring Irish Saints', he had expressed a gripe against nuns for neglecting the names of Irish saints. He attributed this to the fact that many convents were set up by French nuns who had an affection for England since she protected them during the revolutionary wars.[61] In *Vocations* he treats also the taboo subject of the emotional and sexual attractions of priests and nuns.

The Holy Tree is a psychological study of a woman's escape from an unhappy marriage into a doomed love. He is here obviously frustrated by the church's ruling on the indissolubility of marriage. It is strange that one with such liberal ideas and strong emotional attachments should not have made a complete break with catholicism. In *Waiting*, Maurice Blake cannot bring himself to accept the practical advice of a journalist friend to ignore the rules laid down by the Vatican. The traditional and emotional pull to submit to the church, however uncomfortable, is stronger than his desire for marital happiness. Grace in *The Holy Tree* is based on his close friend Rose Macaulay.

Plunkett during the 1920s tried to help his old colleague out with work for the IAOS. He employed him as his agent to search in the USA for a rich patron to endow a research centre for the co-op movement, and also to oversee the publication of some of Plunkett's articles in the *New York Outlook*. O'Donovan failed to engage a suitable millionaire and returned to London in 1928 to work as Plunkett's private secretary. In his diary, Plunkett soon wrote: 'He would not do me permanently as I have not and never shall have enough of his confidence. I don't know him'.[62]

In her short story 'Miss Anstruther's Letters' written, when after World War II bombs had destroyed her flat, and all his letters to her, Rose Macaulay reveals how deep her affections were for him. Her precise relationship to him is more difficult to explain as he stayed with his wife and children, but Rose was a frequent visitor, godmother to his son's child, and a travelling companion of his daughter. O'Donovan stopped writing in 1922, or at least never published any more. He still remained on friendly terms with George Moore. When Moore requested his services as a biographer, however, O'Donovan refused with the excuse that they were too close. O'Donovan believed that Moore used friends to his advantage, and remembered that while he was an editor with Collins during 1917, Moore visited him particularly often.[63] He did however help Hone on the details of the biography. There is much to suggest that had O'Donovan undertaken the work, a far less flattering biography would have emerged.[64]

What O'Donovan worked at between the wars is not clear, even to his children. His daughter Brigid recalls him 'lying on a sofa all afternoon reading his way through the *Cambridge Ancient History* and endless detective stories, one a day.'[65] In 1938 the O'Donovans became involved with helping Czech refugees, this time more successfully than in his earlier effort with the diplomatic service.

On June 26, 1939 while he was on a holiday in the Lake District with Rose Macaulay, both were involved in an accident in which he fractured his skull. His already failing health never recovered from this serious blow. During a long illness, he passed the time by reading Somerville and Ross and George Moore. On July 26 1942, he died of cancer at the age of 71. He was buried in Albany, Surrey where he had lived for some years, presumably supported by his wife's family. A fortnight later, Rose Macaulay, writing as 'a friend', published a short obituary note in *The Times*. She concluded with a telling personal note; 'To know him was to love him'.[66] Beryl died in 1968.

Section Two: Ireland — National Identity, Religion And Land

This section identifies the authors' attitudes to nationality, religion and land. What criteria did these writers apply when examining Irish identity? What assumptions did they hold about national origins? How did they distinguish between the various inhabitants of the island? What shape subsequently did their nationalism take? By what was it inspired? How serious were they about Irish independence? What did they expect for the Ireland of the future?

Daniel Corkery in 1920 asked:

> Who can name a novel dealing adequately with their religious consciousness? Yet this religious consciousness is so vast, so deep, so dramatic, even so terrible a thing, occasionally creating wreckage in its path, tumbling the weak things over, that when one begins to know it, one wonders if it is possible for a writer to deal with any phase whatever of Irish life without trenching upon it .... We may perhaps know that genuine Anglo-Irish literature has come into being when at every hand's turn that religious consciousness breaks in upon it, no matter what the subject ....[1]

George Birmingham, remarking in 1919 on a survey of Mass attendance carried out a year previously in Britain, observed that no one would ever think of it in Ireland: 'the figures would not be worth the trouble to get them'.[2] How integral a part of the national make-up was Catholicism seen to be by these writers? What role do they see religion as playing in the lives of their parishioners? What ideas had they about how a priest should behave and what was expected of him? How did the priest suppose he was seen by the community? Were they happy with the structures of the church? How are bishops depicted? How is the question of anti-clericalism treated?

How many classes did these writers notice in the country? How were they identified? What did they think of the land movement and the social changes of the late 19th and early 20th centuries? What of the texture of everyday Irish life? How are economic matters treated? What of emigration?

4: Sheehan's Ireland

In the general European intellectual context of these years, Sheehan shares much ground with some of the French reactionary thinkers. His guiding mission was to recall the grace and nobility of the last century and more importantly of the eighteenth century. His instinct told him that these values, however, were receding to say the least. He took it upon himself to recall his personal vision of this grand age to inspire all Europeans, and the Irish especially, into reversing the tide of the modern.

The tension between the progressive and the conservative in Sheehan is also peculiar. Like some of his contemporary intellectuals on the continent, he was concerned with the notion of degeneration and progress and had a longing for the recall of some half understood notion of an idyllic past, of grace and stability and grandeur. When this notion of degeneration versus regeneration is applied to the Irish context, his notions become quite tangled. Sheehan tacked a most peculiar line in his approach to national identity. Though he traded liberally off the by now familiar myths and stereotypes of Irishman, he used them as best he could, both for larger purposes and because in many ways he had no choice. While his higher reason suggested to him that it may be unhealthy and even unchristian to have such a strong, absolute, strict image of national identity, the context in which he was writing shaped the figures on his pages. Though Luke Delmege announced that 'only a sheet of tissue paper separated the two races', this attitude is uncharacteristic of the mainstream image of Irishman throughout the corpus of Sheehan's work. The author of all the other works 'always believed that we are a race apart'.[3]

His first attempt at a novel *Geoffrey Austin: Student* (1895), marks an early attempt to break away from stereotype, 'from peasants and policeman' and to set his drama in urban Ireland where he believed 'the best material for Irish fiction lay still untouched'.[4] It marks Sheehan's conscious dissociation from what he called the 'mawkish and ridiculous sentimentality which is so revolting to Catholic instincts'.[5] Apart from the fact that it did not sell, it was in due course as much as hailed as an example of the author's *shoneen* bent by Hogan, then professor of modern languages at Maynooth.[6]

Sheehan himself maintained that the book had been a target of a vicious conspiracy which tried to stop the work from ever reaching print.[7] Because it was a hard hitting critique of the lack of proper religious teaching in Irish schools, it is hardly surprising that it was greeted with some hostility from clerical quarters. Hogan was quick to check Sheehan for the use of un-Irish names in his novels, accusing him of being 'influenced by the vitiated taste of the public', of ridiculing the image of Irishman, and reminded him of his mission to educate and reform.[8]

Another of his clerical critics, the Jesuit mentor Matthew Russell, later warned him against this type of cosmopolitan experiment: 'Remember the holier you are and the more Irish, the better literature comes from you'.[9] And in an otherwise encouraging review of a collection of Sheehan's philosophical reflections, he put it rather more strongly: 'I object to the idea that Canon Sheehan gives of the Irish people, it is not like the people at all .... He pleases English critics too much .... The *Westminster Gazette* says very truly "Canon Sheehan does not like the Irish character"'.[10]

There is evidence in his work of a disdain for 'the Irish character'. In *My New Curate* (1899) he nods knowingly with the comment of a local landlord of Anglo-Irish stock, when he admits 'I have never been able to shake off a feeling of contempt for these poor, uneducated serfs: And their little cunning ways and want of manliness have always disgusted me'.[11]

But this daring revisionist attitude toward 'Irishness' is engulfed in his more popular and better crafted fiction as he bows to the convenient, familiar stereotypes and myths to which fiction readers had become accustomed. In effect, he takes the stage Irishman, modifies him only slightly, and proceeds to identify his peculiar features as precious heirlooms of the Celtic spirit. Though he does not always automatically approve of the uniquely Irish characteristics which he observes, yet somehow owing to their Celtic origin, they seem to be acceptable and forgiven.

His Celt-derived Irishmen are uniformly fatalistic,[12] impulsive and curious,[13] hot tempered,[14] irresponsible with language,[15] embarrassed by silence,[16] naturally poetic and philosophical,[17] capable of the most stupendous sacrifices provided they are out of the common,[18] and the ultimate test: 'No one is a real Celt who would not enjoy hiding under a stone wall on the summit of some Irish mountain, and watching for a whole day the rain blowing up in sheets across the heather'.[19]

The question of the origin and spirit of the race is of course central here. It is obviously not the Irish peasantry which he is trying to convince when he explains:

> Celticism is the cry of the spirit, heard of old in our lonely woods
> and forests, and along our lakes and meres, until the southern

Celticism, breathed upon us, and substituted a more subtle spiritual-
ism for its pagan predecessor, without, however, altogether eliminating the latter.[20]

The more closely he lists the identification marks of the Celt, however,
the more obvious it becomes that he is using his melancholy, reflective
self as a model;

It is the Celtic impulse to get away at all costs from an unendurable
present and to bury the imagination in an ideal past. The Celtic soul
dreads the future and hates novelty .... I doubt if there would be a
word more detestable in the ears of a true Celt than modern progress.[21]

Sheehan shows the Irish as a homogeneous, uniform race. He scarcely
ever draws distinction between the 'Celtic' Irish and the non-Celtic Irish
but assumes that the reader will know whom he means when he refers to
'the Irish people'. It is noteworthy that while the cultural boundaries in his
novels are delicately inoffensive, they are in his pamphlets far more
distinct. Here in 'Our Personal and Social Responsibilities' he urges
Catholics to be more assertive in commerce;

In the agricultural districts, Englishmen and Scotchmen are rapidly
realizing fortunes, where the native peasantry earned a pittance; and
in our great cities, enterprising foreigners are swallowing up com-
mercial wealth.[22]

Sheehan's real worry is that the Celtic gene pool is becoming danger-
ously diluted. It appeared to him however that this was not so much directly
caused by physical interaction or intermarriage, but by the influence of
foreign magazines, novelettes, the songs of the London music hall, and
letters from America.

The Anglo-Irish have a consistently foreign, unhomely air about them.
They appear usually to brighten the plot or as a foil to highlight characteristics or reactions of the native Irish. Of course their Protestantism holds
undying fascination for the author as he plots the most efficient way to
convert them.

However, he was loathe to touch those romantic features of the peasant
which he saw as virtuous — their childlike devotion to the soggarth and
their easy, blurred philosophy of life. His escape world of nineteenth
century literature and world view was, and he knew it himself, a little
far-fetched to be entertained as a viable alternative to the grainy and
rock-hard texture of life around Doneraile. The peasant had many virtues
for Sheehan, which he is quick to list. Ironically, their most endearing

quality is their legacy of the 'peasant mentality' of the nineteenth century. Sheehan feels all this threatened by change, however.

Against this he posed the option of a more vigorous regenerative thinking man, who sought to better his environment and his mind, who was eager to discuss the finer points of religion and still go to Mass every Sunday. His own rationale was remarkably quirky. It is obvious, though always implicit in his writing, that he knew that this transformation was too much to ask for and at times he seems almost grateful for this. Yet time and time again he does ask for it, and then each time recoils, shuddering at the thought. When the issue of a National University was burning, one might expect Sheehan to be in favour of the idea *per se*:

> I am always dreaming of an Irish youth, silent, modest, reserved, reading much, talking little, and trying to bring into daily life some of the graces of civilization. But I am not hopeful. Everyone seems so anxious to rush into print and speak so dogmatically on every subject. Of course infallibility is the privilege of youth: but, what shall we do when the new university turns out three or four thousand such lay popes?[23]

Though he wished for a thinking nation he had very selective ideas about how he wanted it to think. He spoke with loathing of the 'elephantine hooves of democracy' which since the French revolution 'have been trampling out all the beauty and sweetness of life'.[24]

> I am a democrat, a strong advocate of the theory that it is a crime against not only the individual, but against the race, to impede the development of talent, or deprive a whole people of the means of pushing forward on the onward march towards ....
>
> But here the Doctor paused. He was brought up face to face with the sudden question — what was the end to which the race was tending? But he doubled back like a wise man.[25]

In terms of nationalism he felt that the movement once holy and beautiful had degenerated from heroic Fenianism to platform-stomping demagogues. It is most curious that he should exalt the Fenians as saints while never stopping to think of what their ultimate aims were in a free Ireland. They are for Sheehan the utter antithesis of the present nationalist movement. They are heroic because they ignore reality and look to the spiritual. The very absurdity of their pose is their insignia as true Irish rebels.[26]

> Many of them who had been ploughing through life in a broken backed, weary manner, were suddenly stiffened and strengthened into some kind of unnatural vigour, their eyes gleaming with expec-

tancy, as they stood there in the dim light .... There stood a steady
light of their determination, as of men who had deliberately staked
all on some desperate issue, and were fully prepared to abide by the
result.[27]

It was the nobility and idealism which he saw as central to the old-fashioned nineteenth century nationalism which attracted him, and which
made him hope that the same abstract, futile, and safely inept patriotism
would energize future generations of Irishmen. Its function? To preserve
a spirit of sacrifice and civic pride. For Sheehan, and for all his favourite
rebels, 'Ireland' was 'that mysterious motherland for whom all this was
patiently endured'.[28] It was certainly not just a collection of fields and
towns, nor of people, and neither was it to be reduced to a mere politi-
cal/constitutional issue.

One outstanding difference he sees in the new modernizing breed of
Irishman around him is the lessening of national selfconsciousness owing
to emigration and easier communication with the outside world. *Glenanaar* (1905) especially is a celebration of the sturdy peasant values of
prefamine Ireland, which Sheehan imagines included a general honesty,
loyalty and devotion to the motherland;

> And all [conversation and thought] then was limited between the
> four seas of Ireland. America had not yet been discovered, and the
> imagination never travelled beyond the circle of the seas. And so
> there was nothing but Ireland to talk about, nothing but Ireland
> interesting; the Ireland of the past so dark, so tragical; the Ireland of
> the future so uncertain and problematical.[29]

Whilst he claims then that he is not blind to the follies and drawbacks
of the past,[30] yet he 'cannot help thinking that those times were greater
than ours'.[31] It is curious then that alongside his idealisation of the old
peasantry, he should write a novel like *Glenanaar*. Here he details so
closely the harsh punishments dealt to an informer that he barely sup-
presses his admiration for it:

> 'Some people are now gettin' so tindher-hearted that they'll sin Turk,
> Jew, and atheist to heaven. But no wan ever in his right sinses could
> forgive an informer. We have forgot Keogh, and Scorpion Sullivan,
> and the rest of their dirty thribe, but we haven't forgot, though we
> never mintion their names, a Corydon, a Nagle, or a Carey!'[32]

Nowhere does he outrightly condemn their grudgery: 'They feel a kind of
pride and glory in their vindictiveness. It is a remnant, like a cromlech or dolmen,
of that ancient paganism that was so ruthless and uncompromising'.[33]

In 1909 he objected to 'the spirit of the Gaelic League' for its subversion
of the nationalism of his youth:

> By throwing the thoughts of the young in to the far perspective of
> years, it has deliberately blotted out the whole of the nineteenth
> century, '98, '48 and '67, and by the scorn it has cast upon what it
> is pleased to call Anglo-Irish writers, it has wiped out from the
> memory of men such names as Grattan, Flood, Emmet, Tone, Davis,
> Duffy, Mitchell, Martin, Kickham and the rest.'[34]

Despite Sheehan's claims to nationalism he never really wanted it to
work out. When it looked like it was going to work out the idea depressed
him. He had no notion of how an independent Ireland might be governed.
Indeed there is some sense in which he probably saw this as an irrelevance.
In 1904 his old school pal William O'Brien moved to live near Skibbereen
and visited Sheehan regularly. Both of them deplored the activities of the
Irish Parliamentary Party, Sheehan noting that 'political expediency has
taken the place of political morality'.[35] O'Brien won Sheehan's sympathy
for his Cork based All-for-Ireland League which urged the co-operation
of all Irishmen in mapping out a scheme of self-government, and encouraged him to contribute anonymously two lengthy and strongly worded
articles to the first issue of his *Cork Free Press* in October 1910.

This phase in Sheehan's political opinion seems to mark an about face
to the bold 'Fenian' views he had put forward in his fiction and to his
belligerent attitude toward Protestants. When Sheehan analyses, in the first
of these articles the nationalist movement of the last twenty five years, it
turns out in fact to be a tour de force of self-analysis, or at least of the self
of his fiction. He chides nationalists for rejecting practical measures
toward independence because they are too blinkered into wanting one
apocalyptic day of freedom and also because nationalism, he suggests, was
an essential part of their way of life and culture so that they could not
conceive of life without it:

> Whatever measure you can agree upon between yourselves — be it
> land measures, education or even home rule, I, George Wyndham,
> promise with the aid of my conservative government, and with the
> house of lords at my back to pass it into an act of parliament.' Was
> the offer accepted? Of course not. We wanted a little more fighting,
> a little more speechmaking, a little more hunting after will-o'-the-
> wisps, a little more blind trusting in the promise 'To-morrow, and
> to-morrow, and to-morrow!' And we are further than ever from
> national independence today .... A goose does not like to be plucked

but the people like to be deceived. And let them be deceived.[36]

Here he argues for a policy of conference and conciliation. Commenting on his outpouring, to Oliver Wendell Holmes, his American confidante and admirer, he writes:

> I have been for the last few months here in Ireland in a state of silent fury against the insolent domination of the Irish Parliamentary party and their attempt to swamp out all political freedom. At last I was forced to speak, and send you two articles commenting on our political situation, and in favour of a new movement to establish political liberty and break down the barriers between Protestants and Catholics in this country. But whilst I would resent any attempt to interfere with my principles or convictions in political and social matters, or to restrict my freedom in any way, whenever the eternal speaks (and everyday I am becoming more overwhelmed with a sense of his omnipresence) either through direct inspiration or through the Vicariate he has established on this little planet of ours, I am a little child.[37]

Along with this, however, Sheehan did involve himself before and after the Wyndham land act in the business of ensuring that the local changes in ownership were done peacefully and properly; 'it is a league for the pacification of the country by combining Irishmen of all creeds in the cause of their common native land'.[38] By means of Sunday meetings he interpreted the act and gave advice and information to the would-be land owners. In any case Sheehan's contributions to the *Cork Free Press* stopped abruptly. According to the memoirs of O'Brien's wife, Sheehan did not explain the reason and no more was said on the subject.[39] It may have been about this time that he wrote to his friend Russell: 'I think the time is coming when I shall have to say in poetry, all that I want to say'.[40]

Also in his letters he reveals a definite revulsion against Home Rule. Writing to his good friend Daniel Kelleher in 1913, he mentions the excitement and nervousness caused by the expectation of Home Rule and finishes by saying 'but we are on the path of progress and nothing can turn us back'.[41] To his good friend Holmes he writes: 'it will be the worst for Ireland since the act of union'.[42] He could never come to terms with any form of government based on popular rule, as this would inevitably induce a vulgar, ignorant society: 'And who is going to work or fight, my friends, for that abstraction, called Humanity? Not I!'[43]

He cannot abide any thought of a nationalism which might threaten the clerical monopoly. In *My New Curate* he shows how a group of local rebels

are unconsciously influenced by anti-Catholic agencies from the continent
— Jews and Freemasons, when in the interests of Irish independence, they
defy the protective advice of the clergy;

> Lead will do what fine speeches didn't. And if the black militia, wid
> dere ordhers from Rome, attimpt this time to interfere, we know what
> answer to give dem. De West's awake, and 'tisn't priests will set us
> to sleep agin.[44]

An interesting confrontation ensues when Fr Letheby breaks up the
secret meeting of the nationalist conspirators;

> 'The priests are always agin the people', said one keen-looking
> fellow who had been abroad.

> 'That's an utter falsehood', said Fr Letheby, 'and you know it. You
> know that priests and people for seven hundred years have fought side
> by side the battle of Ireland's freedom from civil and religious disabili-
> ties .... You are a constant terror to your mothers and sisters — and all
> at the dictation of a few scoundrels, who are receiving secret service
> money from the government, and a few newspapers that are run by
> Freemasons and Jews.'

> ... 'All the great Continental papers are the property of Freemasons
> and Jews; all the rancour and bitterness stirred up against the church
> for the past fifty years has been their work'.[45]

When Daddy Dan pointed out to Letheby that the same forms of
anti-Catholicism 'namely, the dissemination of pornographic literature'
are at work in Ireland, Letheby grew very quiet;

> As I [the older priest] notice all Irish priests grow grave when this
> awful fact is made plain to them. It is so easy to look at things without
> seeing them. Then, as the full revelation of this new diablerie dawned
> upon him, he grew very angry.[46]

This could be cited as evidence of Sheehan's paranoia about the
modern. It is interesting that Sheehan should find it necessary to *expose*
such agents of anti-clericalism, of anti-religion and of the modern, to what
he saw perhaps as the over-secure clergy who came to his tales looking
merely for light amusement. Sheehan's fear of the modern, however, and
of anti-clericalism which he sees as an integral part of it, is very real. Luke
Delmege explains how the British writer opens the floodgates;

> When he is not shrieking 'Oh heavens', or '*Ay de mi*' he is ridiculing
> the simulacrum of a pope, or screaming about an imaginary 'dirty,
> muddy minded Irish priest', who is supposed to have disturbed the by
> no means normal equanimity of 'his goody'.

What is the result? Voters become smitten by the virus and madness of bigotry; then statesmen are influenced, and Acts of Parliament passed, and the whole thing is liberty and progress.[47]

He is utterly convinced from his first to his last novel that the primary shared ambition of both the 'false liberalism' and the 'orators of socialism'[48] is to subvert the element of the supernatural. One of his later novels was completely devoted to this subject. The heroine of *Miriam Lucas* comes around eventually, after an horrific Dublin strike, to his understanding that the socialist doctrines to which she had subscribed had caused far more problems than they could ever solve:

> She had forced herself to think that it was this perpetual insistence upon eternity, this perpetual undervaluing of time, that was keeping the masses in subjection. Lo! what an evil crop had arisen from a too busy pen.[49]

Sheehan's views form an unusual exhibit of the romantic nationalism of the Young Ireland movement learned at his mother's knee, the highmind-edness of the victorian social critics, a terror of the modern and, amidst all this, a remarkably sane compassion which affords him the occasional grasp of the complexities of sectarian nationalism. Judging by his fiction he was a regressive thinker rather than a visionary, but his more intimate letters and comments in the last few years of his life indicate that he was won over to the peaceful, practical and unfashionable conciliatory policy of O'Brien. While Sheehan may have been swayed by his old pal it is more likely that he lent his support to the All-For-Ireland League because it was the 'outsider' denouncing the 'established' parliamentary party.

Sheehan's identification of Catholicism with Irishness, although every-where in his fiction, is never explicitly stated. In his outspoken article of 1899, however, 'Our Personal and Social Responsibilities', he reports that:

> Irish Catholicism and Irish nationality are interchangeable terms. The one means the other. So true is this, that English converts to Catholicity are known to their compatriots as Irish, so completely wound up is one idea with the other.[50]

He rejoices in the superstitious nature of the peasantry as he finds it consoling to see any old tradition still alive.[51] He has one of the intellec-tuals in the book of that name identify 'the Gaelic race' by its desperate insistence on the operation of the supernatural:

> There's the exact difference between the Gael and the Gall. We believe the supernatural is all around us, that we are immersed in it, surrounded by it, and that it is continually breaking through the thin veil of material

existence, and showing itself to us. When it fails to do so, we go half
way towards it, and clamour for its manifestation.[52]

While he was one of a small minority in clerical quarters of the time
who questioned the condition of Irish catholicism, and was supportive of
the original thrust of the Maynooth Union as a forum of preparation for
challenges in the twentieth century, he was on the whole paternalistic in
his attitudes to the hierarchy of priest and people. He saw the present clergy
as having degenerated from the strong patriotic men of before, to the
contemporary 'coffee drinking, encyclopedic young fellows'. Though he
had many reservations, at the end of the day he was firm in seeing the role
of the priest as the keeper of law, order, and morality.

Sheehan was unusual in bemoaning, or even in recognizing, the slack-
ness and mechanical devotion of many Catholics. Bravely he reveals his
worries about the fragility and inbuilt hypocrisy of the Irish religious
consciousness:

> When I give Holy Communion with you, Sir, on Sunday morning
> [the new curate tells Daddy Dan], my heart melts at the seraphic
> tenderness with which they approach the altar. That striking of the
> breast, that eager look on their faces, and that 'Cead Mile Failte, O
> Thierna!' make me bless God for such a people; but then they appear
> to be waiting for the last words of the *de Profundis*, to jump up and
> run from the church as if in a panic.[53]

> We have amongst us a good many pretty pieties; in fact we are
> bewildered by all these luxuries of devotion ... you have nice
> prayer-books now, in velvet and ivory bindings; but have you the
> melodious and poetic prayers of men and women who never learned
> to write a line ... For beneath these old silvered heads were brains
> that knew and penetrated, by divine faith, into every mystery of our
> holy religion.[54]

The idealisation of the religion of the old people is of course yet another
manifestation of Sheehan's recall to the past. Generally, though he sees
the shortcomings in the religious attitudes of the laity, he realises too that
the situation could be a lot worse. Early in his literary career he lamented
how the upwardly mobile Catholics identified Catholicism with poverty
and backwardness. The French student of *Geoffrey Austin* points out a few
home truths to one of them:

> You boast of the antiquity of your faith, but you are ashamed of it.
> Your semi-educated professional and middle classes would be
> ashamed to be seen at a confessional. In your hotels, not one in a

> hundred would dare make the sign of the cross before meals, in your
> conversation the name of God is never mentioned, and religious subjects
> are strictly forbidden. You pare down and minimize the teachings of
> your church to suit Protestant prejudices.[55]

The issue of the sectarian divide is prominent in most of these novels.
Sheehan is characteristically unsure of his attitudes towards Protestants
and to the relationship of the two communities. Consistently, however, he
shows his frustrations with the diffidence and timidity of Catholics in their
approach towards Protestants. His anger is softened by the knowledge that
he is prone to it himself. He sadly recognizes that he must at least seem to
flow with the tide. He uses in *Dr Gray*, the incident where the old priest
tutors two local Protestant boys in the classics to bring the politics of the
issue to a point:

> The report of what he had done had spread from end to end of the
> parish, and was canvassed with suppressed, but intense, disapproval.
> It was unprecedented and, therefore intolerable. When had he done
> anything for poor Catholic lads? What Catholic boy had he got into
> a situation that would help him and his family on in the world? He
> was always denouncing Protestantism; and now he opens his house
> to two Protestant lads to train them in those classical studies that were
> far beyond the reach of Catholic boys. Where his consistency?
> Where his principle?[56]

Sheehan knows that he must finally submit to the established values or
prejudices of his congregation. Unconsciously however, he highlights the
tendency of Catholics to worship any Protestant who seems to identify
with them. The kindly Claire Moulton of The Big House in *Lisheen* was
'worshipped all the more because she was English and Protestant; and
because, disdaining the gee-gaws of London fashion, she dressed in the
plain skirt and bodice of the natives.'[57]

Though it is interesting that occasionally he offers to see the issue
through Protestant eyes, his attempts are uniformly crude and lazy. The
incredibly humane heroine of *Miriam Lucas* is horrified to discover an
ingrained Protestant prejudice towards catholics;

> 'In that case, Madame, Papists, as you say, are never allowed into
> good' — she gulped down the word — 'Society?'
> 'Never!' said Madame B-, dogmatically. 'Or if ever,' she said,
> settling her hands more comfortably in her muff. 'On account of their
> accidental wealth, or other circumstance, they are merely tolerated,
> never assimilated. But ask your guardian about these things. He

understands them so much better than I.'[58]

The much younger author of *The Triumph of Failure* was even more dogmatic in his understanding of the Irish Protestant psyche. To the question 'Why cannot we get together?' he puppets a most unlife-like Protestant to reply: 'Because we cannot lose our traditions, or change our natures because you are helots ... your servility always repels us. And we hold you in the palms of our hands. Every office in the country worth holding is with us.'[59]

Concurrently, he uses the same specimen Protestant to notice one of the author's most constant worries:[60]'I never yet met a Protestant who was not anxious to talk religion, nor a Catholic who was not anxious to avoid it. Why?'[61]The oversmug answer of the author betrays his panic: 'Because we are so secure of our religion, it does not interest us. You know there must be doubt in order to create interest.'[62]

A later examination of the sectarian issue, again, leads him back to an appeal for the return of feudalism: magnanimously he draws attention to some idyllic arrangements in the west of Ireland where interaction of the two communities runs perfectly:

> In many places along the western coast, a solitary Englishman and his family are often the only Protestants in parishes of three or four thousand Irish Catholics; and, for the most part, they are idolized by the people around. Having no landed interest, they are not concerned about dragging out the vitals of the poor farming population; they often establish valuable industries, inconceivable to the unenterprising Celt; they give liberal English wages; they are benevolent and humane; and they assume a kind of feudal sovereignty, which a people, accustomed to feudal traditions, most readily acknowledge.[63]

Indeed the building of such a community is the happy parting scene of *Lisheen*. Considering that *The Intellectuals* is a self-confessed and contrived fantasy, it is no surprise that the difficulties of Catholic/Protestant relations are effortlessly solved:

> Protestants and Catholics in this country are much like the two old ladies whom a mischievous youngster introduced to each other as stone-deaf; and who yelled and yelled until at last one said, *sotto voce*, 'You're not deaf are you?' and the other, surprised, answered 'Certainly not, are you?'[64]

What is most curious is Sheehan's detour around any explanation of this forked attitude of the community towards Protestants. Though it

plainly annoys him that many Catholics are 'half-ashamed' of their religion, he shudders to inquire into it.[65]Unwittingly, he leaves room for
conclusion that the air of inferiority and obsequiousness of Catholics in
relation to Protestants was as integral a part of being Irish and Catholic,
as it was necessarily never to be acknowledged.Yet, again, in 'Our
Personal and Social Responsibilities' (1899) he speaks his mind:

> However glaring may be these [sectarian] injustices, we cannot fail
> to see that in some respects, we are responsible for them. Our
> supineness and apathy, which we are careful to euphemise as tolera-
> tion, militate against our advancement, and confirm our history in
> our own land.[66]

In the same article he introduces 'the Presbyterians of the north' as an
alien, inhuman army: 'a compact, perfectly united, well disciplined body,
thoroughly organised and moving with the precision of a machine at the
beck or command of their leaders'.[67]

Earlier in *Luke Delmege* he had juxtaposed a savage picture of the 'loud,
blatant, progressives of Belfast' on an intoxicated holiday in Portrush with
a pretty picture of innocent humans picnicking in Crosshaven. This
species, moreover, is human enough to have children — 'a happy, bright,
refined crowd; no hustling or jostling; but Celtic politeness and Celtic wit
and humour'.[68] All Sheehan's Protestants are depicted as temporary
fixtures and are decidedly not part of Irish reality. They are there to be
converted, reformed and eventually nationalised. Their place in the new
state is not examined by Sheehan, but then there is a lurking sense in which
Sheehan neither wanted nor expected an independent Ireland.

Inevitably, a great part of these novels has to do specifically with
clerical life, and for Sheehan and Guinan, almost every aspect of life is
filtered through an individual but basically clerical lens. One of Sheehan's
recurrent themes is the tension between the ways of the older clergy and
the ideas of the 'new', more liberal priests — 'the mighty yet silent
revolution that is progressing in the Irish church'.[69] In his three predominantly clerical novels he tries to come to terms with the changing clerical
order. In the first of these, *My New Curate*, he tries to place what he sees
as the new modernising breed of clergy in context by analysing their
clerical ancestry. These ancestors he divides in two. The first he describes
as 'those polished studious, timid priests,' who, educated in continental
seminaries, had 'a slight compromising tendency' on political matters
owing to their experience of the revolution and Napoleonic wars. 'Slightly

tinged with Gallican ideas, they hated progress and the troubles that always accompany it'.[70] This appreciation seems rather plain when compared with the sketch of the following generation with which incidentally Sheehan identifies himself. These are the priests who protected Irish Catholicism through the perilous Famine years and after.

> Then came Maynooth, which ... poured from its gates the strongest, fiercest, most fearless army of priests that ever fought for the spiritual and temporal interests of the people ... intense in their faith, of stainless lives and spotless reputations, their words cut like razors, and their hands smote like lightning .... In theology they were rigorists ... they had a cordial dislike for new devotions .... I am quite sure they have turned somersaults in their graves since the introduction of the myriad devotions that are now distracting and edifying the faithful. But they could make, and, alas! too often for Christian modesty, they did make, the proud boast that they kept alive the people's faith and imbued them with a sense of the loftiest morality.[71]

His conclusions then on the emerging generation are interesting especially in view of his later opinions:

> Clean-cut, small of stature, keen-faced, bicycle-riding, coffee-drinking, encyclopedic young fellows, who will give a good account of themselves, I think, in the battle of the near future ... they laugh profanely at the aureole of distinction that used hang around the heads of successful students, declaring that a man's education only commences when he leaves college ... and they speak dreadful things about evolution and modern interpretation, and the new hermeneutics and polychrome bibles.[72]

Too glibly he concludes that 'with all my ancient prejudice in favour of my own caste, I see clearly that the equipment of the new generation are best suited to modern needs.'[73]

It is obvious even at this early stage of Sheehan's writing that it is precisely because these younger priests recognise and equip themselves for the 'ugly' modern, that Sheehan cannot fully identify with them. The issue, however, does not clearly end here. Through *Luke Delmege* (1901) and *The Blindness of Dr Gray* (1901) and *The Graves at Kilmorna* (1915), which has as much to do with spirituality as it has to do with Irish politics and nationalism, there runs the same question of choosing between the rigid but safe ways of the old priest and the more flexible but dangerous ways of the new breed. Delmege is recalled ultimately to the old way, having had his 'fling' with the new, but his questions lie frustratingly unresolved.

The character of Dr Gray is a curious mix of the various moods of Sheehan's conscience. On one hand he represents the God-like authority of Canon Law and jansenistic priestliness. He chastises his new curate, Henry Liston, for over-familiarity with the people just as Daddy Dan had done in *My New Curate*. The dignity of the priestly office was a prime point of concern for Sheehan. Daddy Dan was asked to remark in dry tones of experience: 'As if any priest ever went down in language or habit to the people's level who didn't go considerably below it'.[74]

The enthusiasm of Liston in *The Blindness of Dr Gray* receives the same damper:

> But I must tell you at once, and emphatically, that I gravely disapprove of many things I have been witnessing. They may not be sinful, or wrong; but they are unpriestly: ... there was first your order, yes, order, to your pastor to paint and paper your house in an outlandish fashion. Here then are books that should not be seen on a priest's shelf — German romance, German nonsense, a poor substitute for the theology of the Church.[75]

However, this literature is condemned ironically rather for its realism than for its romance: 'there again is its art ... this literature, aping a wisdom which it does not understand, or dealing with subjects that reveal the deformities and baseness, instead of the sacredness and nobility, of the race'.[76]

Here Sheehan is obviously struggling to see the nature of his own sin as an artist: 'But I have the right to indulge in secret a certain morbid if enlightened taste for such forbidden things, that if I were to utter them from the pulpit, I should be stripped of my priesthood and silenced forever'.[77] The argument against the intellectual habits of the young curates, with whom in fact one rebellious side of Sheehan identifies, is that it distances them from 'the plain people': 'An unwise thing for a young man! For he who sups with the Olympians will find it hard to breakfast with *boulevardiers'*.[78]

The stern side of his consciousness then dictates that the priest must at all costs appear dignified and must read only 'some good moral theology books and scripture commentaries'. 'All that rubbish — prose and poetry', (which incidentally the author meticulously copied into his commonplace book), should be taken to the stable-yard and burnt as it is able to inspire a dangerous and futile idealism.[79] It is futile, implies the world-weary pastor, because the vices of the masses cannot be changed, but at best contained. The young priest, however, compromises by locking his books in the book case and merely throwing away the key. When Luke announces his intention to work for 'the elevation and perfection of the race' he is immediately brought up against what Sheehan presents as an established clerical commonplace: 'You saw that cloud, passing there across the black hill?' said Fr Martin. 'Yes' said Luke. 'that is your humanity, its history and its importance'.[80]

Sheehan's hovering affection, however, for the Lethebys and Listons is persistent. His soft spot for them is not merely based on reminiscence of his own early zeal to revolutionise the world, but they represent that awkward but driving force in his personality which compelled him to criticise the establishment and write the books in the first place. Ultimately there is no doubt but that Sheehan would have himself identified with the erring but true Listons and Lethebys.

> Whilst his great pastor kept 'aloof and aloft' administering his parish in strictest accordance with Canon Law and tradition, Henry Liston came down to their level, became one of themselves, spoke to them familiarly, cried with their sorrows, and laughed with their joys. His pastor immediately noticed it and warned him.[81]

One of the strongest inhibitive factors, for Sheehan at least, against straying from the beaten priestly track was the fear that failure would provide the anticlerical gossip vultures with a rich source of amusement. But worse still was the dread that his ventures would be cited as a warning amongst the other priests of the diocese. In *My New Curate* these fears are displayed by Fr Letheby whose ventures to regenerate the local economy have floundered miserably:

> He knew how rampant and unscrupulous was the spirit of criticism in our days and with what fatal facility the weaknesses and misfor-tunes of one priest, would be supposed, in the distorted mirrors of popular beliefs, to be reflected upon and besmirch the entire sacred profession. And it was an intolerable thought that, perhaps in far distant years, his example would be quoted as evidence of folly or something worse on the part of the Irish priesthood 'when Letheby wasted hundreds of pounds belonging to the shopkeepers of Kilkeely' or 'Don't you remember Letheby of Galway, and the boat that was sunk?' 'Oh, he compelled him to leave the diocese!'[82]

The extreme self consciousness of Sheehan towards his priesthood is borne out by his attempts to explain the standing of the priest in the life of the local community. Naturally he was capable of depicting only the way in which he thought he was regarded. It is interesting, however, that as his experience grew, he was big enough to allow into his fiction some negative attitudes as well as the positive. In his second novel *The Triumph of Failure*, the young Sheehan was obviously impressed, although he denies it, by the customary awe in which the newly ordained priest is held: 'but this people, eliminating even that sacred, if human affection, flings around the priest who absolves and sacrifices, a halo of sanctity that might be given to a guardian angel'.[83]

Later, in *A Spoiled Priest*, he admits that it was the same romanticism which first inspired his vocation — 'when he heard his sisters at home discussing the merits of this young student in that shy, half-affectionate, half-reverential manner in which Irish girls are wont to speak of candidates for the priesthood'.[84] Though Sheehan footnotes the title story, presumably for foreign readers, with the over optimistic explanation that 'larger ideas are being developed even on this subject' so that 'not many now believe that no good fortune can ever be the lot of him who has made the gravest initial mistake of his life',[85] he goes on to speak of the 'shattered hopes', 'disappointed ambitions' and the 'stern judgment of the hearth he had desecrated' that mark the aspirant to the priesthood who fails to reach the goal.[86]

The priestly image he implies, is so entrenched in the minds of the community that even the 'spoiled priest's spectacular success in journalism cannot alleviate the family misery'.[87] Just as it is the mothers who suffer most from this trauma, it is they who, throughout his fiction, are the undying defenders of 'the priest'. Though it is very much an undertone in his novels, with the exception of *The Blindness of Dr Gray*, Sheehan admits that a certain unpopularity is also part and parcel of being a priest:

> If they wear a high bayver, they're too grand; an' if they wear a funny hat, they're demanin' themselves. If they're goin' about their duty in the shtreets, they ought to be at home; and if they stay at home, why aren't they walking the shtreets? ... If they take their masheens an' go out for a whiff of fresh air, after bein' cooped up all day in their boxes, pious craw-thumpers an' althar-scrapers won't take off their hat to God's ministers.[88]

There is an implicit suggestion through all his work that the community never completely trusts the priest despite their frequent and eloquent lip-service. In *The Blindness of Dr Gray* he explains at length the difficulties experienced by the old priest in trying to combine the parental, protective role of priest with the loyally supportive one:

> It was also known that he was in *every sense* the father of his people,

and their stern defender against oppression of any kind. It is a
position which, in Ireland, is scarcely understood by those who have
landed interests in the country, or even by the people themselves. If
a priest utters a word in defence of his people, he is at once reputed
an agitator and revolutionary; if he opposes the popular will from
reasons of conscience, he is set down by the people as a friend of
their oppressors, and by the governing classes of the country as a
conservative ally.[89]

The entire plot of *The Blindness of Dr Gray* is evidence of Sheehan's
awareness of the limitations of the local power of the priest. Dr Gray
appointed a young teacher to the local national school 'on account of his
ability and perfect training'[90] who had the misfortune to be the nephew of
a man who had a local farm. However, because the Duggan family had
had their eyes on the farm, the new owner is dubbed a 'grabber', and
similarly, Dr Gray receives a letter demanding that unless the teacher be
dismissed, the parishioners would teach him that 'they might be led but
they would not be driven'.[91] When the priest ignores that threat Duggan
spends the rest of the novel watching for more evidence to convict him.
Soon after Dr Gray offers to tutor two local Protestant boys in the Classics,
Duggan is quick to circulate the rumour that the priest is opening 'a
nightschool for Protestants'.[92] Again and again through the novel Sheehan
shows how easily the peasantry can be misled about the intentions of the
priest. More lightheartedly, he shows them griping about the prohibitive
marriage fees charged by the priests, though these quibbles are inevitably
and instantly refuted by the ever vigilant mothers.[93] When Dr Gray,
however, refuses to clear his character even the mother of the Duggan
family begins to lose faith;

> Although her deep religious feelings would never allow her to take
> part in any unholy remarks about the priests, she still felt, in that
> strange instinctive but utterly irrational manner so common amongst
> the ignorant and uneducated, that they all had a grievance against
> the clergy.[94]

It is interesting also that Sheehan adverts to the refusal of the peasantry
to pay the Christmas dues as the one act of high treason which marks the
bitterest hostility between priest and people in Ireland. 'It is an act of
apostasy, a flinging-down of the gauntlet, the ultimatum, and declaration
of hostilities'.[95] As far as criticism of church structures was concerned,
Sheehan was relatively silent. He permits himself the occasional, and
almost obligatory gripe against the high handedness of the bishop particu-

larly with regard to the appointment of curates — 'as you would pot balls on a billiard table'.[96] He deplores also the attitude of those clerics whose only vocation is to promotion within the church, but these are not common.[97] His most serious source of complaint is probably the regulation caution of the clergy to dodge from thorny, public matters, and the sense of lonely isolation in which those who don't soon find themselves.[98] A rather pompous canon in *Luke Delmege* prompts a favourably drawn Fr Martin to question the traditional hierarchical structures of the church, asking 'who will have the courage to come forward and pulverize forever this stiff, rigid formalism built on vanity and ignorance, and buttressed by that most intolerable of human follies — the pride of caste?'[99]

This is a strange statement on ecclesiastical government from somebody who loathes 'the elephantine hooves of democracy'. Did Sheehan feel that though the masses could never cope with a democratic state of affairs, it would, in the ecclesiastical world, allow the rise of talent?

He sees in the land changes that the peasantry are losing their sweet Catholic resignation in the undignified stampede for mere farms. Security of title, according to Sheehan, has made them 'more abject slaves than ever'. 'The vices forced on them by the colonial power' were now more often called into service in the scramble for land and respectability. The industriousness and frugality which accompanied the old way has now been replaced by 'degenerate public house loafing'.[100]

Sheehan's basic anger at the inequity of the class structure in Ireland is immediately evident. Though it is the deliberately idealistic Luke Delmege who best articulates it, the sentiment underlies all his work: 'he thought with intense bitterness that poor toiler was labouring, not for his own little family over there in that wretched cabin — that meant only bread and potatoes — but for the agent, that he might have his brandy and cigars...'[101]

He finds no fault with stratification in itself but rather in the lack of contact between 'the gentry' and 'the labouring classes'.[102] Sheehan stresses that it is the difference in religion which poisons Irish society. He also takes the equation of Protestants with landlords for granted;

> Here, to his mind, was the radical difference between England and Ireland — that in the former country there was a perfect link between the classes, the nobility and gentry being gently associated with the labouring classes through the medium of the clergyman and his family; whilst here, in Ireland, there was an unspanned gulf between them to their common detriment and disadvantage.[103]

He thinks, possibly because they are a 'royal race', that the Irish view class distinctions more sharply than the British. He explains to the inquiring 'intellectuals' (1911) with an affected blandness, lamenting the sectarian rift of class:

> 'Good' families can trace themselves back to Cromwell or Elizabeth. Some go back to a successful lawyer or doctor about thirty years ago. Some are successful merchants of yesterday, some of today .... In this country a Protestant is supposed to be always more respectable than a Catholic. Our religion, you must know, is the religion of the kitchen, the poorhouse.[104]

Yet Sheehan seems to glory in the triumph of Ormsley's conversion to Catholicism in order to marry Bittra Campion in *My New Curate*. He seems satisfied that at the wedding, 'of course, the front seats were reversed for the gentry .... But behind them, and I should say in unpleasant proximity stood the peasantry'.[105]

The attitude of Sheehan's peasantry to the gentry is mixed of servility and suspicion.[106] Sheehan, and they, delight in inventing justifiable excuses, where they can, for those exceptionally benevolent creatures of the gentry class who are inevitably found out to be crypto-Catholics. The father of Bittra 'the lovely Papist', was 'hated for his iniquity by some, applauded by others',[107] and 'every prayer that went up for the sweet face of his child was weighted with a curse for the savage and merciless father. He knew it and didn't care. For there were plenty to fawn upon him and tell him he was quite right. Ah me! how the iron has sunk into their souls. Seven centuries of slavery have done their work well'.[108]

Sheehan's preoccupation with the world of the gentry, as well as indulging his own escapist bent and that of his readers, also indicates his selfconsciousness in coming from and now representing Catholic, peasant stock. He makes continuing attempts to exhibit what he imagines might be the views of the gentry toward the lower orders. Owing to this, his gentrified society seem to spend an unlikely amount of time thinking about peasants and pronouncing clearly their views on the subject. The effort fails, however, because Sheehan cannot lose himself into the imagination. He cannot lose sight of his personal verdict.

He finds the origin of their attitudes in British imperialist ideology. Allusions to the Indian experience therefore are useful:

> 'It was fortunate for us that the founders of our Indian Empire had none,' said Outram. 'Consciences are all right for full-dress church parade on Sunday morning here in England .... But, by Jove! when you are in the thick of battle, and dealing with rascally natives,

conscience is altogether out of place' .... 'Fortunately, like your good Irish here, they hiss and spit at each other and would sell their fathers for a rupee; and this alone makes their subjection easy.'[109]

The humanitarian impulse of Maxwell, the central character of *Lisheen*, to discover peasant Ireland, is put down to the influence of the 'Christian socialist rot'[110] fashionable in Oxford and London. Rather too deliberately, Sheehan shows how mistaken is the official attitude to the Irish; after countless pages of homage to the Celtic imagination, he edges a lawyer into the following blunder: 'Ah! It is the illiteracy that makes them so dangerous,' said the lawyer. 'They have no imagination; and they cannot see beyond the day.'[111] Naturally the lawyer is blind to the idealism which drives the Irish into rebellion. With suppressed indignation, Sheehan shows how the lawyer sees their rebellion and outrage as a petty, meaningless tantrum.

Maxwell's eccentric voyage provides a link between the two cultures. It is of course imperative that he should be immediately overawed by the virtues of his new world;

> It was clear that here was a world of which hitherto he had been profoundly ignorant — a world where poverty reigned supreme, and yet was but a gentle tyrant, for patience and resignation under hard circumstances made easy a yoke that seemed to one, not inured to hardship, impossible to bear. And what a gulf between his condition and theirs![112]

Though he realises (this was written in 1910) 'what utter and unforgivable idiots we have been' for throwing away 'our country, our race, our happiness', he still holds out a chance of redress: 'The people are forgiving and generous. But can a leopard change his spots?'[113] Happily Maxwell meets with Hemberton, another leopard of changing spots, so that they guide the erring peasantry into a bright, new and safer world. This almost feudal/estate community, is naturally the vision of times gone by, which Sheehan offers as the best solution to the problems of land and Irish society. In his analysis of the damage caused by the land movement, the old Dr Gray observes:

> Up to twenty years ago, in some way those ideals were there, broken perhaps and distorted: but they were there. Then, for the first time, an appeal was made by public men — I won't call them demagogues or even politicians — to the nation's cupidity. Instead of the old passionate war-cry, *Ireland for the Irish*! they sank to the socialist cry, *The Land for the People*! They've got it now! They have the

land; and they fling Ireland to the devil. Each man's interest now is
centred in his bounds ditch. He cannot, and will not, look beyond.
He has come into his inheritance; and he sends his mother to the
workhouse![114]

So long as there was a Cromwellian landlord to be fought and
conquered, there remained before the eyes of the people some image
of the country. Now, the fight is over; and they are sinking down into
the abject and awful condition of the French peasant, who doesn't
care for king or country; and only asks: Who is going to reduce the
rates?[115]

Far from emancipating the peasantry, security of title according to
Sheehan, has made them 'more abject slaves than ever'. 'The vices forced
on them by the colonial power'[116] were now more often called into service
in the scramble for land and respectability: 'In his covetous watchfulness
over Crossfields farm, Dick Duggan had noticed that Kevin was not
drinking himself into his grave half-fast enough for his wishes. He would
have put a distillery at his door, if he could expedite the ruin of this man,
who stood in the way of his felicity'.[117]

The industriousness and frugality which accompanied the old way has
now been replaced by 'degenerate public house loafing'.[118] Yet the writer
helped organise the implementation of the later land acts, and indeed, in
his fiction sympathises with the oppressed tenantry. While he never
outrightly says so, and while he is required by social convention to object
to 'the centuries old oppression' of the peasantry by landlordism, he is
even more frightened of a sudden, revolutionary change in the *status quo*.
It appears that he would much prefer a slow, gradual change and this is
probably why he helped out with the local transactions in land tenure
around Doneraile.

Throughout most of his novels there emerges a sense that Sheehan is
envious of the manners, civilisation and style of the landlord class. He
seems to sigh inwardly that if only the peasantry could imbibe the best of
that culture without losing their 'native spirit', Catholicism and loyalty to
priest, that all would be truly well. He was shocked by the spectacle of his
idyllic, (and largely imagined) sweet, Celtic flock squabbling over land
with each other, as well as with the landlord.

Despite explicit references to the hierarchy of the classes, Sheehan's
fiction shows, in practice, a simple two-way divide. There are landlords
and there are Catholic tenant farmers but there is nothing in between nor
below the level of the tenant farmer.

He is extremely sensitive to the all-pervasiveness of what he terms the 'caste-exclusiveness of Irish society'.[119] Though sometimes he seems to smile on it as a pleasant reminder of the calm days of yore, he is however, generally critical of its unjust premises.[120] Again Sheehan tries to have his cake and eat it. He cannot decide between the gospel of the individual's freedom in society and his imaginative nostalgia for the grandeur of the old order. If he was aware of the ambiguity and incongruities of his attitudes he never admitted to it. He did, however, admit that his social attitudes, ostensibly at least, were necessarily circumscribed by the tyranny of convention. The niece of the old Dr Gray explains to her Protestant male friend how their planned trip to Africa could be frustrated by 'the prejudices of the ignorant'. 'But my uncle is a priest and has to live amongst his people; and he must be careful in these days when people, he says, are so critical'.[121]

The most salient feature of this rampant degeneracy is, according to Sheehan, the complete disregard for the sacred and time-honoured rituals of nationalism. He and Myles Cogan, the very honourable, unselfish patriot of *The Graves at Kilmorna*, are appalled to see the infiltration of 'the empty and vulgar nonsense of a London music-hall' into a rural concert ousting the 'old sweet songs so full of tenderness and sorrow for lost causes'.[122] Some of the base features of the peasantry, however, were there well before the land changes as Myles Cogan sees no change between the Ireland of the late 1860s and that of 1910/11. Reflecting on the behaviour of a recent election mob he concludes:

> Time had made no change. There were the same distorted and inflamed and furious faces he had known; there was the same intolerance, the same bigotry, the same senseless and animal rage that made him weep for Ireland forty years ago. Hot, furious words leaped to his lips; wild storms of contemptuous rage swept his soul; yet in a moment subsided. He murmured mentally; 'Ah, Mother Ireland, Mother Ireland, is this what forty years have wrought in thy child? What hope? What hope?'[123]

There are features of rural life on which Sheehan cannot make up his mind. Gossip, begrudgery, and the quest for respectability are some of these. In *Glenanaar* and *The Graves at Kilmorna* he draws lengthy pen portraits of the local gossip system but refuses either to idealise it as quaint or to deplore it as unchristian.124 He is slightly more firm on the 'trait' of begrudgery:

> 'Tis a little way of our own we have in Ireland, to try and kick the

ladder from under a fellow-countryman who wants to get to the pinnacle of things, careless whether we kill him or maim him for life. But when he comes out safe overhead we will raise our hats and say Huzza![125]

Remarking that 'the distinctive term of popular canonization in Ireland is that word "poor"', he sees this as an inheritance of the poverty which has characterized the race for seven hundred years:

> It was only when you saw beneath the spotless pinafores the carefully inserted patch on the blue serge, or the darn on the sleeve, or the slightly broken shoe, that you knew how gallantly these brave, simple souls were fighting under the perpetual friction and disintegration of great poverty.[126]

Real poverty, however, is carefully avoided in Sheehan. The Syngian west is touched on only incidentally. In *Kilmorna* 'one solitary public-house seemed to have absorbed all the wealth of the place, if one could judge by the exterior'.[127] In the same novel, he lodges an objection to the principles of gombeenist business but sees it as a modern development; Myles Cogan's old-fashioned and honest business methods cannot compete with the 'new':

> 'It appears', he said at length, 'that my shortcomings are reducible to three heads — I don't charge according to my customers; I don't give false discount, and steal from my customers in another way; I don't give drink or bribes, even in the shape of Christmas boxes.'[128]

In *Lisheen* (1907) he shows the awakening of a Protestant landlord to the very contradictory 'reality' of the rural Irish economy:

> These Irish drove hard bargains at fair and market; were economical almost to miserliness in their homes; knew the value of a shilling as well as any other race. But he soon found out that they lent at pleasure and that the poor farmers around were up to their necks in debt for each other in banks and loan offices.[129]

The economy for Sheehan on the whole, however, is of no great importance compared with the spirituality and sentiment of the farmers. He cannot seem to make up his mind between whether the 'poetic, philosophical' nature of the Celt is a vice or a virtue. The wise old parish priest of *My New Curate* warns the young enthusiastic curate who tries to innovate Saxon ideas of industry, thrift and punctuality that 'if you take away the poetry, which is an essential element in the Gaelic character, you make the people prosaic and critical, which is the worst thing for them. Thiggin thu?'[130]

He also argues strongly, however, that the reason for the widespread inertia, is simply, laziness, indolence and fondness of drink. The dire labour shortage in *Lisheen* is put down to 'the common madness, that would exchange for the prospect of gold all the sweetness and beauty of life for all its foulness and sordidness'.131 A picturesque rebel in Glenanaar blames the glamour of the 'returned yank' for depopulating the countryside:

> ... Tis ye, the recruiting sergeants of England, that are sweeping the people away with your letters: 'Come! Come! For God's sake leave your cabins and come out to wealth and comfort.' And *Ye* are patriots![132]

and the priest chimes in, 'They do quare things over there, when they're away from the eyes of the people'. Sheehan is cynical too on reports of Irish success in Tamanny Hall:

> 'How many Irishmen are in the Senate?' was the reply. 'How many Mayors of cities are Irish? What chance is there that any descendant of an Irish Catholic shall ever be president of America?' ....
>
> 'Then you don't think your people wield the large political power and patronage in the States that we have been led to believe? Why, our good countrymen in England are suffering from chronic nightmare on account of the preponderance of the Irish element in American politics.' ....
>
> She shook her head. 'Parochial politics? Yes. State politics? No. Our people are in a state of pupillage, as the Doctor asserted'. I [the author] was genuinely angry with the doctor; but I could not contradict him.[133]

Emigration is frightening for Sheehan, largely because Irish Catholicism, once it leaves Irish shores, becomes consumed by the foul modern. His sympathy for the emigrants is not outstanding. However one wonders how the issue would have been broached if he had not been conscious of his 'half a million readers in America'.[134]

On the whole Sheehan saw his writing functioning as a conservative reminder of a traditional Catholic Ireland under serious threat of extinction by the soulless modern. It was vital to Sheehan's world view that the nationalist flame be kept burning as a symbol of both the subjection and the resistance of the 'race' to whose spiritual survival he tended. It was both Sheehan's priestly and ideological mission to sustain at all costs the tradition in which he was personally and officially invested — and this meant objecting to any threatened solution to Ireland's ills. Sheehan's investment in nationalist energy was not of course consciously motivated by mere self-interest but rather by a desire to reboost the economy of religion, race and nation for the twentieth century.

Sheehan disliked the vulgarity of democracy in practice and called wistfully for a return to a 'gentle' feudalism, where everyone knew their place. He regarded the enlightenment ideas of progress, democracy, liberalism and the natural laws as the errant notions of power hungry demagogues who could not see beyond their noses. For the same reason he saw socialism as a rival which would cruelly raise the aspirations of the lower classes for a heaven on earth and in the process dispense with the mediatory role of the priest. He was convinced that the only salvation to be found was through an investment in the faith of the supernatural.

The patriarchal function of the priest was essential, in Sheehan's view, to holding the fabric of the traditional culture of the nation together. Finding the role of the priest as both master and servant of the flock difficult and lonely, he developed a sympathetic regard for the retiring Protestant landlord class, looking back to them in some senses as the predecessors of the clerical elite which he hoped would continue their mission of social reform. Sheehan wanted to separate and integrate the better influences of English culture with the native Celtic spirit. It was in his view only the low, vulgar, degenerate forms of English culture which he felt had defiled the Celtic inheritance, viewing for instance the attempt of the Gaelic League to 'blank out' the treasures of Irish literature in English as a great loss.

Neither was Sheehan very unusual in his account of Irish gender. He saw woman as the very incarnation of tradition — who functioned to sustain the tradition of the 'race' spiritually as well as materially. Although he would never concede the actual thought, it was his implicit hope that the clergy and women would ally as the spiritual and cultural midwives of the future. While at the same time he shows how each sex could be played off against each other in order to protect the weaker and unwitting 'other' from all outside harm: 'Free masons, Jews, and anti-clericals are a constant terror to your mothers and sisters'.

Sheehan's almost solitary example of an empowered and politicised female character, Miriam Lucas, in the novel of that name, although not portrayed as a conscious feminist (a concept out of Sheehan's view), was conceiving of herself as an autonomous ideologized politicised woman. The whole point of the novel however was to demonstrate flatly how she was no such thing as proven from the outset by her worship of the false

Gods of socialism and egalitarianism.

Having spent most of his life and his writing championing the grand heroic tradition of nationalism, in the latter years of his writing and his life Sheehan became his own best critic as he began to see the limitations of the die-hard nationalist position who tended to 'look step by step measures in the mouth'. As the fiery nationalism of his earlier writing mellowed to a more quasi-revisionist one he also marked a shift in his priestly self-image from his earlier identification of himself as one of the 'robust fighting Maynooth men' to the quieter less ambitious type of pre-Emancipation days. Sheehan seems to have come round however resignedly to accept the ambiguity and inevitable ambivalence of the position he occupied as a man situated between God, government and people.

5: Guinan's Ireland

Of the three, Guinan's sense of nationality is perhaps the most regular. He is the most ebullient, cheerful, inoffensive, unoriginal and yet sincere. He writes untiringly of the many virtues which are unique to the 'Irish people', of the various hardships bravely endured down through the centuries, and of their extraordinary devotion to their faith and country.

It is extremely ironic then that he is the one who shows most awareness of the contemporary hyperbole concerning the national image. In fact, he feels the need explicitly to justify his additions to it; he does this by first fingerpointing to the 'insufferable patriotism' of the Englishman who 'lives, thrives, and grows fat and gross on union Jacks',[1] implying that apart from being silly it may even be counter productive, and then he encourages the same in Ireland:

> The country has indulged to excess, perhaps, in shouting at monster meetings and resoluting and speechifying. All the same we shall never achieve anything without national enthusiasm; and on what is this to be fed? The fuel of national enthusiasm is national pride in our motherland.[2]

Though Guinan uses the Celtic label interchangeably with 'Irish' he does not use it quite as often as Sheehan. His characters are by and large all the same. They are less credible than even Sheehan's worst characters. It is obvious, however, that he had a real interest in and fondness of the common people, calling on almost precisely the same standard identification marks used earlier by Sheehan. They are emotional, impulsive, shy, quick tempered and 'dacent'. Their occasional sins are always of a very venial nature and are related so coyly that they seem almost fetching.

Neither can Guinan escape from presenting stereotyped images of the peasantry. Not alone does he feel it his duty to exhibit their virtues to the world but he genuinely finds it difficult to detect many flaws. It seems that he too arrived at Sheehan's conclusion that 'the best way to make people good is to tell them that they are good'.[3] Throughout he leaves the impression that stock characters are selected from his reading of romances and blended with his reminiscences:

> I gazed at him [an old peasant] in astonishment and delight for some time as he stood before me, a perfect type of the old men of the time; for he looked as if he had just walked out of the plates of Phiz in the illustrated editions of Lever and Carleton, only far more true to the

reality than any sketch ever drawn by the great caricaturist.[4]

Quickly, however, he jettisons any undesirable features from the earlier popular imagery of such writers as Lover, Lever and Carleton. He is particularly irritated by their depiction of Irish funeral frivolities though he is otherwise unusually magnanimous in acknowledging their merit as writers.[5]

Guinan, like Sheehan, has exclusive notions on who is really Irish and who is merely a temporary resident. The real Irish for him are the unpretentious rural dwellers. There is no indication that he was aware of the Protestant Unionists in the Northeastern corner of the island. Though he makes occasional references to farmers of Scotch blood he makes it clear that their culture is foreign and not to be imitated. Though Guinan's 'Saxonphobia' is just as pronounced as Sheehan's, it springs from different reasons. Guinan was in fact the archetypal 'new curate' of Sheehan's stories who returns from England bristling with dynamic ideas to transform the Irish economy and in turn the national character. Though ultimately he was in favour of creating industry and inspiriting Irish life, he did, however, share something of Sheehan's insecurity about the spiritual corruption which would ensue:

> It might well be questioned whether the change would be an unmixed blessing .... Our villages would be more prosperous, no doubt; but would they be happier, more religious, or more simple-minded? Probably they would not. All the same, what small town is there in the land that would not bless the sound of the steamwhistle in its midst, to remind the young men and women that there was employment for them at home.[6]

It is interesting that he attributes the 'Slough of Despond',[7] not so much as Sheehan does, to the unpractical nature of the Celt, but solely to the colonial hang-over in the Irish mentality:

> When I first felt disposed to be vexed at their ignorance and backwardness, and impatient of their slipshod and unprogressive methods, I recalled the fact that until very recently they had been very slaves; and the slave cannot surely be expected to walk after the galling chains have been struck off his limbs.[8]

Guinan consistently blames the colonial experience for any attitude or act which he finds contemptible:[9]

> It is remarkable that, wherever you find a bad landlord or a bad agent, you're sure to meet the informer, and that, too, where you'd least expect to find him, among down-trodden Catholic peasantry. It's a

very humiliating thing for an Irishman to have to admit.[10]

In eloquent and unscrupulous defence of the sense of nationality being promoted by the Gaelic League, Guinan goes beyond the call of duty in juxtaposing a pumped-up, urban, 'whey-faced, imitation Englishman or West Briton, as we say' against a young, virile Aran fisherman:

> Albert Edward de Morphy, whose grandfather from Ballyamadhaun
> in the Midlands began life as a bottle-washer, became a Dublin
> grocer, bought house property and established a living for his golf-
> playing descendants.[11]

He is very obviously to be scoffed at in comparison with 'Shaun O'Flaherty' — 'the living embodiment of the proud traditions of the heroic race'.[12] The recovery of the Irish language, Guinan sees as late as 1913, will infuse a spirit of 'manliness, self respect and business' into the degenerating race.[13] Though the new Ireland will admittedly be profit orientated, it will at least be safeguarded from the ignominy of being confused with England.

In his insistence that the history of Ireland, or 'her record of woes',[14] needs to be repeated *ad nauseum*[15] he betrays his worry that the rising generation may not be fully aware, or sufficiently resentful, of the persecutions of the past:

> Go back on their history for two or three generations and consider
> what it was. Pauperised ... harassed and harried ... plundered ... driven
> from the good land ... taught by the exactions of tyranny to practice
> lying, deceit, evasion, and shifts of every kind.[16]

His very early novels are striking for their depiction of the general contentment of the peasantry. In the *Soggarth Aroon* of 1905 the establishment of a local branch of the United Irish League was a happy, amusing interlude, though here and there are signs of his latent frustration with the rather happy-go-lucky affair that Irish nationalism was. He regrets the sheep-like posturing of the peasantry and townspeople, and their spasmodic nationalist gestures when inspired by 'the pushful, cheeky, self-assertive local leader who read the newspaper'.[17]

His later works of 1907, 1910, 1924 and 1928 have more of the substance of life. Local politics, agrarian discontent and difficulties with the payment of rent, find their way at last into his tales and become more clearly focused as his novel writing continued. Perhaps it was that he became better acquainted with the conditions and grievances of the parishioners or perhaps he simply gained more confidence in his writing.

Concurrently, the fierce patriotism of his younger years and novels mellowed considerably, as he developed a more reasonable perspective on national affairs.

Unconsciously, he refers to the cult of inactive nationalism. By way of excusing a sergeant for working for the crown, he stresses that, afterwards, however, he was, on the quiet, as good a rebel as any.[18] Retrospectively from 1922, he sees the Land League as an ideal compromise between constitutionalism and Fenianism. It provided opportunity for a young, idealistic rebel in *Annamore* with whom the priest admits a certain affinity, to expand his energy without doing anybody any great harm:

> Like many of the best and most selfish nationalists of that period, he was too loyal to his religion to countenance Fenianism, while, at the same time, he inwardly chafed at the over cautious methods of constitutionalism.[19]

But his apparent approval soon developed into hesitation as he fears the land movement may not after all be blessed by God and is unnecessarily lawless, though he remarks that 'it has ever been the fate and experience of our unfortunate country, during the seven hundred years war, that the law must be broken in order to be redressed'.[20]

Guinan's hopes for the Ireland of the future, judging by his fiction, characteristically optimistic. He is capable only of imagining a completely Catholic Ireland. In his scheme of things all her scattered exiles would eventually return, it would merely be a matter of time before Protestants would convert, industry would be revitalized and a stable, vibrant economy would somehow protect the quiet, rural, priest-loving Irish peasantry.

Guinan is remarkable for the strength of his confidence in Irish Catholicism. Having spent his first ordained years 'on the mission' in England he was obviously overwhelmed by the devout Catholicity of his parishioners in the Irish midlands. Whether he believed it or not, however, it was imperative that in his production of a 'literary pabulum for the populace' he should depict an idyllic, rural, Catholic, peaceful world.

For Guinan, the 'memory' of the Irish Catholic experience was the most precious feature of the national identity. He makes repeated references to the 'long, dark centuries of persecution' and purrs triumphantly at the success which Irish Catholicism was:

> Many old men and women shed tears of gladness when they thought of those (penal) times, and of the days of the dear old thatched chapels, and then raised their wondering eyes aloft to the huge campanile tower of St M-'s Cathedral, soaring proudly to the clouds,

while chiming bells filled the air with a melodious clangour.[21]

Fascinated by the persistence of his parishioners in referring to their church as 'the chapel', in order to distinguish it from the Protestant church, he is immediately certain that

> the expression 'going to church' was inseparably associated in their minds with the barbarous penal code, under which the Catholics of Ireland groaned for a hundred and thirty seven years, until O'Connell struck the chains of religious disabilities from their limbs.[22]

He is explicit that Catholicism is the national faith and that it is the faith which holds 'Ireland' together. His often-repeated observations on the role of religion in the life of the peasant confirm, ironically, those of Marx:

> 'His religion is for him, truly, an Aladdin's lamp', by means of which he can possess at will the magic power of transforming his poor lowly cabin into a gorgeous palace of Cathay .... It teaches them to regard trials and sorrows as blessings in disguise, and as sent for their good. It makes them what they are — the most prayerful, spiritual-minded and religiously inclined people on the face of God's fair and beautiful earth.[23]

He reassures his readers that their 'grand faith' will be always safe, 'protected as they are by poverty and persecution, and guarded from contagion by the beneficent genii'.[24] He constantly debated with himself whether it might do more harm than good if this strong, holy stratum, of Catholic peasantry, under his feet, were introduced to the 'sweetness and light', of higher culture:

> Who knows but, maybe, 'ignorance is bliss' in their case, from the religious and moral point of view; for the knowledge 'that puffeth up' might make them less docile to the teachings of the church, and possibly also less vivid and simple their wonderful faith.[25]

Some of the more enterprising menfolk even break into the church during the night in order to be first for confession during mission week.[26] He is, however, alarmed also to see that this simple but sincere Catholicism is seen by 'those rich and fastidious Catholics' as a shameful badge of low social status. These 'are ashamed to do right through fear of miserable human respect, and the world's cheap sneer of sarcasm'.[27] A remarkable volume of Guinan's work is concerned with the image of the priest in the eyes of the community. In fact he sees 'the affection of the simple, lowly Irish peasant for his priest' as 'one of the holiest, sublimest and most beautiful of the many beautiful traits of the Irish character'.[28] He delights in accepting the laurels of the traditional 'Soggarth Aroon'. He reveals the winning formula to those 'non-Catholics' in Ireland as elsewhere who are sorely puzzled to account for the wonderful hold the priest has over his people':[29]

> But let bigotry say what it will .... The simple truth of the matter is, in my humble opinion, neither more nor less than this; the place which the priest holds in the hearts of the people has not been won by tyranny or domineering on his part, or by fear or superstition on theirs, but by the honest services, the unselfish sacrifices, the high character and personal holiness of the So*ggarth Aroon* — the fondest title in any language of the Lord's Anointed.[30]

His, also, it seems plausible to deduce, was a mother-inspired vocation. The ordination of 'The Curate of Kilcloon' means the ordination also of his mother:

> Aware, as he was, of the popular notion in rural Ireland, which invests the mother of a priest with something of a sacred character, he felt convinced that she had acquired a new title to his veneration which made her dearer and holier in his eyes than ever before.[31]

Guinan finds it a struggle to live up to the standards of priestliness expected of him:

> For very shame I cannot but try to deserve the high opinion my simple, religious-minded flock have formed of me, impossible though it is of full realization. How could I have the heart to disappoint their fond expectations, to disillusion them by falling from the serene Heaven to which they have raised me down to the vulgar, common ways of men.[32]

The men in his communities fawn over the priest and ensure that he gets the best livestock at the local auction,[33] and an ample amount from the annual 'voluntary' oats collection, and are generally vigilant in overseeing his material comfort. Guinan shows, scarcely without knowing it, how intimacy with clerical affairs is a local status symbol:

> Cormac was what is known in Ireland as 'a priests' man', a rather strange expression in a country where the people are so passionately attracted to their clergy. However it means no more than a man — usually of standing in the parish — who is on terms of more than ordinary intimacy with his priests, and is more than ordinarily devoted to their interests, which of course are identical with the interests of religion .... They always spoke of him as 'Mr Flaherty' and to be 'mistered' in a rural district connotes a mark of distinction seldom accorded to anyone-outside the charmed circle of 'the qual-

ity' — save the schoolmaster, a prominent shopkeeper, or one having a 'gentleman's place'.[34]

Echoes of the Daddy Dan/Letheby tension abound in Guinan's works also as he compares the two possible approaches of priest to people:

> Although they may like the pleasant, 'gallas' man who sometimes descends to their level in his conduct and conversation, the peasantry reverence and respect more the priest who, whilst being kind, considerate and humble, yet, in his intercourse with them maintains a dignity and a discreet reserve and aloofness. Him they style 'a grand man'; the other perhaps 'a nice man'.[35]

Though he stresses that he never could endure the 'quality' or the 'Inglified' of the towns he admits that at least there, there were some on his own intellectual level,

> whose society was a rare treat for me, people who were, in the truest and best sense, educated, cultured, and travelled. This was one advantage, at least, of which I was deprived in the mountain parish, where few ever journeyed further than the next market town.[36]

He was kept amused, however, in the rural parishes by his many and varied tasks; from curing the sick with miracles to 'adjudicating in cases of family settlements and marriage fortunes', blessing crops and new prayer-books.[37] An acutely embarrassing situation befalls the painfully self-conscious Fr Melvill, the 'Curate of Kilcloon' when the local doctor proposes to marry the priest's sister. Everyone, including his grateful father, thinks the priest has arranged the match.[38] But it is the sniping of his clerical confreres which most upsets his image of decorum:

> Ah, what a fall was there! The brilliant scholar, the literary lion, the learned theologian, lowered from his pedestal of fame to the level of a common, vulgar, intriguing matchmaker for his relatives! Oh, what an odious reputation for the great Melvill of Maynooth who issued from these College gates loaded with laurels.[39]

He takes his duties toward the social life of the community very seriously. It is his open and prompt assumption of authority which is perhaps more interesting than his perplexity over 'what constituted legitimate amusement':[40] 'I believe I could quell a disturbance among them, should the need arise, by a few words of remonstrance more effectively than a battalion of soldiers would do it'.[41]

He recognised both the need for amusement and the possibility that country dances might lead to 'abuses'. In the end he resolves to follow the advice of a local widow 'to check' the dances — 'an expressive and comprehensive term'.[42] In the course of his fifth novel, however, *The Curate of Kilcloon* (1912), he shows he had discovered the basic autonomy of the people when needs be concerning important material issues. When a faked claim is staked on land in which the priest's father had recently invested and the priest supports his father at the local 'league' meeting, his 'Soggarth Aroon' image receives a noticeable dent:

> In the estimation of some few, at least, the patriotic young priest suddenly degenerated from an out and out nationalist to a vile Tory. It required all his philosophy to reconcile to so strange a mutability of fortune.[43]

When he is rudely called 'the son of a land grabber' he responds promptly by striking the culprit. Though remanded by the bishop for this, it was the gesture of self-confidence, at least Guinan would have had it, which ensured that the priest was 'respected ever more'.[44] Very delicately his original notions on the status of the priest are modified as he gains more experience:

> There is a mixture of familiarity and respect, of independence and deference, of audacity and reverence in the Irish peasant's manner of treating his priest which language cannot describe. There is a freemasonry in their relations known only to themselves.[45]

Generally, however, Guinan's problem is that he assumes everybody to be as sincere as he is himself.

The cause of anti-clericalism, though not completely ignored in Guinan's world, meets with short shrift. One real life anticlerical appears in *An Island Parish* (1908) but his 'ideology', as Guinan quickly explains, was prompted by sour grapes over a 'horse-dealing transaction'[46] and in any case the insidious attempts of misguided men, like Bartley Hogan, to stir up revolt against the influence and authority of the priest in Ireland are doomed to failure, for the ties that subsist between him and his flock are too strong and too sacred ever to be rent asunder.[47] Earlier in *The Soggarth Aroon* (1905) the rascally Bryan McEgan, local nationalist agitator, who developed a fondness for the priest's seven year old whisky, and borrowed from him money which he never repaid, causes Guinan to reflect on such roguish irreverence. It is probably the Parnell split which he has in mind:

> I refer to that short season of political madness when a section of misguided Irishmen sought to introduce, in a mild form at least, the war-cry of the French infidels, '*La clericalisme, voila l'ennemi*', a doctrine hitherto unheard of among the peasantry in Ireland .... And yet regrettable instances were not wanting, during that ill-fated crisis,

when the *Soggarth Aroon* was hooted and jeered — ay, and even
stoned — and that, too, in the land of Patrick and Brigid, in the land
of the Gael. Nothing like this, however, happened in the Mountain
Parish .... I do believe that the incidents of that troubled period served
the good purpose of clearing the air, and bringing into the open many
lurking enemies to Ireland's best interests .... It has demonstrated
beyond yea or nay the infallibility (almost) of the judgement of
Ireland's prelates and priests in matters political affecting the sacred
cause of Faith and Fatherland.[48]

Guinan reflects on the various ancestry of clergy in almost the exact
same imagery as Sheehan. The old parish priest was the child of a
generation who had worn the galling chains of religious disabilities, and,
consequently, he inherited a little of their timidity and cautious fear:[49]

> ... He was content to dwell in a humble thatched house, and his fare
> was almost as plain and poor as that of his peasant neighbours.[50] ...
> As a type of the priests of the old school, now rapidly passing away,
> Father Kieran had no equals.[51]

He is also unusually direct in explaining the strain caused the priest by
living all year round in the public eye. He laments that the priest must
watch his behaviour even when on holiday:

> Hence if some will smoke a cigar, take a hand at nap, loo, or poker,
> enter into the spirit of a childish game of forfeits, and join in the small
> talk and badinage of the drawing room — well, what evil have they
> done? None, certainly; and yet they run the risk, possibly of displeas-
> ing a sour-faced, carping critic, who is watching their movements
> with an unfriendly eye, and taking pharisaical scandal from their
> innocent and legitimate amusements. Surely it is only natural that
> those who have passed twelve months in the gloom and isolation of
> their presbyteries in rural districts, where society there is none, to
> speak of, should keenly relish the 'feast of reason and the glow of
> soul', in the society of the cultured and refined who yearly foregather
> in the world-renowned, health-giving resort ... Possibly in 'Lisdoon-
> varna the Gay', some of the raw young curates — the two year olds
> or there-abouts are just a trifle too boyish in their innocent glee; ...
> If they [the simple country folk] will have it that their priest is an
> angel and no mere man, a supernatural being in the guise of a mortal,
> disillusion them not.[52]

Guinan's attitudes towards Protestants were probably more typical than
those of Sheehan or O'Donovan. He was obviously disappointed when he
first went to work in an Irish parish to find that the ready answers he had

learned for the defence of his faith were hardly necessary:

> There was no resident parson in the parish, and no Protestant church;
> and, except for a few uneducated farmers of the nondescript, con-
> ventional type of Protestantism, there was no heretic. These simple
> people were obliging neighbours and skilled in the breeding of cattle
> and horses, but quite innocent of controversial theology — and,
> indeed, of dogmatic principles of any kind — so that Fr Melvill's
> sword and armour might well rust from inactivity before he was
> likely to meet a foeman worthy of his steel.[53]

Also in *The Curate of Kilcloon* he proudly tells the story of Daly, one
of his parishioners who 'nearly killed a Protestant, one fair day, because
the latter, being in a maudlin state from drink, shouted the sectarian
shibboleth, "To h- with the Pope!" in court'.

> Daly's speech was gall and wormwood to some of the justices, just
> as it was honey and sugar to others of them, the people's magistrates,
> who were despised by their aristocratic brothers on the bench, as
> everyone could see.[54]

For a moment he appears to be approaching a more tolerant attitude
towards the end of the same novel when a bicycle mishap 'strands him at
the rector's door' and the previously 'frigid code of social intercourse'
breaks down:

> For in Ireland, as everyone living there knows, owing to the exac-
> tions and persecutions of the ascendancy class in the past, the barrier
> of religious belief has long been as a wall of brass separating
> Catholics and Protestants. There is an ingrained reserve and distrust
> on both sides, the heritage of the bad old times, which it is very
> difficult to overcome.[55]

However, the story finishes with the rector's conversion and entrance
to the Jesuit order — all thanks to Fr Melvill's enlightenment. There is no
evidence that the enlightenment has been mutual if one is to judge by the
much later novel *Annamore*. It includes a story of how a Catholic girl
marries an 'anti-papish' Protestant but nevertheless manages to remain
secretly faithful to her faith. She even incubates their child's Catholicity
by means of a Catholic nurse, and the tacit agreement of the local
schoolteacher, who smiles on her intent keyhole listening while the
religious lesson proceeds. Amusingly Guinan observes that when the 'card
is turned' in the national schools from 'secular instruction' to 'religious
instruction' 'the faces of the little Christians brighten, for now they feel
they are in their own dear Catholic land'[56] while O'Donovan's experience

is that the procedure provoked envy in the majority as they watched the
Protestant children run out to play.[57]

Guinan's attitude to Protestants, on the whole, is remarkably and openly
hostile. He sees the sectarian divide as an occasion of ongoing battle and
hopes his fiction will boost the morale of the Catholic community. Being
at the fore front of the aggressive, Catholic action crusade, his hopes for
the role of Protestants in the future, scarcely need comment. As with
Sheehan, Protestants in Guinan's world will one day be integrated with
the Irish.

Guinan's sentiments on landlords and tenants are both the most un-
equivocal and the most familiar. After dealing a comprehensive list of
retrospective recommendations for what 'the Irish gentry' could have done
for the improvement of the tenant's lot he regrets that

> in the main, they did the very opposite to all this. They rack-rented
> their tenants, and left them to the tender mercies of a griping agent,
> who 'grind the faces of the poor', and extorted the last penny from
> them.[58]

His sympathies are firmly and solely with his peasant flock. He describes the countryside of *An Island Parish* as being one of those poor,
barren districts which parliament did not think it worth while confiscating
at the time of the Cromwellian clearance. In careful neutral tones, he
remarks on the scarcity of gentlemen farmers in the district and excuses
the lack of 'the graces, decencies or refinements of life' with a tired
reminder of 'the struggle for existence'.[59]

Though he speaks admiringly of curates whose ideas of tenant right
were instrumental in 'getting the agent ousted' from the chairmanship of
the Board of Guardians,[60] he prefers to cultivate 'a conservative reputation' for the influence it affords him.[61] The United Irish League, for
Guinan too, evidently lacks the aura of righteousness which the Land
League had enjoyed.[62] Yet, for the entertainment perhaps of those who
had no direct experience of agrarian troubles, Guinan furnishes some
amusing accounts of how the peasantry manage to avoid paying the rent.
Some of these characters resemble in attitude those depicted earlier by
Lover and Lever:

> In truth, he was born in arrears, brought up his family in arrears.
> Indeed, he could scarcely imagine himself in any other environment
> than that of arrears, which seemed to adhere to his bones, and form
> part and parcel of his happy-go-lucky existence.[63]

Much earlier, for *The Soggarth Aroon*, he went to great efforts to simulate typical colourful oratory of a land agitator:

> But fellow-countrymen and country-women, bad and all as the land league are, the land grabber is worse, for he's a mere deceitful, despicable man, that expropriates the results of another's industerin', sweatin' and slavin' for years, by takin' up his farm when he's injected out of it by an inhuman landlord for not bein' able to turn whins into money, and to distract blood out of a turnip.[64]

He lavishes praise consistently on the fairly comfortable, and no doubt, reading class of farmers. As he traces in *Annamore* the fortunes of one such family he leaves no doubt as to what precisely was required to combine Catholicity with respectability. It is interesting that the description of the homestead depicts accurately the homeplace of the author:

> Cormac Flattery, however, was far and away the principal tenant in Annamore. Indeed, he was the second or third largest and most respectable farmer in the whole parish. He wore a good suit of grey tweed; drove a decent jaunting-car to Mass on Sunday, and a well-fed horse under a well-painted cart to market. He was high up on the 'dues' list, had a pew in the 'chapel', and got a 'station' yearly — all marks and token of parochial standing. He had a farm of some 90 acres, and a residence that had an unmistakable air of old-fashioned respectability about it, a long, two-storey, thatched house, embowered in giant, ivy-covered trees of hoary antiquity, that had defied the fury of the 'big wind', and plainly testified that the Flattery family was of no mushroom growth.[65]

He points out that though Cormac went on to marry a local woman it was *not* for money. The children are inevitably sent to boarding school after which (in 1878) a new farm is added to the existing ninety acres.[66] There is no reason to detect even a whiff of cynicism here on Guinan's part, as he cannot be accused of restraining his feeling for those whom he disdains:

> The inspector was a dandified young man, with an English accent, and that peculiar languid, bored expression of countenance which is the exclusive birthright of the class to which he happened to belong — namely, the Castle Official class of moderate means and unlimited gentility and pretensions.[67]

Guinan gripes that there are two laws in the country — one for the rich and one for the Catholic peasant. The respectable Catholic class like the Flatterys are conveniently ignored when it comes to Guinan's explicit divisions between rich and poor:

> Indeed, if the highly respectable drunkards of our hotels and clubs
> were treated with the same even-handed justice as the drunks of the
> inferior order are, sensational revelations might be expected. When
> an unfortunate corner boy or a poor tin-man gets as drunk as a lord
> he is rammed into the black hole; but if a lord, or one of the *seonini*,
> who imitates their ways afar off, gets as drunk as a tinker or a sweep,
> he is worked at by the police, according to immemorial custom and
> the time-honoured etiquette of the force.[68]

He notices how 'a middling farmer's daughter would not think of
becoming a servant in the house of a local strong farmer or shopkeeper',
unless it was far away from home. Her people could then sustain their
respectability in the eyes of the neighbours by circulating the pleasing
fiction that their Mary was a 'lady's maid' or a 'nursery governess', instead
of a common 'servant girl':

> In season and out of season I inveigled against this ridiculous Irish
> pride, saying that these same girls, when they emigrated would be
> glad to get the post of scullery maid or servant-of-all work in a cellar
> kitchen in New York or elsewhere — in the service, perhaps, of some
> upstart 'moneybags', not so decently reared as herself. But it was of
> no avail.
>
> 'You know', they would say, 'we have a bit of a spirit, and sure if
> the neighbours saw one of the girls goin' out to her service, wouldn't
> they say we were beggard and bruck entirely? So there's the way it
> is, your reverence; people like to keep up their respect and daicency
> in the eyes of the country howsoever it goes with them.[69]

In *The Island Parish* Guinan was startlingly frank in detailing some of
the more unacceptable faces of Irish life. When parents of the 'Soggarth'
die, a son-in-law takes over the shop, but falls into gambling and eventually runs away to America leaving a destitute wife. The brother of the priest
tries to rescue the business but develops a fondness for the drink. His son
also falls into temptation, loses money gambling and flees to America
where he contracts tuberculosis. Another sketch tells the calamity which
befalls a household when two brothers are left helplessly on their own,
owing to the death of the housekeeper-cum-sister. The younger brother
exiles himself in order to let the older one marry, but meets with death,
again in America. Another local girl gets pregnant by the master while in
service, has the baby under a false name in the workhouse, after which she
dumps it in the canal, gets arrested, and ends up in a 'lunatic asylum'. The

soggarth, after some time, persuades her father to forgive the master rather than revenge him, but it ends on an ugly note as the girl's brother runs away, this time wisely to India rather than to America. Guinan notes a *mulaheen* had been pronounced on the cabin so that it was ever more avoided by the community.[70]

It is hardly likely that this move towards social realism was deliberate. Guinan may have been merely looking around him for new ideas to vary the theme. In any case, apart from such incidents as detailed above, the book is generally much the same as any of the others. He tells affectionately of the rows and petty bickering between neighbours over turf-banks and rights of way to a spring well — matters in which the priest had to mediate. They know only too well, however, that they need to get along, in order to use each other. As one of them puts it:

> Sure it's foolish, as well as sinful, for neighbours to be fadin' out, and gettin' into varyance over trifles, not knowing how soon they might want one another's help in some way or another.[71]

Another family, stricken by 'a dread malady' were left to their fate as the 'terrible word "faver, the Lord save us" was whispered abroad' so that they were scarcely offered enough help to 'lay-out the bodies or lower the coffins'.[72]

On the subject of emigration Guinan also is frank. He realises and admits that it is the lack of employment in Ireland which causes it, but despite this he feels it would still be better for 'Ireland', if people, though hungry, remained at home. In *The Soggarth Aroon* he persuades a couple not to emigrate:

> I admit I felt no compunction at all in bringing about this seemingly unfavourable turn in their fortunes; for I regarded that humble couple in their hut on the wind-swept mountainside as a valuable asset to the country. A dozen or so years or thereabouts afterwards, when on a visit to the then curate of the mountain parish, I happened to pass by the door of that self-same cabin, I found it alive with merry children, poorly and scantly clothed, indeed, but fair and beautiful, in my eyes, at least, as the dew drenched with flowers of the mountain parish.[73]

Perhaps more realistically he describes one local character who profited well from the visits of Irish Americans, 'who generally have an intense desire to bring home with them a real Irish blackthorn stick'.[74]

The most historically specific of all Guinan's novels, *The Patriots* (1928), narrates local manifestations of Irish national events in the fictional midland town of Druminara from the inception of the Gaelic League to the post-Treaty years. *The Patriots* is probably also Guinan's finest work, as the depth of the author's admiration for the local Longford fighter Sean Mac Eoin, on whom the central character was based, apparently induced Guinan to attempt more indepth and sustained character portrayal. Apart from the obvious factor of Guinan's vicarious pride in a gallant local patriot it was the particular style of Mac Eoin's patriotism, marked as it was by an unwavering deference to clerical authority, which naturally ensured Guinan's deep and enduring appreciation. Mac Eoin's heroic style functioned essentially for Guinan as a dramatic animation of that mixture of romantic nationalism and conservative churchly traditionalism with which Guinan tried to infuse his own priestly and literary practice.

At another level the same tension operates in *The Patriots* to continue Guinan's classical clerical theme of intergenerational conflict between the figures of the wise and experienced fatherly Parish Priest who has seen the realities of nationalist revolution before, and the fiery enthusiastic younger curate who secretly longs for the return of a romanticised Fenian spirit. Guinan frames it visually when two such priestly figures watch in amazement as a newly formed local branch of the National Volunteers practise their drills past the Church gate 'in a manner that left the Canon dumb with astonishment and Father Darragh mute with intense admiration'.[75] And the old Canon trails off:

> But I suppose there is no use in my saying anything publicly about this matter, except to warn the people about the dangers of secret societies condemned by the Church and the folly of thinking of any other means of redress except such as are strictly constitutional.[76]

The tension between the figures of curate and Parish Priest might be read as a dramatisation of the secular/sacred conflict within the figure of the priest who nurtures the nationalist grievance for its history of Catholic identity while at the same time struggling to reserve for himself a position of moral leadership of the flock.

While Guinan shows Seamus McGarry resolving the tension nicely, and while that sense of a clerical moral leadership survived intact in the Free State, it was, to Guinan's deep dismay, radically challenged by the Civil War. It is further interesting that the same tension between the romantic idealist and the sober conservative in Guinan can also be read in Guinan's projection of the forces which caused the Civil War. Despite Guinan's qualified claims in the foreword to set forth a certain clerical objectivity, throughout the book he firmly endorses the Treaty side's appeal to reason over the die-hard idealism of the irregulars. The novel of course coincides with Guinan's deepening experience of life in general and of Irish national life in particular. It seems that the earlier Parish Priestly nostalgic forgiveness of the young curate's rash temperament; 'in all political matters prone to be somewhat impulsive, or maybe imprudently outspoken and impracticably honest, if I might so express it' was definitely limited in the actual moment of crisis.[77] In the foreword Guinan spells out the moral task of the novel:

> In the concluding part of the novel the author enters on a field in which he may fairly be regarded as a daring pioneer, namely, the origin, progress and conclusion of the Irish Civil War in all its sad and painful aspects, which he treats in a spirit of charity and with the restraint, or, rather, reticence of shame, which friends experience in referring to an unhappy family quarrel. Without unduly straining the privilege of fiction, the leading characters, especially the clerical personages, are availed of to give expression to the national voice on the methods of warfare adopted in the fratricidal strife by the intransigents and the moral question involved therein. Who were the patriots, living or dead, who, consistently with loyalty of Mother Church, loved and served Mother Eire more wisely and more nobly? — that is the question this story tries to answer.[78]

Guinan effectively portrays the irregulars as terrorist monsters. De-Valera receives a thinly disguised caricature as an irresponsible, and more especially, cowardly anti-hero to Michael Collins' exalted heroism, as McGarry exclaims:

> I wish I could extenuate the moral guilt of the course of action he seems to have adopted, either willingly, or under a form of duress exercised by his own uncontrollable followers.[79]

And Guinan felt that if DeValera could not handle his followers he should have resigned and everyone would have respected him more. As another of McGarry's comrades declares in *The Patriots*:

> We have a new reign of terror to face, a reign of madness, rather, organised by a few unscrupulous leaders, who hold their deluded followers under threat of death, and are encouraged by wild women who applaud acts of murder and brigandage, in defiance of the Church's teaching.[80]

The trend of events, which culminated in the shooting down of Irishmen by brother Irishmen, had the effect of forcing back Canon

Killian to his old conservatism and rooted pessimism regarding the
capacity of his countrymen to govern themselves. [81]

Canon Killian was always conscious of how the fighting was negatively
affecting the image of a peace and priest-loving Catholic Ireland. Killian
felt that the shooting of detectives for instance:

> betrays a mentality, a vitiated conception of morality which I could
> never have thought possible in Catholic Ireland ... If allowed to go
> unchecked it will, I fear, develop into a passionate blood-lust, that
> may yet sap the instinctive reverence of our people for the sacredness
> of human life — a misfortune too awful to contemplate.[82]

He was ashamed that the children of our 'Godfearing Irish parents could
so forget our careful religious training as they have. I feel somehow as if
it were an impeachment on us, the Irish clergy for neglect of duty in some
way'.[83] Guinan represents the priest's administering of the last rites as he
imagines it would appear to the foreigner:

> He then performed a strange, mystic rite, as it seemed to the Black-
> and-Tans, of which none knew the meaning save the Catholic
> policeman, who was aware that the priest was anointing the man, in
> the hope that life might not yet be extinct.[84]

Killian was also later given to remark sarcastically that the Black and
Tans 'must have felt highly complimented by the aptness with which their
Irish pupils unconsciously imitated the same devilish methods of looting,
burning, spoiling and treacherously slaying their own countrymen'.[85]
Guinan continually contrasts the nobility and glory of the fighting in the
War of Independence with the ignobility of the Civil War. Seamus
McGarry says:

> Jealousy is an Irish failing and always was. It was only when we
> looked on the fight as hopeless that we were united. Deadly danger
> made us all brothers then, ready and willing to die for one another.
> There was a grand spirit of unity in the country up to now with all
> old sores forgotten.[86]

Guinan's vehement disgust for the die-hard extremism of the irregulars
is particularly ironic given that he had earlier spent much time celebrating
the mythology of the lost cause as an endearing national characteristic:

> for faith in the impossible is a strong weakness, as we say, in the
> Irish character. The lost cause, the unrealisable ideal has an irresist-
> ible fascination for the dreamy romantic Celt, which the practical,
> matter of fact Saxon can never understand.
>
> Seamus McGarry: The few brave boys hidin' in mountains, without

enough guns, and our ammunition nearly run out, forced the great
British army to sue for peace and call us an *army*. Hurrah! for Mick
Collins and the I.R.A.![87]

So long as the rebels were all united against the British, Guinan
respected the unselfish manliness of the fight, but when the Civil War
seemed to push the national ideal too far, and moreover threatened
disrespect for the clergy, then the ideal became immoral.

Guinan's commentary prompts one to wonder what Canon Sheehan
might have written of the events had he lived to see them. It seems that
eventually Guinan also followed Sheehan's course in opting for that
mature policy of reasonable compromise which Sheehan espoused in his
latter years. And in many ways both Sheehan and Guinan's path follows
the general graph of the clergy whose position as a national institution
while increasingly legally ensured through independence, was at the same
time practically challenged by the same process, as already foreshadowed
in the Civil War.

An interesting aspect of the working of Guinan's nationalism is his
deployment of gender. Briefly, Guinan ascribes no agency to woman. The
reason for the rebels' fighting was, of course, to secure the proverbial
'motherland' as well as to protect the actual living 'brave, brave Irish
mother'.[88] And the fighting was itself an essential part of the national
sexuality: 'The IRA, indeed, considered armed resistance a patriotic duty;
and tame submission an indelible disgrace to Irish manhood'[89]. For
Guinan, as for Sheehan, woman functioned as a metaphor for the preser-
vation of tradition against progress. Guinan devotes an entire chapter of
The Patriots to 'Woman's Heroism' as defined rather predictably in an
auxiliary capacity to the struggle of brothers, fathers, husbands and lovers.
While Guinan lionized those women who were almost accidentally caught
in situations of heroism he labelled the behaviour of those such as Cumann
na mBan who made a conscious commitment to join in the fighting as
'unsexed, abnormal types' who 'don't represent the God-fearing and
modest womanhood of Ireland'. The passivity of the Irish woman was
obviously a very important part of Guinan's sense of national identity:

> It is now generally admitted that, from the standpoint alike of religion
> and patriotism, it was a fatal mistake on the part of the leaders in the
> fight for freedom to have encouraged Irish women to turn their
> thoughts from the peace and sanctity of the domestic hearth to active
> or sympathetic participation in a warfare of ambush and reprisal,
> with all its inevitable horrors. In the light of after events, the

consequences were deplorable, as evidenced by the deeds of devilry in which unsexed women took part during the fratricidal strife.[90]

Often Guinan measures the courage of a woman by the courage of her brother. He also liked to contrast his male heroes' military machismo and their timidity around women:

> And the giant, who could face a storm of bullets without flinching, seemed quite shy and timid under the gentle raillery of the ladies. [91]

Guinan also congratulates the rebels on their chivalry in protecting Irish womanhood from molestation by the Black and Tans. After Black and Tans killed both a young man who was deaf and dumb as well as his pregnant sister, Guinan remarks:

> Our Irish Irregulars were guilty of horrible excesses, later on, as the Nation admits with shame; but, even in their worst paroxysms of revenge, the woman and the child were immune from harm, in accordance with the chivalry of the race.[92]

Guinan also follows the tradition of blaming on the colonial experience any undesirable features of Irish society. Like Sheehan therefore Guinan is excited by any sign that his fellow countrymen are capable of standing up for themselves with dignity rather than merely returning English volleys.

Compared with Sheehan one immediately notices Guinan's sense of intimacy with 'the people' so that his writing style is more of the folk commentator to Sheehan's intellectual bent. Guinan also lacks whatever historical and international breadth Sheehan had, a factor which accounts in part for the buoyant optimism of his local vision. Guinan echoes more optimistically Sheehan's trust that the political and social economy of the priest-people relationship will capably resist erosion by the silliness of the 'modern world'. Yet, like Sheehan, Guinan is inwardly haunted by the unmentionable feeling that the supposedly unshakable solidity of Irish Catholic identity is under serious threat from all sides. Like Sheehan, Guinan's underlying insecurity about the national identity compels him to repeatedly define the native essence, which is naturally to be found in a spiritual, psychological and cultural residue which somehow managed to escape anglicization and which is conveniently institutionalised in the Catholic faith. Guinan also predictably feels that religion is like an 'Aladdin's lamp' which transforms the lowly cabin into an imperial palace.

Guinan's brief experience in Liverpool had opened his eyes to the reality of how easily the faith could be lost in modern urban contexts making him feel that the strength of the faith in rural Ireland was all the more precious. Marvelling at how strong the faith still was in rural peasant Ireland he gives the lion's share of the credit to the upkeep of the traditional bond between 'priest and people'. Guinan learned that the priest in order to maintain his respectful place must display a certain dignity, discreet reserve and aloofness from the 'people'. However Guinan seems far less pained by the loneliness of the position of the priest in society than for instance was Sheehan. If Guinan's pastoral manner was anything like the majority of his fictional priestly characters one might fairly assume that he was far less formal and serious than Sheehan and therefore he most likely experienced more of the popular 'audacity and familiarity' than the 'respect and reverence' which he himself noted as characterising popular relations with the priest.

On the whole Guinan tries to convince his readers of an ideal rural peasant. Every virtue, and they are in abundance, is attributed to both their Celtic nature and their loyalty to the faith, while any shameful vice such as laziness or a lack of 'manliness and self respect' is of course of more recent and distinctly English origin. Like Sheehan, Guinan in practice finds it much safer and handier to build on the stock images of Irishness than to experiment with reality.

6: O'Donovan's Ireland

Gerald O'Donovan, the youngest of the three, is characteristically also the most intense. He is at once the most idealistic and the most down-to-earth. His practicality lies in his ability to work with what material lay around him, and his idealism in making the effort, where the others had perhaps more sense than to bother.

The effort he expends in his fiction on trying to sort out the problems of Ireland belies a deep romantic feeling for her welfare. He gives the impression that he is in deep personal pain at the condition of Ireland. Like Sheehan and Guinan, he imagines Ireland as an independent person:

> Always in his imagination Ireland had been a woman. In the sad days he remembered from his childhood she was often old and decrepit, sitting by a fireless hearth, forsaken and weary under a broken roof, but always with haunting eyes that looked straight into his soul.[1]

His surface romanticism, however, stops here. Compared with Sheehan and Guinan he is not consciously concerned with the question of national identity. References in his fiction, to the Celtic origins of the race, for example, are rare. He is unusual amongst these writers in having developed a familiarity and sympathy with individual Englishmen, so that the edges of any notions he may have had on Celtic versus Saxon nationality are sensibly blurred. The younger and less travelled author, however, of *Father Ralph* and *Waiting* takes a much narrower point of view on Irish identity and nationalism. Though even then, O'Donovan was too sensible to engage in the listing of peculiarly Irish characteristics, so that his attitudes to nationality are therefore implicit. All round that thinking in his novels is pruned considerably from the rather more impassioned and complex positions he revealed in his earlier magazine articles and addresses.

O'Donovan apparently felt no compulsion to explain, depict or define the 'national character'. Though owing to his mediocrity as a writer many of his characters are slightly stereotyped, they are not the easy-to-hand stereotypes of, for example, Guinan's world. Their credibility is still somehow saved behind their sometimes unbalanced portrayal.

What is most striking in O'Donovan is his great effort to present a representative cross-section of Irish life. He constructs a remarkable diverse world with characters culled from many of the classes, religions, backgrounds and cultures. He is alone therefore, among these authors, in calling a spade a spade in his acknowledgement of the glaring disunity and heterogeneity of the population of the island. His motivation here however is to explain political rather than cultural differences, but as the two quite often go hand in hand, he succeeds to some extent in doing both. In order to explain the factors at play in 'the Irish problem' he tours the reader round the various interests. He has Catholic custodians of the *status quo*, as well as flaming republicans, committed Carsonites as well as indifferent 'Sunday Unionists', dedicated constitutionalists and cynics, cultural revivalists and gombeen men, southern Protestant landlords and snobby Catholic landowners.

Owing to his experience of England and particularly of the Foreign Office, three of his books are rich in analysis of the English dimension of Ireland. While he understands and sympathizes with the tradition of hardline, romantic nationalism, he is realistic enough to query the point of it especially in *Conquest*. Though the novel was published in 1920, the idea behind it was conceived at least as far back as October 1916:[2]

> I'm not weakening, though I suppose I've outgrown the first zeal of the convert. You can't knock down the British Empire with a pop-gun, my dear. But if we only have patience there must be some way of piercing its thick hide or stirring its slowmoving brain ... You won't intimidate England by bashing an Irish policeman.[3]

Yet despairingly he senses that such advice is like 'curing a lovesick girl by telling her to count to ten and draw a long breath'.[4] Though O'Donovan makes no attempt to conceal his deep-rooted nationalism, he makes a brave effort to present a panoramic view of political opinion and prejudice on 'the Irish question'. Coming after his experience with the diplomatic service in Italy, *Conquest* is a perceptive study of nationalism against imperialism, in the Irish context. He remarks on the understandable anti-English paranoia in 'Irish minds'.[5]

> Henry VIII, Elizabeth, Cromwell, William of Orange, are merely steps in your political evolution. You forget their crimes, if they were crimes, in the good they did for England. In Ireland they are murderers and pillagers who have never died .... deep down in Irish minds you are all still the bloody Cromwellian murderers who bore bleeding children through the streets of Drogheda on pike tip, over two hundred years ago.[6]

But he understands also how the British refuse to acknowledge this 'normal condition' of hatred in her own subject countries though she is alive to it in the subject nations of Europe.[7] He tries to enlighten the British as to their true image in Ireland:

> They think you hate them. They can't believe that the cumulation of
> wrongs you've done them can come of anything but an intense,
> persistent hatred — even their imagination fails to fathom English
> stupidity. Oh, I know you don't hate them — you needn't trouble to
> say it. I only tell you what the Irish think — with some reason too.[8]

He succeeds in representing well many shades of the complex of British
opinion on Ireland. One young Englishman sees both landlord and tenants
as children who need 'a leading string',[9] while another is grateful for the
subject of Home Rule as 'a pleasant topic of conversation, as long as he
could remember, and he sees no reason to worry that that convenience
should change.[10]

O'Donovan's ability to see the many differences in view point is
diminished, however, by the far-fetched frankness with which he has his
characters express them. Jim, his own character in the book, poses as an
objective outsider who is in love symbolically with the extreme *Sinn
Feiner*. O'Donovan labours the question of racial memory and the dis-
trusting attitude of the Irish towards England until Jim recognizes that their
generalizations are 'too fluent, too easy'.[11] He laments the unfortunate
image of England in Ireland:

> What the devil is it to an Irishman if the Englishman is as wise as
> Solomon at home? In Ireland he has shown only his stupid tyrannical
> side, and by that he is judged.[12]

It is significant also that his northern unionists are depicted rather flatly
from the point of view of a southern nationalist. Their many points of
opposition to the 1912 Home Rule bill, are splayed with comprehension,
though with a conspicuous absence of sympathy. They have 'a bitter
frightened hate that is capable of any sort of insanity'.[13] Though he calls
for more tolerance in sorting out the sectarian and political problem, it is
obvious too that he feels no sense of common identity with the northern
Protestants, and finds their position puzzling.

O'Donovan's dilemma is compounded of his emotional and humanitarian pull towards nationalism and justice and his more rational, diplomatic
self which is almost paralysed by his affinities with the various sides.
Conquest is the story of the fight between the two sides of his nature and
his engagement in the end to Diana, the Markievicz-like rebel, marks the
victory of his anti-English dimension. It is the analytical basis of O'Donovan's sympathy for Ireland which distinguishes it from the rather more

distinctive and muddled positions of the other two.

Though in his articles he was concerned that Home Rule should not be seen as an end but as a beginning, in his fiction, there is the certain implication that the 'happily ever after' paragraph cannot be attached until Home Rule is conceded. His utter silence after 1922 on 'the Irish question', though partially owing to difficulties in his domestic affairs, probably indicates also a deep sense of disappointment with the course of 'Home Rule' in Ireland.

O'Donovan's basic attitude to Catholicism in Ireland is that the clergy and church structure are moving away from any real sense of religion, though he probably exaggerates the extent to which it is alive amongst the laity, in order to highlight the divergence:

> Under these roofs [of the parishioners] too, were mysteries of faith, hearts through which flowed that living stream that had fructified life ever since man felt the need of religion.
>
> And the church was deliberately putting itself outside it all. For power and money it was sacrificing the heritage of the saints. It no longer made any effort to express this living faith.[14]

Yet he had not given up hope entirely;

> The leaven of holiness still worked in the church, in odd out-of-the-way places, and he has picked up a crumb of food here and there. Decrees and dogmas, and laws, and regulations, had not killed all life. The immense complex machine of pope, cardinals, curia, ecclesiastical officials, bishops, priests, and nuns, dead and mechanical for the most part, had here and there a wheel instinct with the life of the spirit, that kept in touch with the growing needs of humanity.[15]

He points out however the diversity among Catholics in their attitudes to Catholicism and poses a professed atheist to comment on their varying degrees of interest and faith. Dunne, a rare, doubting peasant confides his religious discomfort to Fr Ralph:

> 'Maybe only half-a dozen', he added doubtfully, 'are bothered about it like me. There are a good many that don't believe, and don't care a fig one way or the other'.
>
> 'But there are a good many like Bridget Carey [a remarkably devout woman]', Ralph said smiling. 'There are', said Dunne 'and some of the best too.'[16]

Though O'Donovan is consistently amazed at the diversity of personalities within the church structure, he is shattered nonetheless to discover the rottenness within:

It was a wonderful church, ... with its cruelty, its faith and its
indifference, its piety and impiety! Could the muddy waters ever be
made clear?..Was a synthesis possible?[17]

The overall impression he gives of the clergy is that too many of them
are involved in nepotism,[18] 'keeping their eyes on bishoprics',[19] 'super-
vising' local marriages,[20] collecting local intelligence,[21] and vulgarly
affecting an interest in literature.[22] What he most deplores, however, is
the clerical control of the schools and their seeming delight in tyrannising
the teachers. The schools are dilapidated, the teachers tired, frustrated and
underpaid, and the inspectors too happy with their jobs to object to clerical
manipulations. *Waiting* is the story of one independent-minded teacher
who defies both tradition and the clergy by marrying a Protestant. O'Donovan points to the awful power of the clergy as they stage a mission to
destroy his political career, rousing the petty self-righteous instincts of
many of his old friends and neighbours so that he is shunned and abused.[23]

By the time of his writing *Vocations* (1921) O'Donovan came to pity
those who saw the priesthood as a career:

> He [Fr Burke] never had a moment's regret that he had chosen the
> priesthood as a profession. It flattered his vanity, gave him ease,
> comfort and scope for the prudent gratification of his passions. His
> guiding principle was to reap all the pleasure he could without
> compromising his position, or putting any obstacle in the way of
> promotion to a parish.[24]

This novel is peopled by harsh caricatures of priests who are preoccupied by collecting money 'for masses',[25] teasing the passions of young
girls,[26] and making love with nuns.[27] He is careful to point out however
that this is a minority element; even the womanizing Fr Burke recognizes
that though 'It wasn't a bad world at all, many fools of priests and nuns
didn't knock the best out of it'.[28] Convents sadden him most as he
discovers they are too full of vocationless misfits who live 'in a haze of
ignorance and religiosity':[29]

> They come in for a hundred and one reasons; because some foolish
> nuns have put the idea into their heads; because they're in the way
> at home and it's easier to persuade them that they have a vocation
> than to get anyone to marry them; because a mother or father want
> to make a vicarious sacrifice for their sins; because a vain priest
> wants to boast of the number of vocations he had made; because of
> the sort of education you give girls that makes them bored with their
> own homes and unfits them for making one for themselves. There

are as many reasons as there are nuns, and most of them the wrong ones. And at the end of them all an illusion. The wonder is that things aren't worse than they are .... Thank God you'll find as good women in a convent as out of it. Women with their eyes open who chose a hard life and live it decently. But I'm thinking of them that come in ignorant, and of others, whether they're ignorant or not, who wake up after they come in. Some of 'em get on alright. But the rest — well, well, it's a topsy-turvy world.[30]

It speaks volumes that O'Donovan attributes mainly to convents, these false vocations, despite the obvious similarity which they bear to his own conscription to the priesthood.[31] In *Ralph* he seems extraordinarily forgiving of the overzealous mentality of his nurse and mother who earmarked him almost from birth for the religious life.

O'Donovan's measurement of the status of the priest in the community is the lowest of the three writers. He also refers to 'the spiritual mark' on the priest 'that makes him higher than the angels' and catapults him instantly on ordination past even the rank of 'gentry'.[32] He comments lightheartedly on the supernatural powers of the priest, implying however that it is just a colourful threat used by women to maintain family order.[33] Obedience to the priest was for appearance sake only, it seems, as the people were determined to enjoy themselves with or without the approval of the priest:

I'll take right good care that there won't be any row with the priest on my floor. Haven't I Jim Daly, our labouring man, stationed on the road outside to give warning, if he hears the noise of a car, for fear it might be Fr James going to a sick-call or the like, so that we could stop down the dance and Jim tuck away his fiddle.[34]

The priest's appointment of a relative to teach Maurice, the hero of *Waiting*, prompts the matter-of-fact approval of his nepotism by Maurice's mother:

'Niece, indeed!' Mrs Blake said, tossing her head. 'If she was as near as that to him, he'd have her married long ago to a lawyer or doctor within in Liscannor. She's only a second cousin once removed, or it's not a schoolmistress he'd make of her, and poor at that. It's as plain as two eyes in a cat what he's aiming at in putting her an' you in Bourneen ... It'd be a great back to you entirely to have the priest for a relation.'[35]

It is interesting also that he shows the more lukewarm attitude of some of the educated, middle class Catholics. It is an aspect noted also, though with anger and disgust by Sheehan and Guinan. The mother of Ralph's Irish language enthusiast friend finds a certain crude vulgarity in the priest:

> She had a theory or she developed it at the time, that the priesthood was a special privilege conferred on the lower classes to make them contented with their lot. We had just had the parish priest to dinner, an awful jolly chap, who sopped up gravy with a knife. She drew a lurid picture of the certain degeneration of my manners at Maynooth. She said she respected priests on the altar of course, but one could not have them to dinner except once a year or so, and then only by screwing up one's courage.[36]

O'Donovan is unusual too in raising the question of intra-clerical tension. The Carmelites think the Jesuits too 'worldly' and 'ornamental',[37] the secular priests are careful to watch the Carmelites' mass-offerings and bequests, while 'the bare mention of a friar' makes the heart of Fr Molloy [in *Father Ralph*] 'that low, that nothing short of a stiff glass of punch puts any life in him again'.[38] A concerned nun explains to Ralph that in a village of only four thousand there is a workhouse, a dozen policemen, two convents, a bishop, six secular priests, six Dominican priests and lay brothers and yet 'a woman can live in a house that's not fit for a dog-kennel and die of starvation — we all make some show of doing things when the evil that could be prevented has happened'.[39] Though O'Donovan twice makes the point that 'some priests in Ireland are beginning to see the harm the Church is doing itself', he regrets that 'they're muzzled and daren't open their lips'.[40] A photograph of a bishop in a seminary cloister prompts Boyle, the anticlerical teacher of *Father Ralph* to conclude with more despair however,

> 'Smugness and self-satisfaction in every line of it. That is the Irish church all out ... if not the whole church', he added drearily. 'Nothing short of a spiritual earthquake would make them even question their belief in themselves. They don't know that anything is wrong, and they are unteachable'.[41]

O'Donovan does not hate the clergy as much as he fears for the harm a certain clerical element is unconsciously doing both to itself and to society. His greatest fear in *Father Ralph* was for those uneducated men

> for whom religion, faith, dogma, morality, obedience to priests and bishops, and the most absurd practices of the Church were all so joined together, that a doubt about one led to the denial of all religion. It was almost impossible to bring home to them any real sense of relative values.[42]

The crux of O'Donovan's dilemma is that he himself can see the difference between faith and the malpractice of the clergy. Hence it is his faith in humanity, despite all, which consoles him. Breslin, the crypto-anticlerical newspaper editor of *Waiting* asks Maurice, the hero, where he got his faith:

> a handful of jealous small farmers working together and sinking their differences, an old schoolmaster with ideals, a priest with a love of his people, a few women capable of sacrifice, a growing tolerance of the religious views of others. It may not seem much to you to build a nation', Maurice wound up, 'but it makes my faith unshakable'.[43]

A few pages earlier, however, he revealed how he still felt guilty when he found himself thinking badly of the clergy:

> He stood for a moment at the frowning entrance to a big demesne. He idly wondered who lived there. Then he laughed harshly. It was a convent, of course, or a monastery. All the big places round Dublin were occupied by priests or nuns. The long arm of Fr Mahon stretched everywhere. Resignation was preached from these palaces. But this mood didn't last long. Some inborn instinct of faith or his peasant training, made him take off his hat almost unconsciously and say reverently, 'may God forgive me for criticizing them'. Driscoll [his rebel friend and schoolteacher] often said, too, that 'one wasn't to judge the old faith by its priests, as if it went to that, some of them were as good as you'd meet in a day's walk'.

> All the same, he thought one would have more trust in them if they were a little more like the religion they professed. There he was at his criticizing again! He stepped out quickly to shake off these thoughts. The next convent wall brought them back.[44]

When Breslin suggests a registry-office marriage, as a solution to his problem of marrying a Protestant, Maurice admits that the idea of ignoring the Church had never occurred to him:

> No, you wouldn't think of it. You fellows who kick against the tyranny of the clergy make me sick. You talk, and then lie down meekly under their most extravagant pretensions — you're all afraid to fight them with their own weapons.[45]

There is no hesitation, however, in his criticism of the church's hypocrisy on national questions; in *Conquest* he showed how the bishop 'had a convenient cold' and intended to snub Pierce Daly [an awkward rebel] by not attending the funeral of his brother who was a priest. When the bishop, however, 'got wind of a political demonstration' — a counter-snub in honour of the brother of the deceased — he 'made a marvellous recovery and carried off all the honours'.[46] He observes the same principle at work in the politics of the bishops at national level:

> And to have 'em again a movement at times isn't the worst thing either. They were again the land movement, and a bad fall they got over that same. They were again Parnell, but sure when he got into high power they ran after him, and you'd think from the way they talked that they made him. They have their revenge on him now, since he got into the divorce court, but sorra much good that'll do them in the end either. They did a lot to kill the Irish, but if this move of Mr Charles's and his friends come to anything, you'll have plenty of the clergy going round spouting in its favour. It's a way they have of backing the winning horse when it's well past the post.[47]
>
> ... That a Roman Catholic bishop believing in the present deplorable regime of the Church, as Devoy undoubtedly does, could be a Home Ruler, is a hopeless contradiction.[48]

O'Donovan is noticeably mute on the subject of the history of Irish Catholicism. His despairing preoccupation with its present condition and its bleak boding for the future did not, as might be expected, prompt him to examine its background. He is fascinated, however, by the sectarian barrier and tries hard to expose the myths and 'twaddle'[49] in which it is wrapped. If the childhood of Ralph is a true reflection of his own, sectarianism puzzled and frustrated him from a very young age; but it is more likely that he was trying to convey the sadness of sectarianism to those unfamiliar with Irish culture:

> Ralph thought it a pity that so many of the writers of books he liked were Protestants. He prayed often that they might become Catholics, or that Catholics would write books like *Treasure Island*, and *Quentin Durward*, and *David Copperfield*. He asked Ann [his nurse] why there were no Catholic books so good as these. She was horrified. 'Why, they're nothing but a pack of lies. None of them things ever happened,' she said. 'Catholics write true stories about Lourdes, and St Aloysius, and the like. I misdoubt me but a lot of them Protestant stories were invented by the devil.'[50]

Again in *Conquest*, he reconstructs some questions which might have occupied a child during the Parnell divorce case:

> What was the proper price of black and white rabbits? Why were bishops nearly always fat? Did all Orangemen hate Catholics? Was Parnell a bad man or the best man that ever lived? How could he be

a good man and be a Protestant? Was it only Orangemen who were fried in hell?[51]

By *Waiting* (1914) he was still in two minds about whether Catholic and Protestant would ever come together:

> 'The people seem to have no ill-feeling', she continued, pursuing her own train of thought. 'All the same, there is something — I can't explain it — some feeling that I am different and wrong, and -' she hesitated. Maurice said — 'It's only the memory of old prejudices. I had them myself when I was a boy,' he added, laughing, 'they don't mean anything now.'

> 'I hope not,' she said, looking at him thoughtfully. 'I've said as much myself to Uncle John, but he only shakes his head, says that the priests could arouse bad feelings any day.'[52]

Indeed O'Donovan does not dismiss this hint of clerical bigotry as a piece of Protestant paranoid fiction but has his priests jealously guard those Catholics who mix with Protestants. The bishop of *Father Ralph* is perhaps the most articulate bigot:

> 'I've been ten years in the diocese, and never been in Inniscar before. Your tenants were Protestants! Only too few of our larger places are Catholic. I am glad Inniscar has resumed its Catholic tradition.'

> He laid bare his regular white teeth as he smiled faintly.[53]

In *Waiting* he admired 'the clipped hedges' and well kept farms of the industrious Scots remarking despairingly that it was generally accepted that 'them Protestants have the devil's luck'.[54] By the time of *Conquest* (1920), however, Horace Plunkett's influence is apparent:

> Neither history nor biology was responsible for the myth of the Protestant industrial apprentice ... privilege gave the Protestant in Ireland power and position, but it flattered him to attribute his superiority to virtues of character and race ... Protestants had been protected in their prosperity; Catholics harassed in their pitiful struggle for life by every ingenious device of oppression ... Even the industries of the north were only a happy accident.[55]

O'Donovan is careful to include in the nationalist canon the Protestant heroes from Tone to Parnell who blur the sectarian edges:

> Though they were Protestants itself, they are wearing crowns as bright as St Patrick himself. The pope may deny it to them — may God forgive him from being in the pay of the English — but sure God knows better, and the people know better, being one and the same.[56]

Conquest is an urgent appeal for an injection of common sense into the squabble where 'each attributes to the other some sort of horrible demonology'.[57] Consistently the source of sectarianism is located in those who govern:

> 'If only we could get Home Rule everything'd be alright. The schools'd be taken out of the hands of the Father Melons. There'd be no more breeding of bad will between Protestants and Catholics. No man'd be down on another because of a difference of religion. If you could do something to bring this about, you'd be doing the best work a man could set his hand to.'[58]

Jim's mother in *Conquest* was a convert to Catholicism. Here she argues with the priest for inculcating bigotry into the children through the educational system:

> 'If you get control of the government do you mean to ride roughshod over all the Protestants?' 'What nonsense', he said pettishly. 'then why don't you allow Catholic children to go to school with Protestant children?' ...
>
> 'Now, now, Mrs Daly, we must protect the young from -' 'From having common sense,' she interrupted. 'what has come over you at all?' he said, distressed. 'It can't be that you're not happy in your religion.' 'Perfectly happy. But I wish religion in Ireland, on both sides, wasn't so mixed up with land and politics and racial class hatred,'
>
> 'That all comes from the Orangemen. There's no harm in the Catholics. They use hard words occasionally, but it's the Orangemen -'
>
> She laughed. 'I heard the same words, with the religions reversed, from our record when I was a child.'
>
> 'That's very odd', he said meditatively.
>
> 'I wonder how Jim will turn out,' she said after a pause. 'Oh, he'll hold his own,' the priest said proudly. 'With his size and weight or a bit above it he'll be able to give a good account of himself and his religion anywhere.'[59]

The fortunes of Irish land have not the same sacred pull on O'Donovan as on the other writers. He is alive, however, to what it means to others. He understands, but quietly pities, the mentality of those who are consumed by land feuds, where Sheehan and Guinan harboured a secret respect for feuding families:

> Thank God he [the priest's brother] died like a gentleman, broke his

neck taking the sunk fence in the Dalyhouse demesne, and he following the hounds on a spavined horse. And they called him a peasant. Scovell had sneered at him in the coffee room of the Daly Arms at Lisgeela, and at his mount, had called him 'the peasant Daly', Scovell, the grandson of the upstart who had foreclosed the mortgage in '35 and taken the Dalyhouse and every acre and chattel that the Dalys had to their name except a hundred acre farm Pierce the Rake's wife was able to hold on to — Scovell, a mere Cromwellian settler.[60]

He reports also the intrigue, opportunism and utter selfishness of the United Irish League — 'They talked a lot about patriotism and Home Rule, but sorra much the Bunnahone branch cares for only their own pockets'.[61]

His attitude to the Land League in *Conquest* seems curiously cold. He demonstrates how closely landlords and England are identified with each other by relating the saga of a feud between a Daly and a Scovell. Pierce Daly boasts of his successes to date:

I've hurt 'em in their pride and in their pocket, in their politics and their religion — wherever I thought one of 'em'd feel the blow most. I used to go to repeal meetings and I hardly able to walk the ten mile to Tubber and back because Scovell tried to keep the people from going. I was a Young Irelander in '48 and a Fenian in '65 ... and wherever there was trouble for the English or a landlord I was at the head and front of it ... I never rightly knew whether it was love of Ireland or hatred of the Scovells that moved me most.[62]

O'Donovan is untiring in his *exposé* of the gombeen economy. He is especially appalled at the alliance of the clergy with the local shop-keeper/publican magnates who keep the surrounding farmers and poorer townspeople in their grip. He has a malcontent, 'Jim Byrne', in *Ralph*, explain the workings of 'the divine economy':[63]

There's near three-quarters of the town working for the other quarter at nine and ten shillings a week, and living in houses that aren't fit for pigsties .... The gombeen men pay most of the dues and the priests stand by their friends through thick and thin. If a man won't go to mass Fr Tom abuses him and threatens him to get Mr Darcy or Mr Donaghue to give him the sack. And if a man objects to the wages he gets from Hinnissey, he threatens him with hell and damnation and Fr Tom .... Every time I go into the cathedral and see gombeen publicans' names tacked onto every stained glass window and every seat — advertisements for porter and whiskey every one of them — I see the whole place red with the sweated blood of the poor.[64]

Persistently he shows the clergy draining the town of its capital:

> 'The church lets Hinnissey bleed the people and the priests bleed
> Hinnissey'.[65] The clergy have a finger in almost every aspect of the
> economy. A schoolteacher cannot be appointed until his father
> makes a donation to the church spire.[66]

Later in *Vocations* (1921), he shows how convent snobbery conditions
even the daughters of thriving shopkeepers to feel ashamed of their
background. Sr. Eulalie warns the mother of the two heroines that they
must be discreet about the family business when starting in boarding-
school:

> 'Not enough', Sr. Eulalie shook her head emphatically. 'A brewer
> or a distiller or a big wholesale house in Dublin, with the owners
> living, say in Rathgar, is, of course, different. But a mixed wholesale
> and retail in a country town — and living over the shop too! It's
> unheard of.'
>
> ... 'It'd be quite easy, too, to pretend that the shop wasn't there',
> Johanna's retaliatory laugh had in it a shade of malice.
>
> 'Oh, no, no, no pretence, Johanna. That would be sinful. In view of
> all the special circumstances, however, Mother O'Neill thought the
> rules of the convent could be relaxed if the shop were never men-
> tioned.' Sr. Eulalie said hastily, 'they needn't be ashamed of the shop
> or anything like that — just silence and a discreet tongue, with now
> and again, perhaps, a little mental reservation'.[67]

O'Donovan is equally vicious in showing the greed of the nuns for
property. Like the legend of St. Brigid's knack for acquiring land, the nuns
in *Vocations* similarly throw holy medals into desired fields and after
offering novenas, the land falls into their hands.

The manner of fulfilment varied. A recalcitrant owner died, and his heir
was moved to a sense of his religious duty by a substantial price. A novice
brought in a field as a dot. Bankruptcy made another possible. But the
greatest marvel of all was longest in coming. The old reprobate, who for
fifty years forced the nuns to walk to the parish church by the public street,
died intestate, and his property all came to Sister Angelica, his niece, to
whom he had frequently sworn he would never leave a cent:

> Sister Angelica never walked the gravelled path from the convent to
> the parish church, without meditating on the justice of God, mani-
> fested all the more strikingly as her uncle David had left an unsigned
> will bequeathing, in a long clause of derision of the convent, the
> coveted field to a cat's home.[68]

It is O'Donovan's real awareness of the diversity of economic means which prompted him to promote the cooperative movement both in life and in fiction:

> Bourneen was a comparatively rich parish of tillage land, pasture and grazing. The majority of the farms ranged from 20 acres to 50; a few were close on a hundred acres, mixed land for the most part, good, middling and poor, but capable of yielding a comfortable existence. Along the bog, however, on the east of the parish, and stretching up a spur of Slieve Mor, were many small holdings of reclaimed bog and mountain on which life was a constant struggle. And, by the sea, twenty or thirty families depended, half on miserable strips of bottom, half on precarious fishing in small boats on an unsafe shore. The Land Purchase Act had done something to better the conditions of all the farmers, but it had done least for the poorer, and nothing at all for a score of landless labourers.[69]

Soon after Ralph forms a working-man's club, it is secretly but firmly suppressed by the clergy. Suddenly the committee echo the verdict of the parish priest — the club is 'anti-national', or 'irreligious', 'anti-clerical' or 'opposed to the best interests of the town'.[70] O'Donovan reasons that the clergy oppose these regenerative clubs, co-ops and schemes because they 'give the people airs of being able to do things without the help of their parish priest'.[71] And, of course, the co-op scheme flies in the face of the powerful shopkeeper/parish priest *entente*.

In *Ralph* O'Donovan points to the disdain of the Dublin middle class Catholic for their Gaelic-speaking rural heritage. When the attendant in the Dublin museum hails the Celtic exhibits as being 'all the work of Irish speakers', Ralph's nurse assures him that 'most likely them things were made in Johnson's in Grafton Street. No person I ever knew could make the like of them; hard set they'd be to mend an old gate, let alone make them grand things'.[72]

The question of emigration scarcely features on O'Donovan's list of preoccupations. Apparently he was too busy pin-pointing the root causes of it to give the issue any explicit consideration. O'Donovan was a broken idealist. Disillusioned by a less than perfect world, he stopped writing after 1922. Nevertheless his particular contribution to the idea of Ireland and its fate amongst the reading public, sharpens the picture of that island itself.

O'Donovan had a genuine interest in reconciling tensions in Ireland through understanding the fears, passions, and insecurities of history. On the issue of national stereotypes for instance he was remarkably willing to acknowledge the heterogeneous humanity in both nations: 'England's stupid tyrannical side is just *one* side'.

O'Donovan's basic complaint is that the Church was a powerful machine which needed to become more responsive to both the emotional and material needs of its modern people. He also took a more detached, wryly cynical look at people/priest relations. The main difference between O'Donovan and Sheehan and Guinan is that O'Donovan was resolutely of the modern, facing boldly into the twentieth century while the other two would have preferred rather to turn the clock back.

O'Donovan, perhaps predictably, also has the most liberal approach toward the equity of the sexes endowing his female characters with a refreshing complexity, individuality and power.

Section Three: The Reception

7: Sheehan

In 1895, M.H. Gill and Son published *Geoffrey Austin, Student*, Sheehan's first novel. It was issued anonymously and lay on the bookseller's shelves for two years.[1] It did however find favour in the American Catholic press — specifically the *Catholic World* and the *American Ecclesiastical Review* — which fact was called to Sheehan's attention by Fr. Russell of the *Irish Monthly*.[2] Heuser, the editor of the *American Ecclesiastical Review* suggested to Sheehan that he write some sketches of priestly life, 'as a great number of the American priesthood were of Irish birth or descent, a popular atmosphere would be created for such stories'.[3] Within a few months the first ten chapters of the serial were submitted. The sixth however began to wander into Celtic romance, with a priest banishing a witch and fairies, so that Heuser advised him that such elements 'however familiar to local readers' might be out of place in an American review.

The edited sketches, appearing in the May issue of the *American Ecclesiastical Review* in 1898 as anticipated, were an immediate success amongst the American clergy. By the end of the year Marlier, Calenan & Co. of Boston had published the series in book form. In January 1900 the reviewer in the *Irish Monthly* rejoiced that the work had at last 'reached our shores after keeping us waiting so long that already the book is in its fourth edition in the U.S.'[4] He prophesied that it would be a 'record-breaking and epoch-making book'. He noted that though it was meant more directly for priests 'it would do the laity no harm to study it, as they are sure to do'. It was distributed in Britain and Ireland by the Art and Book Company of London. Sheehan had again left *My New Curate* anonymous, but when he discovered that some of the Irish bishops, including his own bishop of Cloyne, had taken to it, he claimed it.[5]

The *Irish Monthly* notes that with the success of *My New Curate*, 'orders by the hundred have poured into Messrs M.H. Gill & Son' from the priests of the U.S. enquiring about *Geoffrey Austin*.[6] Gills subsequently twice reissued the novel now with the author's name on the title page. Heuser tells how 30,000 copies of *My New Curate* were sold within eighteen months, not including translations.[7] It was probably Russell who in the *Irish Monthly* expressed astonishment 'at the welcome accord to such a book':

> For instance, in a dull English town like Hull the managers of the
> public library were compelled to supply their patrons with four
> copies of *My New Curate*; and these we have been told are never
> allowed to repose for a moment on the shelves.[8]

This raises the question of readership in England. Though Irish emigrants were probably responsible here, Sheehan may also have had an
audience amongst English Catholics and amongst interested English Protestants. English reviewers of O'Donovan's works in 1913 and 1914,
however, saw his 'inside' explanation of clerical life in fiction as a new
departure.

Meanwhile *The Triumph of Failure* published in 1898 by Burns, Oates
and Washbourne of London had attracted little attention. Fr J.P. Hogan
who was to watch Sheehan's career closely in the *Irish Ecclesiastical
Review* saw it as unreal and exaggerated with the philosophical element
too obtrusive for fiction. He gave *My New Curate* unqualified praise
however 'trusting that Sheehan's example might stimulate others to labour
for the same good cause in fields that are still unexplored'.[9] Heuser notes
it was not long before ecclesiastics of distinction from 'the colonies and
the states' descended on Doneraile to see the author of *My New Curate*.
Sheehan recorded in his diary such names as Dr Yorke of San Francisco,
Dr John T. Mullen of Hudson, Massachussets and Dr James Cotter of Ohio
(author of *Shapespeare's Art*, 1903).[10]

In a letter to Longmans of London (30 Sept. 1901) Sheehan explains
that it was 'the request of S. Brown, and the necessity of immediate and
simultaneous publications in London and New York, that influenced me
in deciding to place the book *Luke Delmege* at your disposal'.[11] Apparently having some difficulty in reaching an agreement on colonial sales,
Sheehan reminds Longmans of his popularity:

> Perhaps I should have mentioned before that this book was sought
> by Marlier, Boston and Herder, St. Louis, who allowed me name my
> own terms. Also the following London publishers solicited the book:
> Messrs Burns and Oats & Washbourne, The Art and Book Company
> [who acted as London agents for the distribution of *My New Curate*],
> T. Fisher Unwin who would have purchased the copy-right .... Father
> Luke seems an imitation of R. Buchanan's Father Anthony, and
> would challenge comparison, though I anticipate for my book far
> greater popularity. ... These chapters now have to run in the *American
> Ecclesiastical Review*. Twelve months ago orders were placed in the

hands of Boston publishers for this book from the leading book-sellers of America. I think you would do well to notify to the American and British public that the book will be published by your firm in November or early December.

Yours truly, P.A.S.[12]

One month later Heuser sold the copyright of *Luke Delmege* to Sheehan for one dollar.[13] Sheehan was to get 15% royalties on the first 7,500 copies sold and 20% on the price of the English edition sold beyond that.[14] It was first issued in an edition of 10,000 copies, ten times more than the typical average number per edition. The following year, Longmans agreed to have a French translation published entitled *Ames Saxonnes et âmes Celtiques*.[15] It was translated into German in 1904.[16] It was hailed in the American publication *Catholic World* as 'one of the finest works that the art of fiction has ever given to the world'.[17] Bibliographical articles by Mathew Russell about Sheehan soon appeared in *The Dolphin, Catholic World* and *American Ecclesiastical Review* and his sermons were printed in the *Homiletic Review* of New York.[18]

J.F. Hogan in the *Irish Ecclesiastical Record* wrote an extremely lengthy review of *Luke Delmege* and Sheehan's progress to date.[19] He was astonished that Sheehan, though claiming to be a supporter of the Irish language movement, could not find Irish names for his characters. He pointed out that Sheehan's clerical personages are not typical of the Irish priesthood but then typical priests would be of little interest in fiction. Having approved of *Luke Delmege* at the beginning of the review for its contribution towards stemming the tide of corrupt literature, he continues to tell of its reception in Maynooth:

> We have heard of persons who think that in all this Fr Sheehan has dealt an unnatural blow at the reputation of his *Alma Mater*. There are few, we imagine, so narrow minded as to share in this view. We prefer to think that the interest of the author of *Luke Delmege* in his own college is not the less warm and sincere because he has spoken so freely of what he regards as some of her shortcomings. Whether he is justified in his strictures is a matter that we would like to leave to others to decide. All we can say is that to us they appear supremely ridiculous .... If she has turned out a 'Luke Delmege' has she not also turned out a parish priest of Doneraile? The greatest tribute to her position in the ecclesiastical world is that so many persons should be concerned about her merits and defects. She has in hand, in truth, an undertaking that is serious and weighty enough not to trouble

herself about trifles.

It is probable that in the future, as in the past, the Irish clergy will look for the ideal in such matters to St. Charles Borromeo and St. Vincent de Paul, to Jean Jacques Olier and the Council of Trent, rather than to the lofty personages created to give them hints and suggestions by the author of *Luke Delmege*.[20]

In Sheehan's interview for the student magazine *St. Stephen's* (1902), he pointed out the 'certain importance attached to my writings with having now half-a million readers in America alone'.[21] The interviewer notes the figure was attested to by the *Boston Pilot*. In 1904 the reviewer in the *Irish Monthly* was much relieved to see at last his collection of essays, *Under the Cedars and the Stars*, published in book form, noting many Irish readers had already enroled themselves in the literary supplement to the *American Ecclesiastical Review*, *The Dolphin*, where it was first serialised:

It has the one charm in particular of revealing to us more of the author's personality than his novels; and who amongst us is without that craving to see 'behind the veil?' Many have quite a morbid curiosity concerning the inner life of a man whom they admire. Whether he be a Napoleon, a Leo XIII or a Tennyson, they like to know everything about him, down to his very weaknesses and hobbies. Are we not then privileged in being allowed to penetrate into Fr. Sheehan's sanctum?[23]

The first edition of the collection however sold only 2,500 copies, though there were at least 4,000 copies first issued. Apparently Sheehan held high hopes for the collection, adding to the contract that the agreement with Longman's could be terminated after seven years, and reserving to himself all rights of translation, reproduction, serial and dramatic rights.[24]

Glenanaar (Longmans, 1905) sold 11,500 copies in its first year. The *Irish Monthly* hoped it would soon overtake *Luke Delmege*, then in its twelfth thousand.[25] The *New Ireland Review* observed that an interesting feature of the book was 'the prevalent Irish-Ireland tone, the occasional Irish phrases and the spirit of the *Sinn Féin* policy with which it is strongly infused'. It also predicted for the novel an enormous popularity.[26] Though it was well reviewed generally the *Irish Ecclesiastical Record* included a notice, by Edward Nagle, regretting Sheehan's 'new departure'.[27] The story he thought was too 'grim' and 'sombre' with scarcely a trace of that 'innocent drollery flavoured by the introduction of the clerical element in a manner that [before *My New Curate*] has never hitherto been approached'. He had hoped Sheehan would break the 'sombre' tradition of 'the Irish novelists' — the Banims, Gerald Griffin and Kickham.

Indirectly criticising *Luke Delmege* he approves in *Glenanaar* of the 'bold, clear outline of character types rather than the introspective attempt at psychological realism — better to be up and doing than turning a search-light upon their own inner selves'. He congratulates Sheehan on dispensing with the long, erudite passages of philosophy and excuses him for depicting a wealthy, returned emigrant because at least if he is himself affluent, he is not 'discreetly silent' about his less fortunate fellow-Irish-men, as are some of his type in real life'. The *New Ireland Review* of 1907 was grateful also for the new light in which the Irish clergy were drawn:

> The electioneering curates, and the foxhunting parish priests (whose prototypes never probably existed in fact) have had their day in fiction, ... Canon Sheehan has come forward and introduced us to a galaxy of genial, good-humoured priests.[28]

Lisheen (1907), first appeared in the *Catholic World*. The first book edition (Longmans, 1907) sold 11,600 copies, about the same number as *Glenanaar*. J.F. Hogan in the *Irish Ecclesiastical Record* felt 'that some-how it is not the thing'.[29] Oliver Wendell Holmes agreed with him that Sheehan's 'fashionable people' were not quite so real as his peasants.[30] Soon after it was serialized in the *Catholic Times*, Sheehan received at least one cheque for his novel of £152-9s-10d.[31] Curiously *A Spoiled Priest and Other Stories* (1905) was published by Unwin and three years later *Canon Sheehan's Short Stories* by Burns and Oates. These were not widely received, however, and no sales records survive for them.

Returning to Longmans and the 'clerical novel', the *Blindness of Dr Gray* appeared in 1909. The *Spectator* thought this 'profoundly interest-ing'.[32] Longmans halved the number of copies of the first edition from, for example, the first printing of *Luke Delmege*.[33] Hogan found the 'old gentleman rather gloomy and depressing'; his curate 'rather priggish and pedantic' and his niece 'anything but convincing in her relations with the Wycherleys'. He thought the gypsy and Romany subplot 'forced upon us a little more than is needful'. However, he added:

> There is not a time we visit the continent that we do not meet with scholars, both lay and clerical, who have been deeply impressed with the culture and education of the Irish clergy, as evidenced by the works of the author of *My New Curate*. For this, if for nothing else, all Irish priests owe him a deep debt of gratitude.[34]

The *Irish Monthly* reviewer though he understood the novelist had to be careful 'to represent persons and things in such a way that they are no longer recognizable by those who live amongst them', intimated that Sheehan had perhaps this time gone a little too far:

> No doubt there are great differences of character and custom in different parts of Ireland, but many will dispute the correctness of some of the impressions about our priests and people that strangers will carry away from these brilliant pages.[35]

The Blindness of Dr Gray like most of Sheehan's works had already (in 1908) been serialised in the *American Ecclesiastical Review* and *The Dolphin* as 'The final law'.[36]

The Intellectuals or The Sunetoi as Sheehan preferred to title it, first ran in the Irish Rosary (1910) where it was immediately unpopular with the readers and soon terminated. Longmans published it, however, in 1911.[37] Predictably it did not prove nearly as popular as his novels. In the same year Sheehan wrote to Longmans with reference to a new edition of his *Early essays and lectures*, first published in 1906 at a loss.[38] He suggests the first 200 copies could be royalty free — 'As I would not like to see any of my books going out of print during my life-time'.[39]

A year later, preparing Longmans for *Miriam Lucas*, he writes:

> I have a novel in manuscript dealing with socialism: and although written some years ago, it has a graphic picture of the present strike in Ireland. It could be published in time for the Christmas markets, but our postal service is completely disarranged just now.[40]

Miriam Lucas was published towards the end of 1911. Selling 11,300 copies in the first edition, it was acclaimed by the *Irish Monthly*.[41] 'M' in the *Irish Ecclesiastical Record* observed that although 'we cannot deny the author the right to exercise his art in fiction of this class, we can deny his claim to originality, or even to pre-eminence in it'. He declared that 'the vitality of literature must be maintained from local sources, [Miriam Lucas travels to New York and back] it fails when it relies upon art alone'.[42]

Sheehan's death in 1913 provides the opportunity to see what those besides reviewers thought of him: The *Catholic Bulletin* regretted that 'not until Ireland realises herself can we see the products of native genius in proper perspective'.[43] *The Triumph of Failure* was here judged to be his greatest work and 'should be seen in the hands of every Irish student at the most impressionable period of his life'. The *Irish Catholic* remarked that all Catholics should be grateful for him as he proved that 'essentially Catholic themes have in them all the elements needed for pure literature'.[44]

Of the English papers, *The Times*,[45] *Morning Post*[46] and *Westminster Gazette*[47] all paid tribute to him, the latter observing that Sheehan's death 'breaks the quartet of popular novelists who are priests of the Catholic Church: Mgr Benson, Dr William Barry, Mgr Bickerstaffe-Drew — better known to the reading public as 'John Ayscough'. The *Cork Free Press* published tributes to him for the entire week after his death with appreciations from the Gaelic League, All for Ireland League, and from many of his (mostly clerical) friends.[48] The chairman of the local Libraries Committee told 'how no author was so much sought after as Canon Sheehan'. A letter from the Dublin Corporation revealed that Sheehan's name had been before the Council with a view to being placed on the list of the Freemen of Dublin, but owing to the author's humility, they had lost the opportunity of honouring him.[49] The honorary treasurer of the Cork G.A.A. Board remembered a match in Fermoy, which was vividly described in one of Sheehan's books [*Glenanaar*]. One American priest wrote a poem on Sheehan and his works which was also published here.[50]

Selling promptly 13,000 copies, *The Graves at Kilmorna* was published by Longmans in 1915, two years after the author's death. The *Irish Book Lover* observed the 'vein of pessimism' running through it and thought 'Myles Cogan' must have been an exceptionally sensitive individual as the reviewer knew an old '67 man' who had gone through precisely the same trials and yet 'a merrier man he never met'.[51] Later biographers such as Boyle (1957), Linehan (1952) and Houlihan (1971) blame Yeats for stealing Sheehan's thunder, recalling how after 1916, *Kilmorna* was regarded as the vision of more than a prophet but then 'Yeats with his ingrained arrogance' took all the credit for inspiring the rebellion.[52] Heuser comments on his widespread popularity on the continent and indeed nearly all his works were translated. Sheehan is quoted as having written in a letter to Holmes, that his books had never 'caught on in France' — 'because I have written somewhat enthusiastically about Germany, but in the Fatherland and especially Austria and Hungary, these books are great favourites'.[53] John Horgan (author of *Great Catholic Laymen*) wrote Heuser from Madrid that in Spain and Portugal his works were looked upon as classics of Catholic Literature.

In 1917, four years after Sheehan's death, he was accorded three lengthy assessments. The first in the *Irish Ecclesiastical Record*, expressed astonishment at the rapidity with which he acquired the mastery of his art. Michael Phelan S.J., the reviewer, put him in a category of genius all his own with the observation that 'to all great artists, Newman, Gibbon, Michelangelo, Sheehan formed unique exception in never having to rewrite a line'. Phelan noted that *The Triumph of Failure*, his favourite, was then in its fifth edition. He was angered by what he called the inconsistency of the 'gratuitous criticism' received by Sheehan, citing J.F. Hogan's faultfinding with *Geoffrey Austin* and *Luke Delmege*. He wondered why at the annual meetings of the Catholic Truth Society and sometimes at the Maynooth Union there is a cry for great Catholic writers and when such a writer does appear he is 'assailed by his own co-religionists'. He concludes that Sheehan's real crime lay in his success.[54]

John D. Colclough, who taught in Gayfield Seminary, Donnybrook — the 'Mayfield' of *Geoffrey Austin* — contributed an article to *Studies* in June of that year regretting that Sheehan had not confined himself to devotional works:

> Here Canon Sheehan was in his true province .... But injudicious and undiscerning critics took him in hand, hailing him as the pioneer of a new world of Catholic imaginative literature. He was not a great literateur. He was a great priest. He possessed every priestly virtue.
>
> The next generation may know the titles of Sheehan's novels. They will not know their contents.[55]

Soon after, again in *Studies*, Professor George O'Neill, S.J., M.A. explained the melancholy of *Kilmorna* owed much to Sheehan's intellectual frustration:

> A man of high ideals and sensitive spirit who never found a congenial and sympathetic *milieu*, who received praise indeed, but seldom the right kind of praise, who always hungered for the spiritual gains and pleasures of a university life and found they were always denied him — such a man sees perhaps too readily, his own peculiar tragedy reflected in a larger tragedy of national history ...
>
> ... The mind of the author was one that encompassed much but grasped little.[56]

Sheehan's great patron, Herman J. Heuser brought out a biography in 1918 (New York), *The Story of Canon Sheehan of Doneraile as told chiefly by himself in his novels, letters, memoirs and autobiography*. Stephen Brown in his *Ireland in Fiction* (1919) was generally most approving of Sheehan's works. He saw *Luke Delmege* as 'One of the best, if not the best, of Irish novels' but as a problem novel it was 'strangely inconclusive'. He was slightly negative in describing Sheehan's last two volumes, *Miriam Lucas* and *Kilmorna*. In the former he thought the author raised more problems than he solved, in the latter the plot and incident were but slight and he disapproved of the author's gloom and pessimism about modern Ireland.[57]

There was a silence with regard to Sheehan until the late 1920s when there seems to have been a resurgence of interest in him and in his novels. 1927 saw the publication of a simple biography by Fr Francis Boyle, C.C. A morose reviewer in the *Irish Ecclesiastical Record* found it difficult to believe that there was 'need among the reading public of Ireland for a volume of this kind on the late Canon Sheehan' as twenty years ago Canon Sheehan's life was common knowledge:

> And now he is almost forgotten. His writings are no longer in favour, and are relegated to the top shelves of the parochial lending-library or presented on prize-day in convents to successful students who think them too dull to read. ... One must admit that Canon Sheehan has nearly passed into oblivion when Fr Boyle considered it necessary to publish these facts and views of his life and writings. His writings are probably passing through their most trying phase at the present day and will, later on, be accorded the place they merit in literature, but to rehabilitate them just now would require a better informed and more interesting volume than the one before us.[70]

In 1927 Longmans wrote to the Bishop of Cloyne, to whom Sheehan's royalties were now due, informing him that they would publish in New York a new edition of *Intellectuals* if he agreed to reduce his royalty from 20% to 15%.[58] The royalties on *Kilmorna*, however, as it was published posthumously, remained with the author's brother Denis. The London branch of Longmans in the same year wrote to the New York branch with a view to reissuing *Kilmorna*: 'Mr. D.B. Sheehan, as usual, seems very unwilling to reduce the royalty upon the *Graves at Kilmorna* but I am writing to him again and hope he will give way'.[59] Meanwhile the *Catholic Times* was given permission to serialise *Intellectuals* for the sum of £25.00.[60]

Concerning a reissue of *Parerga*, a collection of essays originally published in 1908, the bishop was informed that they were selling 30 to 40 copies a year: 'and if 1,000 copies were printed they would probably be sold in course of time. It would not however be possible to pay 25% but maybe 15%'.[61] In 1930 *The Queen's Fillet* was reissued in a series called 'Longman's romances'. Though this time the bishop received only

10% in royalties, he was assured of a large sale.[62]

In 1928, by special arrangement with the bishop, *My New Curate* was eventually published in Ireland by Talbot. Also issued was *Tristram Lloyd*, an unfinished manuscript of Sheehan's. It told the story of a Geoffrey Austin-like Irish Journalist and his unhappy sister who dies before Tristram discovers his own happiness. It was finished by M.H. Gaffrey O.P. who was commissioned by the executors. He also edited the *Irish Rosary* and dramatised some of Pearse's stories.[63] The *Dublin Magazine* thought it should have been left unfinished — 'a relic of a great Irishman'. The one interesting feature of the book, they added, was the biographical introduction by Heuser.[64]

Easons drew attention in 1928 to *Tristram Lloyd*, a new edition of *Kilmorna* (1925) and to the much lower price of the Talbot edition of *My New Curate* compared with the current American edition.[65] A few months later they reported in their Monthly Bulletin that both Talbot books were meeting with 'a very good demand'.[66] Meanwhile the *Catholic Bulletin* had, in 1926 another article praising *Geoffrey Austin*.[67] *Studies* had a contribution from Sophie O'Brien, wife of William O'Brien, reporting on a Gaelic League lecture in Mallow of that year which was devoted to Sheehan:

> The lecturer so carried his hearers that when he had done speaking, there was a suggestion of raising a monument in Mallow to Canon Sheehan and the other two illustrious Mallow men whose names the lecturer had brought together — Thomas Davis and William O'Brien.[68]

P. Ivers Rigney subjected Sheehan's suggestion on the educational system to detailed scrutiny in a 1930 issue of the *Irish Ecclesiastical Record*, implying that Sheehan's ideas were élitist and impractical.[69]

Dr William Stockley, ex-Professor of English at University College Cork, and nephew of William Smith O'Brien, followed in 1933 with a short, but telling biography of Sheehan. He remarks that if Sheehan suffered from 'irritated *confrères*', 'he has certainly suffered now from those who think to raise him, by turning him into an idol'. He makes a most interesting reference to a comment of Fr Russell's but, alas, cites no source:

> Yet Fr Russell came to say, 'I object to the idea that Canon Sheehan gives of our Irish people. It is not like the people at all, as far as I have seen them.' And the Irish Jesuit critic continues: 'he pleases English critics too much' adding that the *Westminster Gazette* says

very truly; 'Canon Sheehan does not like the Irish character'.[71]

Many of Sheehan's novels were translated into Irish during the 1930s. *Glenanaar* was first translated and published in 1931 as *Gleann an Áir* and reissued in 1937. *Uaigheanna Chill Mhoirne* (*The Graves of Kilmorna*) appeared in 1933, *An Sagart Óg* (*My New Curate*) in 1936, *Filead na Bainrioghaine* (*The Queen's Fillet*) in 1937 and *Lisín* in 1939. Agreements for the translations of *The Queen's Fillet*, *Glenanaar* and *Kilmorna* were made with the Minister of Education, the first costing £20 with no royalties due.[72] *Gleann an Áir* sold 2,099 copies, *Lisín* (Lisheen) a mere 150, *Filead na Banrioghna* only 110 and *An Sagart Óg* a redeeming 1,175.[73] The first and last were more probably deemed more suitable as school textbooks, owing to their lighter nature and stronger plots, so that this may account for the large difference in sales. Generally however it was these two novels, in both Irish and English, which Irish readers preferred.

Neil Kevin in 1937 dedicated 'To Maynooth men all over the world' his happy memoirs of Maynooth (*I remember Maynooth*). The last chapter he devotes to a scrutiny of *Luke Delmege* in order to show that the character was very much ficticious. He had no memory of the novel ever being discussed though he had 'a real affection' for all Sheehan's novels. Regretting that Sheehan was never fêted in the halls of his *alma mater* he would have been comforted to think 'that no one there had said or written anything to make greater that dull pain'.[74] Kevin's attitude towards Sheehan, and *Luke Delmege* in particular, was as ambivalent as that of Hogan, Professor of Modern Languages in Maynooth who reviewed many of Sheehan's works in the *Irish Ecclesiastical Record*.

Again in 1939 M.H. Gaffney complained that Sheehan's books were on the verge of being forgotten — 'They share that dismal fate with the books of Lever, Kickham and many other writers who wrote to the tempo of their generation'.[75] Yet the 30th impression of *Knocknagow* was printed by Gill in 1935.

The Capuchin Annual of 1942 included another long essay on Sheehan's achievement by Fr Michael, O.F.M. Cap. 'Great was his wonder' that Daniel Corkery did not condescend to mention Canon Sheehan in his hard but just words about 'This submerged world of Anglo-Irish literature'. Fr Michael comforts himself that 'it must be because Canon Sheehan is unique, in a class by himself'. He remarks that Corkery was not sorry that *Knocknagow* was unknown except to the Irish. Fr Michael, irate that

Knocknagow got a mention and Sheehan was ignored, points out that Sheehan is known all over America and Europe: 'His work has wrought conversions to the faith'. He points out that eight of Sheehan's novels have been translated into German, three into French, some into Dutch, Italian, Hungarian and Slavonic as well as Irish. He continues to apply Corkery's thesis of 'Land, Religion and Nationalism' to Sheehan's work, proving that Sheehan's novels were immersed in all three elements. 'Sheehan', he remarked, 'like every priest is savagely attacked by his own'. Scathingly he remembers 'Fr Russell's lady critic' (Katherine Tynan) who would not review *The Triumph of Failure* 'saying it was too high for me'. He continues in the same vein:

> A priest, and a Canon at that, and 'first of first' in his diocese exclaimed to me once; 'Sheehan, Pshaw! He never wrote anything worth while except one poem — *Senan the Culdee*' ...
>
> One might not go too far in saying he created the clerical novel in the English language. Clerical is a word enough to make even some Irish men froth at the mouth and to make even the Catholic nowadays nervous because the half believes the clergy have undue influence. Most men would not worry about the word as applied to *John Inglesant* or *Barchester Towers*. But these are very small beer beside the sparkling champagne of Canon Sheehan.

Even Frs Heuser and Russell were suspected by this reviewer of being 'conscious that the glamour of editorship of his work would give them a reflected glory'. He reports in the *Capuchin Annual* (1942) how 'a North Monastery boy' (a reputable Cork Secondary school *cum* seminary) reported that he had read all Sheehan's novels. It was noted that Sheehan was a favourite topic for theses amongst German university students and indeed, 'our students in the national university and in some of our ecclesiastical colleges are still presenting their theses on Canon Sheehan for the M.A. degree'. Indeed Sheehan's very substantial body of writing continues to provide rare documentary insight into some of the processes through which Irish Catholic identities were formed.

The Blindness of Dr Gray was translated into Dutch in 1946.[78] *My New Curate* and *The Triumph of Failure* were still selling in Eason's, in the company of the works of Rosa Mulholland, E.J. Edwards, Cecily Hallack and F. Parkinson Keyes.[79]

In a 1947 article of the *Irish Bookman* Declan Meehan remarks on the loneliness caused Sheehan in his childhood years by his perception of himself as being 'different from the average'. He traces to this the cause of that 'faintly puzzling indefinable attraction which, after we have read the novels, lasts longer than our irritation with the, at times, altogether misplaced erudition in which they abound'. He observes that Canon Sheehan remains 'more than a moderately successful Irish novelist, read and re-read by a considerable number of Irish people. He remains a "must" for anyone setting out to make a study of literature in Ireland'.[80]

What appears as a most realistic observation came from the special 50th anniversary *Annual of the Catholic Truth Society* in 1949. It was Canon Sheehan's pamphlets and short stories only, however, which were circulated by this organisation:

> Apart from the 'holy' stories, others in our series have come in for criticism — the simple stories of such writers as Canon Sheehan, Katherine Tynan [who thought Sheehan 'too high for me'], Rose Mulholland and Canon Schmid. We utter no *mea culpa* for these, for though it must be conceded that they are altogether too simple for the sophisticated world of today, they were written in a world that had not even dreamed of film or radio, and for a population that had hardly even been touched by foreign press influence. The contempt heaped upon them today by so many is merely a measure of the change that has taken place in the mind and manners of our people.[81]

In 1952, the centenary of Sheehan's birth, M.P. Linehan (in whose uncle's house Sheehan had found the newspaper back issues reporting the Doneraile conspiracy trials) brought out a biography. Perplexed to find Sheehan's name absent from the roll call of Irish literary greats, he embarked on a lengthy explanation. The reasons essentially were threefold according to Linehan. They were not to be found 'in the deficiencies of his art, but in its very qualities, in the historical background against which he wrote and others in the psychological makeup of our modern world':

> If it is accepted that Irish culture, or lack of culture is the culture, or lack of culture of a Shaw or a Joyce, then we must reorientate all our sense of values .... The Ireland painted in *Luke Delmege* is not the Ireland portrayed on the boards of the *Abbey* or the *Gate*, but it is infinitely a more real Ireland. Visit Gardiner Street Church on the night or morning of any novena and you will find the scenes witnessed by *Luke Delmege* ... Sit in any village church on Hallow E'en and you will hear the same remarks that *Luke Delmege* heard when he was preparing the altar list for the dead in Rossmore.[82]

Linehan asserted that the odds were against Sheehan owing to his subscription to the conciliatory policy of the All-for-Ireland League:

The minority party which Sheehan supported was originally brought into being because anybody with a Cork accent was refused a hearing at an All-Ireland Nationalist Convention. Canon Sheehan had a Cork accent and his reputation in Nationalist circles suffered accordingly.[83]

It is doubtful if Sheehan's support for 'the minority party' (*i.e.* William O'Brien's section of the All-for-Ireland League) amounted to any more than his fiery anonymous address in the *Cork Free Press* and his pastorly supervision of the Wyndham Act in Doneraile. But if it did, all account of it was effectively suppressed. It could well have been that what the author described to Russell as 'the few exciting episodes' in his memoirs which were 'never intended for print' were to do with activity such as this, but these he instructed his brother to burn before his death, fearing 'they might do harm to others'.[84]

Linehan regrets that Sheehan, a cultural revolutionary whose *Kilmorna* (1915) inspired Sinn Féin, was forgotten after 1916 when 'the political circumstances of the time threw the spotlight on the writings of the men of Easter Week'. The disillusionment and cynicism of the early years of the Free State — 'The age of jazz and chromium', the 'speed, noise, and vulgarity' of the 30s ensured that a generation had grown up ignorant of Canon Sheehan. Another reason he feels was that the 'all out drive for the restoration of the national language' meant that literature in English was relegated to a minor place so that Sheehan was 'hidden in the consequent black-out'. Further back, the purpose of the Celtic literary revival was, Linehan saw plainly, to obliterate all Ireland had learned from Greece, Rome and Judea and this was after all what Sheehan most cherished. Because 'Irish thought' after his death 'was completely occupied by things political and economic' ... it left a clear field to the paganism of Yeats, the Theosophy of A.E., or the socialism of Sean O'Casey.

> The clique which had arrogated to itself the function of dictating to Ireland in all things literary was drawn from a class who a few generations before, in the words of Edmund Burke, had created 'a machine of wise and elaborate contrivance, as well fitted for the oppression of a people, as ever proceeded from the perverted ingenuity of man' .... The braggadocio of Lever and Lover might be played out, but there still remained the superstitious peasant, living a lotus life and enshrouded in 'the mists that do be on the bog'.

> Anybody, least of all a Catholic priest, who dared to suggest the contrary, was to be discredited and disowned. It would never do that

Dublin should be shown to the world through the cultural and religious life described in *The Triumph of Failure*, that the fisherfolk should be painted as they are in *My New Curate*, that the rural dwellers should be described as they are in *Lisheen*. Rather must the world's impression of Ireland and the Irish be gathered from *The Shadow of a Gunman, The Playboy of the Western World*, or *John Bull's Other Island*.[85]

Linehan singles out unusual Sheehan readers for special mention. These however, demand introduction, so that the purpose is defeated. For example, Msgr William Barry of Dorchester:

— himself a writer of such standing that he was chosen by the editors of the Home University Library of Modern Knowledge to write for them on 'The Papacy and Modern Times 1303-1870' ... While the Countesse Costa de Beauvegara [of Italy] paid tribute to the effect on the religious life of her children's nurse from the reading of *My New Curate*.[86]

Also in 1952, the ever-faithful *Capuchin Annual* marked the centenary with an essay competition on the subject of Canon Sheehan. Adjudicated by Fr Henry, O.F.M. Cap., Chevalier Thomas MacGreery and Sheehan's old friend from Cork D.L. Kelleher Esq. The first prize went to Miss Winefride Nolan from Co Wicklow. Born in Wales of an Irish father, in the year Sheehan died, she was then married to a Wicklow farmer and awaiting the publication of her first novel in the Autumn of 1952 — *Rich Inheritance*. She considered how the complexity of Sheehan's plots were 'woven into a harmonious whole' and found that Sheehan evoked a pleasantly romantic past:

One remembers with nostalgia, in this age when the spurious internationalism of the cinema and chain store is imposing a drab uniformity of sophistication upon the characteristics of nations, the individuality of his Irish people.[87]

L.J. Wrenne, the winner of the second prize started out life as a national teacher, joined the civil service but, refusing to take the oath of allegiance, had left to become news editor of the *Cork Examiner* during the War of Independence. He was, in 1952, manager of a printing press in Midleton, Cork. The only interest of his essay is in his plea to the Irish Tourist Association to produce a booklet for the benefit of tourists in Doneraile to be entitled the *Spenser-Sheehan Country*.[88] Other competitors included Liam Brophy — 'one of the most prolific, popular and authoritative writers on Catholic topics'. He laments that since Sheehan 'The liturgical movement has made pathetically little headway in Ireland'. Noting how the contemporary laity 'seal off our spiritual life from the mere secular levels' he traces the origin of this 'habit of mind' to 'the dualism of our former Lutheran rulers'.[89]

Pádraig O Dargáin, a journalist with the *Enniscorthy Echo*, was a grandson and grandnephew of two farmers who belonged to the society Sheehan established to oversee the smooth running of the Wyndham Land Act in Doneraile. He was first prompted, he explained, to study Sheehan's writings after hearing a lecture by Daniel Corkery.

O Dargáin pointed out that it is easy for people nowadays to praise the Fenians but not so easy was it in Sheehan's time 'when the memories of the Fenian Rising were fresher and when those of power and influence discouraged such sentiments'. He asserted that Ireland's youth could 'make Ireland a great nation spiritually, culturally and even materially, if ever a worthwhile majority could be persuaded to assist at Holy Mass daily and to recite the Rosary daily'. The first step in this direction would be 'to persuade them to read and re-read the writings of Canon Sheehan'.[90]

A nun, 'B.M.', sent in a tribute to Mother Ita O'Connell who died in 1950 and had encouraged Sheehan's literary activities, reading his manu-scripts before dispatch to the publishers.[91] The Very Rev. John O. Bucha-nan, an Irish American, described as a builder of 'million dollar schools in America', was grateful for the insight in Sheehan's novels to the private life of the priest which 'is shrouded in deep mystery for the average man, especially the non-Catholic'.[92] Mrs O'Brien, wife of William, contributed yet another account of the author's close friendship with her husband. A similar article had already been published in the *Annual* three years previously on this subject.[93]

Gladys V. Towers reported in the *Irish Monthly* (1952) that Sheehan's picture held a place of honour in many homes and 'his sayings are constantly repeated'.[94] Fr S. Rigby, impressed by Ó Faoláin's *The Great O'Neill* referred to the pioneering stance of James Fitzmaurice, the six-teenth-century Munster rebel, in identifying Ireland with Catholicism, 'Faith and Fatherland'. But Rigby points out Sheehan's Ireland was not a Fatherland but Motherland as 'Myles Cogan' had revealed:

> A woman beneath a round tower and ruined abbey, a harp by her side; a wolf-dog at her knee; all looking towards a sunrise or a sunset above an illimitable ocean.[95]

The Blindness of Dr Gray got another lease of life in 1953 when it was reissued by Talbot. However, Longmans at this point felt the market for Sheehan's work had disappeared. Corresponding with Talbot, the director wrote:

> Thank you for letting us know re reprint of *The Blindness of Dr Gray*. Judging by the other two novels which we reissued some time ago, I think it is unlikely that we should feel like importing sheets from you, should this possibly have occurred to you.[96]

'With St Patrick's day just around the corner' Easons' bulletin warned booksellers in 1954 that 'the following very popular titles will almost certainly continue to be in demand and you should check your stock against the list':

> *The Irish Republic* — D. Macardle
>
> *The Fight for Irish Freedom* — D. Breen
>
> *Political Writings and Speeches* — P. Pearse
>
> *Jail Journal* — J. Mitchel
>
> *Speeches from the Dock* — W. Tone et al
>
> *Death Sails the Shannon* — Griffin
>
> *Stories of Frank O'Connor* — F O'Connor
>
> *Lisheen* — Canon Sheehan
>
> *The Graves at Kilmorna* — Canon Sheehan
>
> *The Blindness of Dr Gray* — Canon Sheehan
>
> *My New Curate* — Canon Sheehan
>
> *Sally Kavanagh* — C.J. Kickham
>
> *Ireland and the Irish* — C. Duff.[97]

Clonmore and Reynolds reprinted *The Triumph of Failure* and *The Graves at Kilmorna* in 1956. Easons were still selling Sheehan's novels up to the late 1960s but sales records are not forthcoming.[98] The Talbot edition of *My New Curate* at any rate was reprinted for the tenth time in 1958.

Linehan contributed again three consecutive articles on Sheehan to the *Irish Independent* of November 1968. He claimed that in the hospitals of Salonika and the trenches of Adrianople during the Balkan wars of 1911-12, Slav translations of Sheehan's works were popular with the Bulgarian and Servian soldiers. Linehan also asserted that the popularity of the novels 'has lasted almost down to our own day for until its copyright exhausted a new edition of at least one of his novels was brought out every second year since his death.[99]

From the 1930s until the 1970s the Phoenix Publishing Company, an off-shoot of the Talbot Press, took sheets of Canon Sheehan's novels from Talbot, bound them specially and circulated them in uniform editions at reasonable prices. They were sold all over the country from door to door, on the street, to country school masters for school libraries, and by mail order. Those in the trade estimate that they sold approximately 1,000 copies a year in the 30s and the figure hardly climbed in the later decades. Then it was regarded as one of the livelier activities of the Talbot Press which normally confined itself to liturgical publishing.[105] Many houses and libraries around the country still keep one of these sets, regarded by older generations as a treasure.

Linehan speaks of how Sheehan 'anticipated spiritual problems and foresaw Ireland as a religious sanatorium to which would come those suffering from a spiritual leukaemia resulting from the scientific splitting of the human personality.'[100]

Linehan pointed to the utility of Sheehan's 'spiritual medicine for the new paganism of 1968', pointing out that democracy has resulted merely in the anarchy and revolt at authority of the 1960s. *Glenanaar* he suggested might be profitably televised by *Teilifís Eireann*, and a school of Sheehan studies would make a valuable contribution to present day thinking. This would be far more edifying than schools such as those celebrating 'Merriman's genius'.[101]

The series of articles inspired the establishment in the following year of a 'Friends of Canon Sheehan Society'. With membership at 10/- and chaired by Mr. Robert Walker, its aims were

1) To extol Sheehan and popularise his writings here and abroad

2) To have his novels adapted for T.V. and radio

3) To have his writings readily available in cheap editions if possible

4) To set up a summer school in Doneraile

5) To develop Doneraile as a tourist attraction with the aid of Bord Fáilte.[102]

Through the *Catholic Standard* members were found in Spain and Britain. Though the Phoenix Publishing Company was still issuing his work in sets of twelve volumes, the society wanted this supplemented with some of Sheehan's less popular works — *Under the Cedars and the Stars*, *Parerga*, *The Intellectuals* and *Geoffrey Austin*. Dr Liam Brophy wrote in the newsletter that *Kilmorna* 'is really a man's book,[103] which of course it is in the sense that women were assigned no active role in the national struggle. Was it merely coincidental that it was a woman who was deluded by socialism (Miriam Lucas) whereas Myles Cogan's manly Fenianism was as sane and respectable as his Catholicism?' Sheehan was of course by no means unique in infantilizing 'woman' as innocently and naively in over her head in politics — the obvious dupe therefore for the false Gods of socialism. Sheehan's perspective on the inappropriateness of women taking any political initiative is suggestive also of his reservation about their sharing in any priestly power.

R.T.E. dramatised *My New Curate* for radio in 1969 and Eamon Keane read (on radio) quite a few of the novels. The impulse came from within the organisation, officially at least, and though producers remember them to be 'tremendously popular', evidence of reruns is lacking.[104]

Con Houlihan reassessed the image of Canon Sheehan in the *Irish Times* in 1971: 'He is remembered, I suppose as the gentle moralist whose best-known passages were in our parents' readers in the national school.' Asking 'Why is his star so low now,' he admitted, 'there is, of course, something in Sheehan's work that makes it seem attractive at first sight — it reeks of that dark past, of an age that melancholy seemed to have marked for its own'. He notes that while his best books, in terms of technique, were *The Queen's Fillet*, *Miriam Lucas*, and *Dr Gray* yet these did not make the same impression on the Irish mind as some of the others, less acclaimed in Britain and on the continent. *Glenanaar* he rightly described as 'a great basket into which Sheehan threw pieces of history, social commentary and short stories .... But it has found a deep place in our minds'. He sees Casey's reaction to the knowledge that his grandfather was an informer as 'typical' as was the 'cruel snobbery' depicted in Irish life. On the self pity and apathy of the peasantry in the novels, Sheehan knew that 'like long term prisoners they feared the day of their release'. He identifies also in Sheehan, the begrudgery directed towards the minorities, as a constant feature of Irish society:

> Had he lived he would have understood Béal na Bláth all too well ...
> *Kilmorna* is, God knows, as 'modern' as the latest bulletin from the
> Shankill road or Ballymurphy. ... All the same I don't expect to see
> hordes of American scholars throwing back pints in the pubs of
> Mallow or Doneraile or roaming with their notebooks around the
> fields of Ballyorgan or Twopothouse. Sheehan's work is too lucid
> for thesis hunters.

(He had already made a slighting reference to the 'silent and punning Joyce').[106]

Folens of Dublin reproduced the Longman's edition of *Luke Delmege*, as it was then out of copyright, in a paperback series of fiction republications in 1973.[107] As late as 1980 the Mercier Press (Dublin and Cork) reprinted *Glenanaar* in a version abridged by Lorna Gault. Although Sheehan deliberatley isolated himself from any literary community, his work was well noted by fellow Irish men writers who frequently shared his interest in 'national' themes.

Frank O'Connor remarked whimsically, that he learned German in order to read the quotations in Canon Sheehan.[108] Francis MacManus observed that though Sheehan's reading was wide he did not read enough fiction. He saw Sheehan as a trapped artist; from the literature-shy Maynooth, to the cramps of pastoral duties, to Heuser whose influence he deemed 'possessive and directive, confirming the incarceration of the artist', Sheehan was 'jolted, reminded, warned, and informed that there was serious business to be done'. MacManus sees even the William O'Brien connection as a cramp to his style reminding him always of his duty, as a priest, to 'inspire nationalism; if you could only realise your first postulate — viz. that a tolerant and sympathetic-minded priest should be the inspiring force of the reunion. Alas and alas! That postulate is the hardest to supply.'[109]

Benedict Kiely (writing in 1957) pointed out that 'accidental considerations often draw attention to a writer who would otherwise have been included in the general neglect' — Kickham's claim to literary fame, he supposes, was his association with 'the Fenian revolution': and Sheehan's 'the fact that a Catholic priest was writing capable and penetrating novels'.[110] In a later article (1957), Kiely thought it very ironic that the *non serviam* which *Geoffrey Austin* timidly flirted with was the making of James Joyce. 'Was he or was he not aware,' he asks, 'or would he have seen it as comic, that George Moore (who, Kiely later states, never read Canon Sheehan) 'had written one of his pseudo-confessional passages to prove that a young man of feeling could not bother himself with a woman unless she was over thirty and married to somebody else?'

He rates Sheehan's denunciations of 'the people and country' as more severe than the harshest of the later realists:

> But the Irish take a masochistic pleasure in having themselves called
> names by priests and patriots, and by nobody else; Canon Sheehan
> ... is regarded as a smiling national piety like the coloured label on
> a box of shamrocks; while Yeats, who lamented the past glory of the
> Fenians as much as Sheehan ... is considered no Irishman at all and

no better than naygur or a black heathen.[111]

Kiely marked the liberation of Sheehan from 'the monstrous carapace that the state of being a national piety imposed upon him' — 'it is now possible to see that one should read him because he is a considerable novelist'. Kiely, however, has a soft spot for almost any fiction about quiet, rural Ireland.[112]

Sean O'Faoláin, comparing Sheehan with Gerald O'Donovan noted in both, an obstacle 'inherent in their professional exclusiveness', which prevented them from coming to grips with the church in their fiction.[113] Fr Peter Connolly in a masterly review of the fate of 'the priest in modern Irish fiction' considered for once the priest in fiction *after* Canon Sheehan:

> Sympathetic novels on the whole have been characterised by an inability to pass beyond Canon Sheehan. They have neither discovered nor borrowed a new convention of writing by which to imagine the inner drama of the priest or, more accurately, the possibility of such drama. It is mere literary naiveté to say that only the priest can do this.

He is the first to point out that Sheehan's much-vaunted 'insight' into the 'inner clerical life' is in fact no insight at all:

> Though Canon Sheehan had inner access he did not choose — he probably could not in his day — to reveal more of his priests than could be observed by any member of the parish committee, namely, the priest's pastoral methods and some of his intellectual worries.

Sheehan's constraint however on this, as on many issues, is not insignificant. Canon Sheehan always *necessarily* managed to keep the Fr Letheby in him in check. It must be pointed out though that the balance was, to the last, delicate. Peter Connolly concluded: 'His ideal image of the priest, nowadays discernibly Victorian, so often puts itself outside the range of modern sympathy.'[114]

It is eloquent that almost all of his recent literary critics are forced to examine the writer's personality and disposition rather than individual novels. Jeremiah Lovett observes that as Sheehan chose the position of a writer of the nineteenth century it is in that context, with Griffin, Carleton, Kickham, Lever and Lover that he must be viewed and not with Moore and Joyce. Comparing him however with Carleton, he regrets that Sheehan's mind was so preoccupied with a wider range of social concerns that he did not have time to observe 'the small, simple facets of life' from which Carleton made his 'compelling picture of the age'.[115]

Anthony Coleman notes that Sheehan had no *Irish* literary model and identifies George Eliot as his major influence which could well account for his poor imitations of the world of the gentry.[116] Oliver MacDonagh in *The Nineteenth Century Novel and Irish Social History: Some Aspects*, has recognised the richness of *Luke Delmege* as a social document. Though he observes that the author unwittingly describes the maturing of Irish peasant society, Sheehan's consciousness of the changes was all too evident. Rather more unconscious was his revelation, as MacDonagh notes, of the shift in the centre of the local power structure from the (shrinking) Big House to 'the graceless residence of the parish priest'.[117]

Kenneth H. Connell uses only *My New Curate* to pack the last punch in his essay 'Catholicism and marriage in the century after the famine', where the two priests agree that the old, sudden, dowry-proposition of the nineteenth century resulted in happier marriages than the 'lurid and volcanic company-keeping before marriage' of 'recent times'.[118]

Pádraic O'Farrell attaches great importance to Sheehan's novels:

> The beliefs, value judgements and disposition of Sheehan are scarcely less important than Pearse because Sheehan both formed and reflected the clerical and popular mood and conscience in Ireland, and, obviously, he had accepted the redemptive necessity for a rising long before it came. Sheehan's novels widely read in the 1890s to 1920s suggest that at least a part, perhaps a substantial part, of thinking, religious, non-revolutionary Ireland dwelt imaginatively in the realm of rebellion before 1916.[119]

Kilmorna, it must be remembered, was only published in 1915. Sheehan hardly either 'formed' or reflected' 'the clerical mood' and as for the popular mood, it is more likely that his works merely satisfied, though very effectively, sentiments already formed. Tom Garvin draws on Sheehan's thinking to illustrate what he assumes was a widespread fear of the modern. There is hardly evidence to support his view that Sheehan 'was a guru of sorts in his last years'. Though he was invited to speak to the Maynooth students in December 1903 there is no reason to believe that anybody was impressed.[120]

Lovett also discerns Sheehan's true influence as 'political and cultural':

> He fixed in literary form the blend of cultural and political and religious nationalism on which this state was founded. To him we can trace the sacrilisation of the political and the secularisation of the religious which are the most notable characteristics of modern Irish Catholicism.[121]

Garvin however would have it that 'the state was founded' on Sheehan's brand of cultural nationalism *despite* the best efforts of the patriots of at least the pre-1914 period.[122]

At the time when he was writing the novels almost every section of the reading public would have found something of interest in at least some of his works. The novelty of a priestly-writer may have attracted some, but it was, in the final analysis, his attitude, choice of subject material and style which sustained interest. Many readers it seems did appreciate a light-hearted alternative to an English fiction reflecting a culture of which the newly literate Irish peasant had no experience. His hordes of Irish American readers both clerical and lay, had an obvious need for such fiction as a prop to their somewhat insecure cultural identity. Whatever little realism was to be found in Sheehan's work there was more of it there than in earlier 'novels of Irish life'. His blend of frank drollery with the more familiar, luscious imagery in defining 'The Irish Character' had an inevitable appeal. It was, as J.F. Hogan observed, so much better than anybody else was doing at the time, that 'it could be disposed of with almost unqualified praise'.[123] Sheehan managed somehow to express, almost despite himself, a set of familiar, catholic and patriotic values, but in a strikingly refreshing new way. Many must have read his novels, as he early suspected, purely for light amusement, oblivious to the warnings and admonishments of contemporary Irish life, the redemption of which was ironically the author's professed purpose in writing them.

Sheehan characterised his Irish audience and their motives in reading his work, more accurately than they characterised him:

> For we [he observed in 1909] have a curious reverence for the opinion of outsiders; and a nervous dread lest we should figure badly in their sight.[124]

His readers selected and cherished those images of themselves which they found flattering and were all the more grateful to Sheehan for advertising their Catholic respectability abroad.

Sheehan's audience, both at the time of his writing and since, was very fragmented. When his devotees speak of him as being 'forgotten' they most probably mean by the younger generation and 'forgotten' in comparison with Yeats and Joyce 'who should never have written'. It is ultimately fitting that such a fractured thinker as Sheehan should gain the ear of many diverse types of readers. Highly educated readers overlooked his literary faults if they agreed with what they deciphered as his message.

Many read his novels for amusement, nostalgia, curiosity and any number of reasons, satisfied that 'a priest's novel' could hardly be harmful, and the clergy had a look for obvious reasons. There was not a great selection of light novels on familiar Irish life to choose from and Sheehan had the decided advantage of writing a set. Had he written only two or three works, he would have been much more easily forgotten. But for a priest to be a fully fledged novelist and a very readable one at that, was spectacular.

A random check amongst seminarians in Maynooth College in 1986 revealed that full sets of Sheehan's works were held by the libraries of the local, diocesan seminary colleges. Some seminarians still read such of his novels as *My New Curate* and *Luke Delmege*. Over the decades Canon Sheehan became very much a household name. His works were the ultimate in 'acceptability' by those Irish with a strong sense of Catholic morality. Since the 1950s apparently his novels were read largely by women. They were frequently borrowed and reborrowed from local libraries, by the same readership, and recommended repeatedly to daughters and granddaughters as wholesome, humorous and safe. By the 1960s however daughters found more exciting things to read. The novels are still to be found in local libraries (the favourites being *My New Curate* and *Glenanaar*), and are still regularly borrowed, but it is safe to assume that they are now read mainly by elderly people. The obstinate apologists of Sheehan through the century, and they are a sizeable minority, share Sheehan's repulsion from the loud modern however, and continue to hope for a revival both of popular interest in his writings and of the prescribed values therein, in that order.

The fixed image of Sheehan today is widely inaccurate. Readers took from his work what they chose, and promptly formed an image of the author to match. He is still seen by many as a friendly, fatherly 'Soggarth' who delighted in scribbling happy tales of the people and for the people. The worrying, lonely, wary priest who did not know quite what to make of himself either as priest or artist, was from the beginning, generally ignored.

In the decades after his death Sheehan's writing continued to command a loyal following of support from people who saw values in Sheehan's writing which they felt ought to be reinculcated in following generations through establishing Sheehan more securely in the national literary canon. The regularity of the attempts to launch various commemorative events and summer schools etc. indicates a certain consistency to his following from one decade to the next which continued to be easily revivable in certain circles. It also suggests however that such support was finally too thin to sustain effectively such ideas. As might be expected such proponents were often, though by no means always conservative lay cultural ideologues as well as nuns and priests. And what is further interesting (though not perhaps unpredictable) is the domination of male voices in the various campaigns to revive Sheehan's literary reputation despite the apparently considerable extend of his female readership.

Not least amongst Sheehan's critics and admirers were his clerical colleagues. The conspicuous lack of warm applause with which they received Sheehan's work is curious. As well as the scepticism, and slight embarrassment at the way in which Sheehan somewhat humanized the image of the priest, there was possibly also a little jealousy, resentment and schadenfreude. Yet the popularity of Sheehan's novels on the continent also excited those colleagues of his who took an interest in the international image of Irish catholicism and the Irish priest. For such Irish priests as Msgr Hogan, reviewer in the Irish Ecclesiastical Review, Sheehan's novels were very exportable advertisements for the specialness of the institution of the Irish priest and Irish Catholic culture to both clerical and lay populations abroad.

Finally there is no doubt that it was the Irish-American Catholic audience which established Sheehan. Perhaps it was that very tendency in Sheehan's work to flirt unintentionally with the audience's desire for a humanised priesthood which attracted an Irish-American reader eager to Americanise and refresh the image of the Irish Catholic priest. The fact that the author was an Irish priest himself lent his works an unpassable stamp of validity.

The timing of Sheehan's launch was just right to capture a certain slice of a highly literate Catholic Irish-American market; the post-famine time period in which Sheehan generally set his novels was accessible and nostalgically plausible to the imaginations of that generation of immigrants who formed his readership by the turn of the century. Further, Sheehan's denunciations of democracy and his sadness about emigration were likely to have validated whatever segment of the emigrant population was similarly disillusioned with the fabled democracy of the USA. Some emigrants would therefore have appreciated Sheehan's celebration of the sense of social sturdiness and wholesomeness of the old way which they were forced to leave behind. Finally, Sheehan's literary craftsmanship was respectable enough for Irish-Americans to be proud of, in a literary market in which the Anglo-Irish literary accomplishment was yet far from established.

Amongst the 'high' literary critics of that tradition in Ireland it continues to be Sheehan's personality and his priestly-writer image which continues to account for his stature as a literary phenomenon rather than the power of his novels as such. Few such critics are still calling for a reevaluation of Sheehan's work. As Jeremiah Lovett has pointed out, even as social documentary Sheehan's work is limited by the absence of such telling detail as characterised for instance the work of Carleton. It is now, finally, the tradition of his popularity itself, amongst quite different Irish and Catholic cultures which continues to propose his body of writing to be such an interesting cultural institution.

8: Guinan

Joseph Guinan's first novel, *Scenes and Sketches in an Irish Parish, or Priest and People in Doon* (1903), was reasonably successful, going into its sixth edition by 1912.[1] It was published by Gill and Duffy simultaneously in Dublin, New York, Cincinnati and Chicago and by Benziger in New York. All records of M.H. Gill & Son Ltd. were unfortunately destroyed by fire at the O'Connell Street premises in September 1979.[2] Neither are those of Benziger any longer available.[3]

All the reviewers were unanimous in their emphasis that the sketches were 'true to life'. A reviewer in *New Ireland* was grateful for its treatment of 'all the typical events of Irish life', remarking that 'we need such pictures, such refreshing baths of reality, such faithful realism composed with the integrity of a witness on oath'.[4] The *Irish Monthly* was more reservedly ambivalent: 'The author writes simply and earnestly about what he knows and says what he feels'.[5] The *Irish Times*,[6] *Freeman's Journal*,[7] *Westmeath Independent*[8] and *Cork Sun*[9] recommended it fulsomely, while the rather irritated reviewer of the *Leader* observed that 'it brings out to the full, the place occupied by religion in Irish life'.[10]

The *Irish Independent* predicted that it would quickly be greeted with 'a cordial welcome across the seas in far distant lands wherever our kith and kin have found a home'.[11] Indeed the reaction of the American Catholic magazine, *Ave Maria*, proved this correct:

> Homely are the incidents which the author relates, but they illustrate a side of the Irish peasant's character little known, and unfamiliar to thousands who bear Irish names. Let us tell more about it and quote from its fascinating pages.[12]

The editor, Father Hudson, also wrote to Guinan:

> I assure you I have shed tears over your pages. Your book deserved to have as many readers as there are letters in it. I am more glad than I can say to hear of its success. It will do a world of good. I have ordered a hundred copies to supply to prisons, hospitals, etc. The extracts I copied from your book were reproduced in Catholic papers all over the United States. With all my heart I congratulate you.[13]

Exported also to Australia, the Adelaide-based *Southern Cross* deemed it 'as faithfully and as distinctly and beautifully Irish as Sullivan's graphic verse in "Canadian woods", ... it is probably the best portraiture of West Leinster Life'.[14] The Catholic journals, of course, approved wholeheartedly of the effort, the *Tablet* granting that the sketches 'may be accepted as faithful transcripts of life in an Irish parish.[15]

Guinan's second novel, *The Soggarth Aroon* was his greatest popular success. Published again by both Gill and Duffy in 1905 it had reached four editions by the end of that year and was reissued in 1906, 1907, 1908 and 1912. Benziger in New York also issued several editions, and Burns, Oates and Washbourne of London published it at least once. Predictably it was received with a chorus of approval from the Catholic press including the *Catholic Watchman* in far-away Madras.[16] The reviewer in the *Southern Cross* (Adelaide) appreciated it as 'The best possible antidote to such books as those of Mr MacCarthy'.[17] The editor of *Ave Maria* enthused once more,[18] and the *Boston Pilot* quoted some passages 'which will make their own appeal to an exile from Erin'.[19]

The *Pall Mall Gazette*, in a lengthy and favourable review, observed that it was 'a new departure' in Irish literature, noting it as the first time a priest had treated the relations between priest and people, though of course it was not.[20] In the same line, a writer in the *Glasgow Herald* hoped it would redress the 'abject and humiliating' picture drawn by Protestant controversialists, of the submission of the Irish peasantry to the priest. Guinan's book would reveal 'how much of tenderness, chivalry and fervent devotion it includes'.[21] The *Liverpool Daily Post and Mercury* advised:

> Shut the door upon all such hard material influences as political economy, and the troublesome attitudes of the Saxon, and let Father Guinan lead you into the wholly delightful land of which he tells ... most readers will put it down with a better comprehension of the Irish character, and a greater respect for the troubles of Erin.[22]

A solitary note of scepticism appeared in the *Manchester Guardian*:

> He always speaks well of his flock, and we are led to consider the typical Irish parish a very happy place, guarded by a 'trinity of good angels', of whom the dispensary doctor is third, the school-master second, and the 'Soggarth Aroon' an easy first.[23]

Reviews in the Irish press were solidly supportive, including even the usually fairly critical *Irish Monthly*. Rosa Mulholland found Guinan 'delightful': 'Oh, that more *soggarths* would write out of their hearts'.[24]

The Moores of Glynn appeared in 1907. Though it was not nearly as successful as *The Soggarth Aroon* it nevertheless reached four editions in five years. Though it was noticeably more disciplined than the previous two, the *Irish Monthly* was the only journal to mark the rise in artistry.[25] The *Irish Daily Independent* predicted for it 'a place among Irish stories second only to *Knocknagow* and the *Vicar of Wakefield*' and wished to see a copy in every village library and convent library in Ireland.[26] The *Irish News* in Belfast declared:

> Not even the marvellous idylls of Tipperary life that came to us from Kickham's loving fancy are more absorbing, interesting, or surrounded by a more delightful atmosphere of reality than the series of pen-pictures in the *Moores of Glynn.*[27]

The *Irish People*,[28] *Irish Ecclesiastical Record*,[29] *Ave Maria*,[30] *Irish Rosary*[31] and other Catholic journals greeted it with the usual unqualified approval. Though it was noted generally that Guinan was moving more towards realism, *The Freeman's Journal* pointed out however, that his was of 'a healthy, innocent, elevating, edifying kind'.[32] The *Tablet*, this time, was conspicuously unimpressed:

> If not exactly the book of the year, the *Moores of Glynn* (a story of the early land war) is likely to be very popular with advanced nationalists.[33]

In Australia it was recommended to the children of emigrants as 'a veritable mine of information'.[34] Both the *Catholic Herald of India*[35] and the *Bombay Examiner*, evidently already well acquainted with Guinan's work, were appreciative, — the latter remarking that

> Some critics have objected to the too strong feelings shown against the Saxon in certain parts of this book; but we do not think that English readers who have any insight into the feelings of the Celt, or the historical causes of them, ought to be offended thereby.[36]

The Island Parish, published in 1908 by Gill, went to a second edition only. This may have been because it revealed, however delicately, more of the scars of Ireland, such as alcoholism, gambling and pregnancy outside marriage. This novel was apparently not published in America unlike the first three. It was also less widely reviewed. The *Irish Independent*,[37] *Catholic Weekly*[38] and *Irish Monthly*[39] however found nice things to say about it. The *Freeman's Journal* expressed 'intense satisfaction' that at last, 'otherwise intelligent folk in the other island' would see the real Irish peasant, as distinguished from the 'Mickey-Free' of Lever;

> The great charm of *The Island Parish* is the interesting sidelights it throws on the moral and social life of a peasantry that has suffered so heavily from the unsympathetic, if not malignant Hogarths and

Peniers of Irish literature.[40]

Neither is there any evidence that Guinan's next novel was published by the American publishing companies. *The Curate of Kilcloon* (Gill, 1912) was not however as sad. This time it took twelve months before a second edition was issued. Perhaps the novelty of the priest-writer was wearing off. The *Irish Ecclesiastical Record*, though remarking that it lacked 'the dramatic unity and force of *My New Curate*, with which it has a family resemblance', advised that 'anyone who has read and appreciated the former will not fail to be charmed with *The Curate of Kilcloon* and should hasten to place him on his bookshelves beside his compatriot'. It was also valuable as

> a pleasing antidote to the morbid, unreal, though realistic trash, with which the minds of the people are being poisoned. .... There is one note in the book, common to the author and his hero, which will appeal to many of his clerical readers, and that is the deep love and attachment shown to the great Alma Mater of the Irish priesthood ... May the product and the market increase Do cum gloire De agus Onora na hEireann.[41]

Reviews generally were unremarkable. It was regarded simply as a welcome addition to the list of harmless, national fiction.

When *Donal Kenny* appeared in 1910 the *Freeman's Journal* predicted 'a hearty welcome for the gifted author of *The Moores of Glynn*'[42] although he had two novels published in the interval. A year after publication (by Gill) it was issued by Benziger of New York and reached a second edition in 1912. A new edition to the usual chorus of praise this time came from the *Canadian Messenger*.[43]

Guinan, curiously, had no new novel published until 1924, fourteen years after *Donal Kenny*, which was not very different from any of its predecessors. *Annamore, or The Tenant-at-Will* was published by Benziger in New York, where it reached a phenomenal sixth edition in the course of one year, and by Burns Oates and Washbourne of London ('publishers to the Holy See'). Its success in America may be partially explained by the good press given 'The Returned Yank' who, in having made his fortune, solves all the family difficulties of land security, marries the president of the local branch of the Ladies League and brings her back to America with him. There is no trace of an Irish edition of *Annamore* nor of *Patriots*.

Stephen Brown's conclusion in *Ireland in Fiction* was coy:

Of both [priests and people] he has intimate personal knowledge, and for both unbounded admiration. He writes simply and earnestly. To the critic used only to English literature, his work may seem wanting in artistic restraint, for he gives free rein to emotion. But this is more than atoned for by its obvious sincerity.[44]

It is remarkable that in 1925, The Talbot Press of Dublin and Cork brought out new editions of both *Doon*, Guinan's first series of sketches, and *The Soggarth Aroon*; a front page blurb on the latter ran:

> *The Soggarth Aroon* which passed through many editions and has been long out of print, is now republished at the request of supporters of the good literature crusade — the great need of our time.[45]

They were included in a Talbot advertisement with such literary weapons as the works of Gerald Griffin, Daniel Corkery, Kickham, Standish O'Grady, Seamus O'Kelly, Eimar O'Duffy, Peadar O'Donnell, Annie M.P. Simthson, Lynn C. Doyle, James Murphy (*The Priest Hurlers*) and K.F. Purdon *(The Folk of Furry Farm)*.[46] *The Soggarth Aroon* was selling for 3/6 but *Doon* for just 2/6. *The Soggarth Aroon* eventually reached its ninth printing in Dublin in 1940.

The Catholic Bulletin in the November issue of 1926 drew attention to 'A library of Irish fiction by Irish priests' comprising *The Island Parish* (3/6); *The Curate of Kilcloon* (3/6); Sheehan's first attempt — *Geoffrey Austin, Student* (5/-); and *Inis Fail, or Distant days in Tipperary* by Rev. P. Hickey (3/6).[47]

Hickey was an Australian priest whose novel was set 'in the early days of the Parnell Movement' and treated of the horrors of landlordism and emigration, with verse by Fanny Parnell, Fionnbarra, Clarence Mangan and Dalton Williams. Reviews of the works followed, seeing Guinan's work as 'a picture brimful of the familiar experiences of nigh three-quarters of a century which should awaken cherished memories in every Irish heart'.[48] *The Moores of Glynn* was also republished in 1928 by Burns Oates and Washbourne Ltd., London.

While there is no information available on the reception of *The Patriots*, in the USA, the style in which it was marketed conveys something of the appetites which it was intended to satisfy. In the introduction, the Archbishop of Baltimore, Michael J. Curley, D.D., described the novel to American readers as:

> a synthesis of more than a quarter of a century of Irish history ... a story of butchery and brutality on the part of an alien power that kept poor Ireland crushed and bleeding under its savage heel during a

woeful night of seven and a half centuries . . . The Irish Ireland
movement — the Gaelic League — the rebellion of 1916 — the
Anglo Irish War — the defeat of England's army — the treaty —
the evacuation of alien troops. . . . Guinan's latest novel ought to be
read by every American interested in the history of a truly unique
nation that in all its sufferings and woes never forgot God and never
surrendered its claim to freedom.*(Michael J.Curley,* The Patriots, *intro.
pp 4-7)*

Curley also noted the therapeutic effect of such novels in their detailing
of the pain of emigration:

When Kathleen [an emigrant in *The Patriots]* reads the story of it
all, she too is not ashamed to add her tears to those shed all over
America by the exiled readers of Canon Guinan's Irish stories. We
love him more for the tears he made us shed than for the merry
laughter he caused by his inimitable analysis of the insuppressible
fun in many of his characters.*(ibid. p 4)*

Accounting then for his sales, his works were evidently widely circulated amongst both the Irish and Catholic clergy abroad. They sustained
on the whole a steady sale in Ireland amongst the laity, a certain section
of which apparently had a steady need for a consoling read about the 'old
Ireland of priests and people'. In America although the *Ave Maria* was the
first to publish his work in serial form, Fr Heuser, Sheehan's benefactor
in the *American Ecclesiastical Review,* had no apparent relations with the
much less skilled Guinan. One emigrant, Katherine Hearne Kelley, wrote
vividly however of the uplifting experience his works caused her:

His stories and sketches hold more than my alien eye can know.
Those who live in Ireland, in the country of youth's immortal
simplicity, will see without effort the vibrant health and goodness of
the author's work ....

... Father Guinan's works have for me an afterglow, and I have a
haunting reminder of the hold on life his creations have. His people
I can no more forget than the old neighbours of earliest memory. He
has photographed Ireland in the morning light of charity ... I have
found his books improve on re-reading, and especially on tasting
small portions of them, not as parts, but as wholes, ... I have been
reading them slowly, letting fancy play round his paragraphs, looking up at the round towers and down into the holy wells of his
sentences.

... And I shut the book and look towards Tir-n'an-Oge, and I hear
dimly the voices of home. I am in exile, thinking of my own people.

> They are sighing and fearing and crying; they are saying the evening
> Rosary; they are laughing and dancing and trusting in God.[49]

Guinan obviously hoped to inspire recruits to sustain his crusade for Catholic literature, when he willed to his executor, James McNamee, bishop of Ardagh and Clonmacnoise, all his rights to his books published to provide prize books for St Mel's College, Longford, the college where he studied before going to Maynooth and taught for a short time afterwards.[51] Guinan does not feature in the *Dictionary of National Biography*[52] nor even in J.S. Crone's *Dictionary of Irish Biography*,[53] in Hickey and Doherty's *Dictionary of Irish History since 1800*[54] nor in Hogan's *Dictionary of Irish Literature*.[55] Brian Cleeve notices him briefly in his *Dictionary of Irish Writers* but lists only four of his novels.[56] It is interesting that although Sheehan features in Crone's dictionary, O'Donovan, like Guinan, is not mentioned while Guinan and Sheehan only are included in the *Guide to Catholic Literature 1888-1940: An Author-Subject-Title Index*, published in Detroit, 1940.[50]

Guinan was reasonably successful in his mission to supply a literary pabulum for the Catholic reading public. His winning formula was the intimacy he showed between priest and people, an intimacy which both in fiction and in reality was an important security blanket to many ordinary Irish Catholics. Novels about themselves, and, on the whole, flattering ones at that, were bound to be popular.

Amongst the clergy in Ireland his works were probably sampled but hardly devoured. Most of the Catholic clergy abroad, if they did not have a direct connection with Ireland, had an interest in and a fondness for Irish Catholicism, so that Guinan's novels reawakened happy memories, reinforced them in their mission and appealed to their sense of root. Those Irish-Americans who were wont to read such fiction had apparently very definite ideas on how they wanted to imagine Ireland. They had little desire to read about the cruelty and ugliness which was, naturally, a part of Irish reality, irrespective of whether or not they acknowledged it. No doubt some emigrants had no interest whatever in Irish affairs, but to the overwhelming majority a nationality of which they could be proud, was essential.

9: O'Donovan

Father Ralph (1913), Gerald O'Donovan's first novel, at 6/- was double the price of Guinan's works selling at the same time. It was bought steadily for 18 months. From April to December 1913, 5,000 copies were printed at intervals with another 2,000 in the following year.[1] Macmillan, the publishers put a preliminary notice in the *Pall Mall Gazette* announcing it as 'an indictment of Irish Catholicism which is bound to arouse considerable discussion'.[2] A month later the *Irish Times* reviewer regretted Macmillan's notice as it 'made the bristles upon the necks of all the controversialists in the three kingdoms erect themselves'. The sympathetic reviewer observed that it was not an indictment but 'a story of a religious man rebelling against a system'.[3] The *Church of Ireland Gazette* pointed to it as confirmation of their view that 'the inhabitants' of 'southern Ireland' were 'slavishly submissive' to an 'unscrupulous church'.[4]

The reviewer in the *Northern Whig* regarded it as the first serious attempt by any Irish writer to treat of the clergy in fiction and noted that it was all the more remarkable for being an inside view. Though he thought O'Donovan had exaggerated in his picture of the clergy it was preferable to the caricatures of earlier fiction.[5] The *New Statesman* reviewer remarking on O'Donovan's appreciation 'of the native mysticism of the peasant — still pagan in certain aspects', noted that the writer had *not* intended to minister to the hopes and self-satisfaction of the propagandist of Protestant theology in Ireland'. The earlier chapters of *Ralph* reminded him of George Birmingham's 'Irish *romans à clefs* in which the various regenerative and degenerative influences of Irish life were personified by well-known Irishmen under thin disguises ... Mr. Birmingham did this sort of thing excellently, but his imitators have been too many'. Interestingly, the reviewer observes that the general preoccupation of Irish writers with matters national is restrictive;

> When the Irish Turgeniev arrives he will certainly convey an impression of contemporary Irish types, forces and institutions; but the impression will not be less true because he will be primarily inspired by life in general, and not by Irish life in particular.

The reviewer agrees with Father Duff that Irish Catholicism was better served by the priests before it had acquired sufficient wealth to plant the country with local seminaries, such as the 'Burrahone' of *Ralph*, for their training.[6] The *Irish Book Lover* thought it 'severe, but at the same time dispassionate, just and scrupulously reverent towards the essentials of religion'. They implied that if the picture of seminary life seemed harsh, this was because seminary life *was* harsh, and the Maynooth scenes were 'refreshingly true to life'. This critic was glad to say that 'venomous enemies of the Catholic church' would find it disappointing.[7]

A writer in the *Times Literary Supplement* recognised *Ralph* as a further addition to the campaign of the lay, Catholic *intelligentzia* which included W.P. Ryan and 'Pat'. Though the reviewer regretted that it was a true picture, he remarked that it would hardly be believed in English Catholic circles.[8] A writer in *Truth*, perhaps having been impressed by M.J.F. McCarthy's work, was grateful for the explanation it offered to the contrast between the imposing churches and the humble homes of the parishioners.[9] The *Nation*,[10] *Spectator*[11] and *Daily Chronicle*[12] did not venture to assess its authenticity but found it generally interesting. The Irish Catholic journals were eloquent in their utter silence. No doubt aware that any publicity was good publicity, they chose to ignore it, though it must have been met with intense interest in clerical circles. Their British counterparts, however, were vocal and hostile. The *Tablet* described it as a 'grotesque libel'.[13] The *Catholic Times and Catholic Opinion* agreed.[14] The reviewer in the *Catholic Herald* surely voiced the thoughts of Joseph Guinan, Canon Sheehan and the Irish Catholic press in advising O'Donovan not to waste his time in trying to imitate the 'Modernist and free-thinking productions of a continental press'.[15] The Salford Diocesan Federation complained to the editor of the *Manchester Guardian* for allowing the book to be reviewed in his paper.[16] The *Church Times* however cautiously implied some sympathy with O'Donovan's frustration. The writer remembered Newman's manoeuvres on the University question, and thought the church in Ireland unnecessarily harsh in its attitude to internal dissent.[17]

A year after *Father Ralph* first appeared an 'Irish Nationalist' reported to the *Freeman's Journal* that it was being used as propaganda by the Unionists.[18] The *Sunday Observer* had recently published a letter from one explaining that the 'atmosphere' depicted in the book was precisely the reason why Ulster Unionists wanted nothing to do with the priest and the 'gombeenman'.[19] A sub-leader in the same issue of the *Freeman* described the book as a gross libel on both the Irish priesthood and on the Irish people. O'Donovan was accused of trading off both his high profile in the cooperative movement, and that of his friend, Horace Plunkett. The writer agreed with the 'Irish Nationalist' correspondent that Plunkett should distance himself from the book.

O'Donovan was approached by a Canadian Orange newspaper that wished to serialise the novel, but this venture apparently did not material-ise.[20] The New York branch of Macmillan refused to publish *Father Ralph* owing to the hostility it aroused in Catholic circles. In correspondence with John Quinn of New York, an American enthusiast of Irish literature, O'Donovan said that the book was a success in England, was still selling well, and that a large colonial edition had also been sold.[21] He pointed out that, apart from the Catholic press the book had been well received. Other American publishers evidently having refused it, O'Donovan regretted the loss in the 'interest of truth' apart from any financial loss.[22]

Putnams refused it on the same grounds as Macmillans, who having been attacked in the U.S. press for connecting its name with *Father Ralph*, had been repudiating O'Donovan and the London branch.[23] Quinn, im-pressed by the book, advised O'Donovan to try Mitchell Kennerly for publication — 'a courageous man'. Quinn, who thought it good for the church, had no objection to being thus quoted in a letter to Kennerly, but did not want his views made public.[24] During the following year a Rev. T. Connellan reported to the *Catholic* that Roman Catholic societies, resenting the frankness of the book had lobbied American publishers to suppress it.[25] A month later Connellan reported that *The Record of Christian Work* having enquired for copies of the novel, had failed to trace any. He claimed also that O'Donovan's second novel, *Waiting* had been similarly boycotted by the American press at large but that the *Churchman*, in New York, had arranged to fill orders for both novels.[26] Mitchell Kennerly did eventually publish *Ralph* in 1914.

George Birmingham, writing in 1917, implied that O'Donovan's pic-ture of the clergy was just, Fr Duff representing the kindly side and Fr Molloy the other:

> Those who know Ireland recognise him as surely as they recognise the other. The man is essentially a bully. He finds himself in possession of a power which no tradition of the class from which he sprang has fitted him to use .... He is impervious to any sense of the ridiculous .... He is capable of saying that Ireland is 'at the present time being daily douched in a cataract of English literary filth' when he means that Sunday newspapers are on sale in Dublin. ... It is men of this type who constitute the real danger of the power of the Roman Catholic Church in Ireland. They are a new type. A few years ago they could not have existed. The Protestant aristocracy possessed a

power which rivalled and curbed theirs in secular affairs. It is the fall of that aristocracy which has made them possible.[27]

Macmillan of London obviously expected *Waiting* to be equally successful. They first printed 4,000 copies in April 1914 where they had merely printed 1,000 at a time of *Ralph*. In June of that year however they reprinted 2,000 copies only and no more subsequently.[28] The *Irish Times* reviewer was disappointed that *Waiting* did not fulfil the high expectations aroused by *Ralph*: although it was no worse than *Father Ralph*, neither was it any better.[29] The *Times Literary Supplement* regretted O'Donovan's tendency toward 'theatricality' but remarked that the priests' supper scene in Chapter 23 was 'a piece of satirical bludgeoning not unworthy of Swift'.[30]

The *Irish Book Lover* saw *Waiting* as much less bitter than *Father Ralph*: 'but it remains for him to show the reading public that he is something more than a man of one idea'.[31] Irish newspaper reviewers[32] were at pains to point out that O'Donovan had caught a true picture of rural Ireland while the English reviewers were explicit that, as outsiders, they were unable to judge the accuracy of the book.[33] The better acquainted reviewer with the *Manchester Guardian* appreciated the book as 'an honest contribution to the new spirit in Ireland, the spirit that will save it without either moonlighting or gunrunning'.[34] The reviewer in the American *Catholic World*, however, was not surprised that 'an apostate' portrayed Irish life so unfairly. He was noticing the book merely to warn readers of the kind of man O'Donovan was.[35]

Stephen Browne's *Ireland in Fiction* (1921 ed.) included descriptions of *Father Ralph* and *Waiting*.[36] O'Donovan's 'general view of Irish Life' in *Ralph*, Brown remarks, 'is seen from the standpoint of such writers as M.J.F. McCarthy, W.P. O'Ryan, and 'Pat', but clerical life is depicted with far more minute knowledge than by any of these'. 'Sensational features such as the amours of priests and nuns' Brown is glad to see absent. However, 'scarcely a page of this book does not appeal to non-Catholic prejudice'.

Waiting it seems did not create quite the same shock as *Father Ralph* had. Whether it was that readers were simply prepared for the second assault or whether it was seen as milder is not clear. As Maurice, the hero of *Waiting* had no direct connection with the priesthood, there were fewer ugly scenes of clerical life, which may have softened the impact of the book, in Ireland.

Conquest, published in 1920, this time by Constable, London, and in the following year by Putnams of New York, met with an interesting response in England. The reviewer in the *Manchester Guardian* remarking on the 'cold, sawdust romance' of the book thought O'Donovan was 'adopted' by Ireland 'because the story, in spite of everything, — its setting, its dialect, its knowledge of certain sides of Irish life — does not impress us as distinctly Irish'.[37] The *Times Literary Supplement* was exasperated:

> Mr O'Donovan's evident intention was to write a propagandist novel, but he has done much more than to defeat his purpose of showing that the most tolerant Irishman must in the end turn against England. He has, indeed, come very near to writing the one book which justifies England's failure with Ireland. One can imagine the intelligent foreigner, at the end of the third or fourth dinner party, laying down the book in despair of ever understanding the awful complexity of opinion and hatred among Irish political parties who, Mr O'Donovan is careful to assure him, are 'racially as like as two peas'.[38]

In another review however, transferred from the *Times Literary Supplement* to the *Irish Book Lover*, it was recognised that O'Donovan's main thesis was that 'priests, Englishmen and Irishmen are neither all good nor all bad'. Noting that many of the priests in the book are not religious, this was regarded as a touch of verisimilitude, as 'many priests are not religious in fact'.[39] *Truth* described it as 'waterlogged' with offensive politics and went on to deplore any nationalism which inspired hatred of other countries.[40]

An enquiry by Constable in 1920 revealed that *Conquest* had sold up to 5,000 copies in America.[41] Norreys Jephson O'Conor in *Changing Ireland: Literary Backgrounds of the Irish Free State 1889-1922* (1924) wrote that *Conquest* might become the *Uncle Tom's Cabin of Ireland*. He pointed out that though much complicated by religion, the Irish question was not fundamentally a religious issue. He recommended the novel to all thoughtful people as 'a penetrating, lucid, and impartial analysis of the Irish question.[42]

Vocations (Martin Secker, 1921) not surprisingly was received with hostility in Ireland. In a letter to the *Observer* O'Donovan wrote:

> Even in Dublin it is to be had, though, in the bookshops patronised by girls from convents, by some slight finesse. I am told that in these wonderful shops, although it shares popularity with the lives of the

saints and other less edifying works of fiction, it is not displayed, and can only be purchased (promptly, however), by a whispered conversation with the shopman.[43]

Another reviewer for the *Irish Book Lover* observed 'the ex-Reverend Jeremiah O'Donovan goes from bad to worse' in his unworthy efforts to besmirch the church of which he was once a member: 'Would an honourable man not feel happier earning his bread as a labourer than by the promulgation of such scandals?' He was not surprised that O'Donovan had to seek a new publisher. Referring to O'Donovan's letter to the *Observer*, it seemed to him that O'Donovan rejoiced in the fact that it could only be obtained surreptitiously.[44] The next issue of the *Irish Book Lover* however carried an extract from the *Times Literary Supplement*, 'Some novelists', comparing 'the national question' in the work of O'Donovan, Daniel Corkery, Conal O'Riordan and Aodh de Blacam.[45] The impartiality of O'Donovan's artistry is stressed here and the theme is seen to be the pity of self-deception.

> His thesis, if he had a conscious thesis, would be that neither the Roman nor the Protestant church can now afford a satisfactory medium for the religious passion. They do their best, but the result is waste and perversion, which he describes, as an artist should, in terms of men and women. The women do not get rid of sex by becoming nuns, nor the men by becoming priests. If anyone says they do, the answer is — not in this novel, which by its excellence proves that it is the result of real experience. And it is common knowledge that one may mistake the love of men or women for the love of God; one may deceive oneself even about the highest matters.

In the *Dublin Review*, C.C. Martindale S.J. considered it an unjustified smear of vulgarity and wondered why the Irish had come to rely on those modern anti-clerical novelists who had an appetite for the sordid.[46] *The Times* was supportive, agreeing that 'there are few sins more sinful than the deliberate shepherding of girls into "professions" before they are able to make for themselves a mature choice'.[47]

A most perceptive criticism came from the *New Statesman*.[48] This writer saw that *Fr Ralph* was not a rebel, but rather a conformist — to the church of St. Dominic, St. Francis and St. Ignatius. Patronisingly however, he pointed out that

> it had not been given to him [O'Donovan] to understand that the common sensual man prefers that any such teasing discussion, with its threats of increasing austerity, should be abandoned save when

there is a great saint to make his blood run so hotly that he can face
necessity for reform ... and that to him a man who talks of the need
for holy and rigorous living, with no other inspiration than conviction
of the utter necessity of holiness is as little winning as one who
because of some hygienic theory urges his fellow creatures to bathe
in cold water.

Though the criticism is perhaps more appropriate to *Conquest*, the
reviewer adds:

There is something profoundly wrong with a country whose population is so penned together by their need to assert their nationalism
in the face of England's denial, that they look on each other with that
dislike and irritation which one feels for one's companion in a
railway carriage on too long a journey.

The reviewer for the *Times Literary Supplement* thought it unreal, the
'horrible things' [licentious priests, gluttonous bishops, secret sins within
convents ...] 'being presented, not as exceptions but as the rule'.[49] Most
of the other British papers however found it successful as a work of art,[50]
except the *Observer* which saw in it propagandistic intentions.[51]

George Moore, as might be expected, enjoyed *Vocations* and urged
Horace Liveright of New York to publish it;

I have just read a book which I think very well of. It tells the truth
in so interesting a way that I could not put the book down, but kept
on reading it for three or four days .... If it were not for my own work
I could write a prodigiously favourable article about it.[52]

The book was accepted by Boni and Liveright and appeared sporting
Moore's endorsement on the jacket in 1922. The *Boston Evening Transcript* pointed out that this might not be an advantage in view of Moore's
'pronounced individuality'.[53] Louis M. Freed of the *New York Times Book
Review and Magazine* echoed Moore's opinion.[54] However the endorsement of Moore prompted the *Nation* (New York) to compare both writers
and saw O'Donovan as sharing Moore's 'unrivalled firmness of touch,
faint steady luminousness and surgeon-like union of precision and cool
tenderness'.[55]

What then did later generations think, if at all, of O'Donovan's novels?
In the obituary notice in the *Times Literary Supplement* of 1942, it was
observed that because they could not be regarded simply as fiction the
reader's reaction to them depended on his attitude to life.[56] Though it was
remembered that George Moore had once considered him the most powerful force in modern Irish fiction, this was hardly surprising owing to

what the reviewer saw as their common concerns. Hugh Law in 1926, thought the historical student of the future might learn as much from Sheehan's *My New Curate* as he would from 'those less agreeable, though indisputably, powerful, books', O'Donovan's *Father Ralph*, Conal O'Riordan's *Adam of Dublin* or George Moore's *The Lake*.[57] Seán O Faolain thought of O'Donovan as 'a romantic sport' — out of the boglands defying Rome, writing so well'.[58] Benedict Kiely sees in *Ralph* some considerable documentary value but summarises it as 'sour, unbalanced pampleteering'.[59] Frank O'Connor remembers how as a youth he was excited by O'Donovan's picture of Ireland, capturing the 'practical forward-looking excitement of the period with its subsequent disillusionment'.[60]

In *A Guide to the Best Fiction English and American Including Translations from Foreign Languages* compiled by Ernest Baker and James Packman (London, 1932), both *Father Ralph* and *Waiting* are listed, the former recommended to provide a valuable picture of Irish life. Meanwhile in the *Spectator* O'Donovan was, with Edgeworth, George Birmingham, Conal O'Riordan and Joyce, considered to have made 'novels of national life'. These writers were at once living, and, in their respective fields true to life'.[61]

The utility of *Father Ralph* as a social document illustrating the ways of the clergy in Irish life has only fairly recently been recognised. K.H. Connell however draws on *Ralph* perhaps a little too extensively. However much O'Donovan admits the healthy features of clergy and laity, the strength of his depiction of their ugly side is such that it dominates all.[62] O'Donovan's work constitutes a striking, but exceptional, counterpoint to Irish priestly fears of the modern.[63] A. Norman Jeffares in *Anglo Irish Literature* recently answered Hugh Alexander Law's query in his work, which coincidentally bore the same title, by rating O'Donovan's work far ahead of Sheehan's in their respective fictional treatment of the clergy. He is hopeful that O'Donovan is now beginning to be reassessed.[64]

Peter A. Costello drew attention to O'Donovan in *The Heart Grown Brutal: The Irish Revolution in Literature from Parnell to Yeats* (1978) hoping O'Donovan would be seen disinterred from his dark burial place in the Yeatsian shadow of Ben Bulben.[65] Not until 1983 however was a full study undertaken on O'Donovan's contribution to Irish history.[66]

As all of O'Donovan's works had a point to make, once made, the books could be safely put aside. His are not the kind of novels which reward reading, nor are they the kind which were likely to find a place in the heart of the reading public. He probably appealed most to those who already bore grudges against the clergy, both abroad and, more discreetly, in Ireland. They were welcomed abroad as a window on to the colourful puzzle which 'the Irish question' was seen to be, their frankness and clarity distinguished them among more romantic and deluding analyses of the time. In the context of the Irish bookshop also, they were different. In comparison with the work of F.H. O'Donnell, M.J.F. MacCarthy and the like, they were well written novelties, with a story and a refreshingly drawn picture of Irish life.

Closing Comments

It is hardly surprising that national identity was a prime concern of three Irish Catholic writers at the turn of the century. There is a sense in which Sheehan, Guinan and O'Donovan were all trying out variations on old themes in the hope of constructing a serviceable national image. It is interesting and eloquent in itself that though strong views are very often put forth emphatically, they are often modified, or contradicted outright a few pages later.

Because these writers had such different aims, methods and audiences, it is naturally difficult to generalise. One of the more obvious features to emerge from this study is the ambivalence and the inconsistency of the writers from the moment they begin to consider 'Ireland'. One common denominator of these three writers is their insistence on narrowing their focus exclusively to Ireland. They rarely venture to compare or speculate on comparable problems within other cultures.

Compared with the complexity of the debate in recent years on the question of national identity, these three articulators were quite definite as to what constituted Irishness, though of course their definitions vary. The dogmatic definitions offered by Sheehan and Guinan probably betray an underlying insecurity however, O'Donovan did not feel the need to 'protest too much'.

All four intimate a sense of Ireland as an abstract, animate being, or spirit, which survives independently of changing political definition. Ireland is referred to in terms of its potential, its past, or partially in terms of its actuality. 'The Irish' emerge as a fairly singular homogeneous community, rooted indefinitely far back in history, whose characteristics have in the main, remained marvellously intact. Though some more obviously than others, all of their expressions of Irishness were intended as medicinal rather than descriptive. Yet in order to create a wished for Ireland in fiction, they had to show or suggest in tandem, the miserable alternative which lay actually around them. This they do sometimes by accident and at other times they cannot help but cry out in pain.

It is hardly surprising that they built in the main on a composite of an imagined past, outer legend and selected bits of cliched imagery from abroad. Sheehan and Guinan both are remarkable for the consistency and forcefulness with which they insist on the phenomenon which the Irishman is. At certain points it is apparent that Sheehan has managed to convince himself of this fiction, while at others he lays it on so thickly that he must have been aware of a grain of salt. Guinan, however, never could entertain any other notion, while the rather more cosmopolitan O'Donovan, exasperated by such blinkered thinking, tried to shatter that illusion.

O'Donovan is odd in his mix of hopeless romanticism and his often quite sound realism. The best gymnastics, however, are performed by Guinan. Almost unconsciously he paints himself into and out of the trickiest corners in his presentation of the 'beauties' of Ireland. Features which to most might appear shameful, Guinan argues as creditable.

Sheehan comes out of it as a secretive, confused and often harsh man. He tries to see Ireland as a poet's refuge and says it is so while all the time crying that the nation had derailed. Guinan worried that it might happen in the future, while O'Donovan believed Home Rule and a few technical adjustments could right matters. Theory aside, however, when it came to actually writing, despite Sheehan's outright claims to the certainty of stereotype, he is helpless in trying to weave these ideal types into the novel. All too often the real world disturbs his attempts at idylls. Guinan, by contrast, the far less skilled writer of the trio, manages to stay on course.

It is ironic that it was this combination of idyll and reality in Sheehan's fiction which was to prove the corner stone of his popularity. It was the touch most cherished and enjoyed by exiles and by readers in the middle years of the century because it allowed them the mix of soft, harmless nostalgia about the way things were, alongside what they seized on as his 'authenticity' — his knowledge of 'the real Ireland'.

It may well have been that Sheehan himself duplicated the confluence of the nostalgic and bitter elements in the average emigrant's emotional attitudes toward Ireland. This feature worked doubly to win him a modicum of respect from the literary community, marking him off as a refreshing antidote to the stacks of the third rate, lush, almost voyeuristic works about 'Erin's Isle' — a category in which Guinan's work fits more easily. By accident as it were, Sheehan therefore combines a traditional song of praise for the stereotypical Irishman with an underlying note of disgust for the actual Irishman. Often he describes what ought to be as though it were actual, while on the next page he might describe the actual, showing his disgust with it. So, the stereotype is constantly undermined by the aberring 'modernizing' Irishman.

Had he not stressed the contrary one might assume that he simply saw his project to be a spiritual one and above the issue of national image. But

Sheehan, like Guinan, saw the spiritual and the national as one. Clearly Irish Catholicism was for them, as for many others, national identity. Their lyricism of the peasant can in one sense be explained by Sheehan's comment in *The Graves of Kilmorna* that 'the best way to make people good is to tell them they are good'.[1] This twosidedness of Sheehan encouraged the peculiar split image which he developed amongst those who read his work, the ambivalence of the criticism which he attracted and the curiosity value which he held for many. People who were never quite sure quite what to make of him simply gave him the benefit of the doubt. He never obliged by clarifying his position, partly because he was not aware of the extent to which it mystified his work and partly because the gentleman and businessman in him prohibited it.

Perhaps this credits Sheehan with more sensitivity than he deserves. Much of his commentary can be seen to be operating under no less an ordinary principle than putting one foot in front of the other, and then not always in a straight line. It is hardly likely that he ever got round to considering the issue from the point of view of sales, or to realizing that the struggle against stereotype just was not worth it or, that the short term advantages in 'vitiating the taste of the public' outweighed the long term disadvantages of perpetuating prejudice and misunderstanding. This never arose as an issue for Guinan while O'Donovan was far too concerned with the actual condition of life in Ireland to worry about the popular national image. At any rate as he continued to write, Sheehan found himself subscribing to the notion that the Irishman was built according to a unique design.

Sheehan presents a pastiche of stereotypes but mixes them in very differing situations while Guinan's characters are distinguished only by the incidents in which they are involved. Though O'Donovan often seems to be no more than a clever caricaturist, nevertheless, in terms of Irish fiction, they were new caricatures. On the issue of sectarianism, Guinan emerges as the most confidant bigot, while Sheehan blames the obsequiousness of the Catholics for much of the problem. O'Donovan despairs at the cultural and political impasse between the two communities.

Sheehan's picture of class, land and society does not wildly differ from Guinan's. Yet Guinan haplessly vacillates between presenting an idyllic countryside and pathetically sad situations. O'Donovan is the only writer to refer explicitly to the class of landless labourers — and to include them in his scheme for a new Ireland, while Guinan's gaze rarely transcends the 'respectable class of tenant farmers' and the adventures of their families.

For O'Donovan, the health of the rural economy was a linchpin of the new Ireland — releasing the poor from the grip of shopkeepers and priests. For Sheehan, and to an even greater extent for Guinan, the economy is peripheral to the well being of their flock. Though they would dearly like to see spinning wheels buzzing in the cottages, they are ultimately wary lest the reality of an industrial revolution might suddenly engulf the land.

It is interesting that the Cromwellian land transactions are such a strong motif in their thinking about the origins of Irish nationalism. While Guinan and Sheehan alike see the event as the turning point in modern Irish history, O'Donovan adopts a more open-minded 'revisionist' position. The other two resign themselves to accepting the myths and most of the old inter-pretations of Irish nationalist history, whether or not they approve or believe them, as though they recognised them by then to be so entrenched that there was no point in holding out any hope for their modification, much less their disposal.

Guinan, Sheehan and O'Donovan were unusual in facing up to the fact that Ireland appeared to be caught on the edge of a new and threatening world. They recognised it as a time when urgent action needed to be taken. These writers were gingerly anticipating a new Catholic Ireland, so that an interesting combination of the obligatory ecumenism is supported by an undertow of Catholic triumphalism. Alongside this triumphalism in Sheehan and Guinan however, there is a motivating undercurrent of worry that this new, buoyantly prosperous Catholic laity might soon outrun the clerical leadership.

Though it would be an exaggeration to say that Irish Catholicism at this time was shaken, there was nevertheless in small pockets of clerical Ireland, a nervousness for its future. A study of these three ideologues indicates the complexity, hesitancy and flexibility of both the individual and the group in forming any attitude to the modern. Where Sheehan worries and warns about the exposure of Irish Catholicism to foreign influences, Guinan presents a far more secure front. Though he knows the disease is virulent, he is convinced too that it will hardly be allowed gain a toe hold in Ireland. O'Donovan, by contrast invites the modern and locates the threat of irreligion within. His only hope is that the new state might usher in a new, reformed Catholicism, formed of the virtuous points and 'good men' amongst the clergy.

Writing apart, all three were activists to some extent. Even Guinan set up a somewhat out of the ordinary school of domestic economy in Longford. All three were breaking ranks with their massed colleagues who abided by unwritten understandings about the limits of clerical normality.

This literature was prompted by the confluence of many factors: the encroaching modern; emigration; the stirring effect of all that counter productive Protestant energy; and the expanding market for reading material. So that there emerged a branch of Catholics who founded the Catholic Truth Society of Ireland, the Catholic magazines, the Catholic social organisations, and who encouraged the writing of, and then the consumption of books such as these, all in a thinly veiled bellicose pose. Some tried to give the impression that they were doing it for no more serious a purpose than to provide some wholesome light entertainment for people of the same faith and values, when at the same time, however, one gets the impression that privately they felt it had better be done 'before it was too late'.

Irish America established Sheehan and Guinan. In the post civil war period the United States saw a proliferation of new Catholic journals, vigorously supported by the American bishops. It was through the *American Ecclesiastical Review*, its literary supplement from 1902, the *Dolphin*, and *Ave Maria*[2] that Sheehan and Guinan first found an outlet for their work. This is evidence of the 'symbiosis' of the Irish at home and abroad. It also suggests that even Irish American Catholics and clergy were far less inhibited about the reading of novels than their Irish cousins.

In Ireland at the close of the last century, the moral health of anybody who engaged in such literary activity was automatically and generally suspect. In the cloisters of Maynooth, this was especially true. The writing, or reading, of literature beyond the bounds of the prescribed texts by the clergy was not only frowned on, but silently prohibited, as Sheehan capably illustrated in his later novels.[3] Most of the fiction at the time was seen as morally harmful, 'putting notions' into the heads of otherwise sensible young women, and even young men. At the least, fiction was frivolous and vain and worthless. The novel was, after all an English institution which sprang to life with the putrid smog of industrialisation. Novels, like drink, scientific inquiry, the music hall and subsequently films and jazz, were under a cloud of suspicion and carried overtones of naughtiness or even damnation for respectable Irish Catholicism. People who had scruples about reading 'profane' literature could read Sheehan and Guinan with good conscience. And priests inclined to interdict all novel-reading would have had to make an exception of Sheehan and Guinan. Some few Catholic writers, such as Kickham, enjoyed a similar exemption from the 1880s onwards. The works of these writers, and of Sheehan in particular, with the phenomenal *Knocknagow*, became steady favourites to be read, reread and passed down to children.[4] As well as being selfconsciously Irish, they were entertaining, safe, and in English. They provided an easy to read, Catholic, and, at one level, cheery story.

These writers are interesting also in that they always had to deal with the public image of being a priest. The sustained popularity of Sheehan and Guinan can be put down largely to their daredevil element as priest writers. Though priests were never discouraged from writing *per se*, they were clearly expected to use the medium for missionary purposes, so that anything which appeared to violate the assumed rules was exciting. It is interesting that in the first issue of the *Furrow* (1950) Archbishop D'Alton noticed an increasing interest in writing 'on the part of our younger priests' and promptly instructed that their themes should be drawn from 'life in the priesthood and Christian culture'.[5] At the turn of the century, there was an ambivalence at the heart of the clerical attitude to Ireland and the modern world, and that same split attitude marks D'Alton's comments in the 1950s. Though he remarks that cinema and radio brings 'our people' constantly in to contact with an alien and materialistic outlook — 'despite that, I think it is the general verdict that, where their religion is concerned, the heart of our people is essentially sound'. Then and before, 'the flood of the modern' somehow was a threat, yet Catholicism was seen to be 'sound', and there was no need for worry. Sheehan was exceptional in probing the spirit of the Catholics to which he ministered, so too O'Donovan; Guinan and the bulk of the clergy were happy with a head count. Sheehan was at war with Maynooth complacency as surely, if not as openly as O'Donovan. This anti-intellectual bent on the part of the authorities was easily colonised through the parishes of the country. The real damage was believed to be done when fiction carried potent ideas, to the Irish peasant.

There was apparently a real hunger for fiction about 'the inner life of a priest' in early twentieth century Ireland. Obviously Sheehan and Guinan satisfied the need to some extent, but stopped short of revealing what the audience most wanted to read. The human side of the 'Soggarth' was read with great interest, but then again the gritty clerical humanity which O'Donovan promptly provided was not generally welcomed either. There was a quick curiosity and delight in discovering how the priest saw the community and how he distinguished between the various types.

Underneath the dominant image of priest and people as being inseparately bonded, as presented by Sheehan and Guinan, there lurks a suspicion that their authority may be conditional. Through all of the works, though particularly in O'Donovan's, it is clear that the position of an anticlerical was a very lonely one indeed. In any matter relating to sex on which the clergy made known their disapproval, the vast majority in the community were careful to disapprove too. On matters non-sexual, however, and concerning the interest of the majority, there was a tacit but established understanding on the right of 'the flock' to veto.

O'Donovan was not writing for an audience in the way that Sheehan and Guinan were, which may have been partially responsible for his lesser success. He was not obviously or consciously writing anti-clerical or anti-Catholic propaganda, though occasionally he came close. He was simply hoping that his disgust with matters clerical would be an eye-opener for those, both inside and outside the church, who had unshaken confidence in the system as it was. The generally hostile reception of O'Donovan's work in Ireland prompted Joseph Hone to write naively in the *London Mercury* of 1921 that such novelists as O'Donovan rarely received the credit they deserved in Ireland and were accused of 'writing down' Ireland for the British public. This is because the majority of the nineteenth century writers usually *were* aiming to please, at all cost, English taste.

Though these are just three writers with varying degrees of success, together they indicate the perplexing variety of ways in which images of Ireland could be selected and merged for various purposes. More significantly their record demonstrates the efficacy of the novel and the real need it satisfied during this period as a comforter against the passing times. Could it be that the popular Catholic writers considered here mark a deliberate changing of course from the writing down of Ireland for the English market, to the *writing up* of Ireland for the Irish?

Appendix I

Figures are given below for the known editions of the works of Sheehan, Guinan and O'Donovan. The figures given for the three writers are uniformly modest as they exclude translations, circulation in serial form, reselling, borrowing and incalculable reprints.

The total number of copies of the novels can be estimated only by some printing figures for the first editions and by estimating that a minimum of 1,000 copies were printed for each further edition. On that rule of thumb the following figures emerge as minimum:

CANON SHEEHAN

My New Curate	Marlier Boston 1900:	30,000)	
	Talbot (1928-58):	10,000)	40,000
Luke Delmege	Longmans 1st ed.	12,000)	
	Folens (1973)	1,000)	13,000
Glenanaar	Longmans 1st ed.	11,500)	
	Mercier (1980)	1,000)	12,500
Lisheen	Longmans 1st ed.	11,600)	
	Clonmore & Reynolds		
	(1956)	1,000)	12,600
Dr Gray	Longmans 1st ed.	18,400)	
	Talbot (1953)	1,000)	19,400
Miriam Lucas	Longmans 1st ed.		11,300
Kilmorna	Longmans 1st ed.	13,000)	
	Talbot (1925)	1,000)	
	Clonmore & Reynolds		
	(1956)	1,000)	15,000
			———
	TOTAL:		123,500

A sample indication of the turnover of the Phoenix editions can be seen from their sales account of their reprint of the 1928 (Talbot edition) of *The Triumph of Failure*.

STOCK		SALES
2000 copies printed	13 April 1933	714
	31 May 1933	37
	30 Nov. 1933	60
	31 May 1934	33
	13 Nov. 1934	167
	31 May 1935	36
983 copies	13 Nov. 1935	To be destroyed

Though Phoenix engaged in reprinting Sheehan's novels from the early 1930s, the Talbot papers (P.R.O.I.) are not available beyond 1937, and those before are not very informative.

JOSEPH GUINAN

Editions Known			Estimated copies
Doon	1903 (2 editions)	Gill & Duffy	
	1906	Gill & Duffy	4,000
	1912	Benziger	
	1923		
Soggarth Aroon	1905 (4 editions)	Gill & Duffy	9,000
	1906	Benziger	
	1907	Gill & Duffy	
	1908	Gill & Duffy	
	1912	BOW	
	1946 9th printing	Talbot	
Moore of Glynn	1907	BOW	5,000
	1908	Pratt (N.Y.)	
	1912	BOW	
	1915	BOW	
	1928	BOW	
Island Parish	1908 (2 editions)	Gill	2,000
The Curate of	1912	Gill	2,000
Kilcloon	1913	Gill	
Donal Kenny	1910	Gill	3,000
	1911	Benziger	

	1912		
Annamore	1924	BOW &	6,000
	1925 (four editions)	Benziger	
Patriots	1928	Benziger	Unknown

| | TOTAL: | | 31,000 |

GERALD O'DONOVAN

Fr Ralph	1913	Macmillan	
	1914		7,000
Waiting	1914	Macmillan	6,000
Conquest	1920	Constable)	5,000
	1920	Colonial ed.)	
	1921	Putnams (New York))	
Vocations	1920	Martin Secker	2,000
	1921	Boni & Liveright (NY)	

| | TOTAL: | 20,000 |

These figures may appear to be very small scale when compared with Ireland's most popular novel, *Knocknagow*, which sold an estimated 100,000 copies between 1873 and 1887. However *Knocknagow* was such a phenomenon that between Kickham and Sheehan for example, in the popularity ratings, contending novelists would be scarce indeed.

Appendix II

Advertisement Circulated by M.H. Gill & Son 1912

M.H. GILL & SON, LTD., DUBLIN.
List of New and Recent Editions of Our Popular Presentation Series.

Special attention is drawn to this List of Books, attractively issued in UNI-FORM crown octavo size.

	s.d.
ANNUNZIATA. L.S. Oliver	1 6
ESTERINO ANTONIO. Translated by Lady Herbert	1 6
LEO	1 6
THE SMUGGLER'S REVENGE. Lady Lentaigne	1 6
STEPHANIE. Louis Veuillot	1 6
DONAL DUN O'BYRNE. D, Holland	1 6
HUMOURS OF SHANWALLA. Patrick Archer	1 6
A HAMPER OF HUMOUR. Liam. Net	1 6
WITHOUT BEAUTY. Zenaide Fleuroit	2 0
CHASED BY WOLVES. Trans by H.J. Gill, M.A.	2 0
JOLLY HARPER MAN.	2 0
COINER'S CAVE. W. Herchenbach	2 0
MARTYRS OF CASTELFIDARDO. Trans. by a Presentation Nun	2 0
FARLEYES OF FARLEYE. Rev. T.J. Potter	2 0
SIR HUMPHREY'S TRIAL.	2 0
PERCY GRANGE.	2 0
THE KNOUT. Mrs. J. Sadlier	2 0
SISTER ROSALIE. M. Le Vicomte de Mileau	2 0
RUPERT AUBREY. Historical tale of 1681	2 0
FERRYMAN OF THE TIBER. Madame De La Grange	2 0
TOLD IN THE GLOAMING. Josephine Hannon	2 0
LITTLE HUNCHBACK. Countess De Segur	2 0
GEOFFREY AUSTIN. Very Rev. P.A. Sheehan	2 0

TRUE HEARTS' TRIALS. T. O'Neill Russell   2 0
SCENES AND SKETCHES. Rev. J. Guinan   2 0
SPEECHES FROM THE DOCK. A.M., & T.D. Sullivan   2 0
GEMS FOR THE YOUNG. Rosa Mulholland   2 0
LINDA'S MISFORTUNE. Clara Mulholland   2 0
STORY OF IRELAND. A.M. Sullivan   2 6
IRISH READINGS.   2 6
SHAM SQUIRE, OR THE INFORMERS OF '98.
                              Fitzpatrick   2 6
IRISH FAIRY TALES. Edmund Leamy   2 6
KATHLEEN MAVOURNEEN. Randall MacDonnell   2 6
MY SWORD FOR PATRICK SARSFIELD.   2 6
IN SARSFIELD'S DAYS. L. MacManus   2 6
HERMIT OF THE ROCK. Mrs. J. Sadlier   2 6
OLD HOUSE BY THE BOYNE. Mrs. J. Sadlier   2 6
UNA'S ENTERPRISE. Nora Tynan O'Mahony   2 6
SHAN VAN VOCHT. James Murphy   2 6
WILD ROSE OF LOCH GILL. P.G. Smyth   2 6
ANNALS, ANECDOTES AND TRADITIONS
OF THE IRISH PARLIAMENTS   2 6
TEMPTATIONS OF NORAH LEECROFT.
                              Francis Noble   2 6
SOGGARTH AROON. Rev. Joseph Guinan   2 6
THE WONDERS OF IRELAND.
                   P.W. Joyce, LL.D. Net   2 6
ENGLISH AS WE SPEAK IT IN IRELAND
                   P.W. Joyce, LL.D.   2 6
GILL'S IRISH RECITER. J.J. O'Kelly Net   2 6
LIFE OF THE BLESSED VIRGIN. Abbe Orsini   3 6
LIFE OF OUR LORD. Rev. H. Rutter   3 6
LIGHT OF THE WEST. Lieut-Gen. Sir W. Butler   3 6
LECTURES OF A CERTAIN PROFESSOR.
                              Rev. J. Farrell   3 6
RAMBLES IN EIRINN. William Bulfin   3 6
TRUE MEN AS WE NEED THEM. Rev. B. O'Reilly   3 6
MIRROR OF TRUE WOMANHOOD   3 6

PERSECUTIONS OF THE IRISH CATHOLICS.		
Card. Moran	3 6	
CANONISATION OF SAINTS.		
V. Rev. T. Canon Macken Net	3 6	
OLD AND NEW. Rev. N. Walsh Net	3 6	
FOR THE OLD LAND. C.J. Kickham	3 6	
ARMOURER OF SOLINGEN. Trans by H.J. Gill	3 6	
GOOD AND PLEASANT READINGS.	3 6	
CID CAMPEADOR	3 6	
SCHMID'S TALES	3 6	
CASTLE OF COETQUIN. A.W. Chetewoode	3 6	
CASTLE OF ROUSSILON	3 6	
TREASURE OF THE ABBEY	3 6	
RESEDA	3 6	
A STRIKING CONTRAST. Clara Mulholland	3 6	
PHILIP'S RESTITUTION. Christian Reid	3 6	
VICTIMS OF THE MAMERTINE. Rev. J. O'Reilly	3 6	
JOHN CANADA	3 6	
ALICE RIORDAN. Mrs. J. Sadlier	3 6	
WALKING TREES AND OTHER TALES.		
Rosa Mulholland	3 6	
MARCELLA GRACE	3 6	
A FAIR EMIGRANT	3 6	
THE CURATE OF KILCLOON. Rev. Joseph Guinan	3 6	
AN ISLAND PARISH	3 6	
FORGE OF CLOHOGUE. James Murphy	3 6	
OLD CELTIC ROMANCES. P.W. Joyce, LL.D.	3 6	
CROMWELL IN IRELAND. Rev. Denis Murphy	3 6	
PRIVATE OWNERSHIP. Rev. J. Kelleher Net	3 6	
POEMS OF THE PAST. Moi Meme	3 6	
POEMS OF JAMES C. MANGAN. D.J. O'Donoghue		
Net	3 6	

END NOTES

Introduction:

1. Patrick J. Corish, The Irish Catholic Experience: a historical survey (Dublin, 1985), p.209.
2. Sheehan, Preface to Intellectuals, (London, 1911), p.iv.
3. Review of Vocations Spectator 14 Jan. 1922 p.55.
4. Claude Cockburn, Best Seller: the Books that Everyone Read 1900-1939 (London, 1972), p.8.
5. Oliver MacDonagh The Nineteenth Century Novel and Social History; some aspects (Dublin, 1970), p.29.
6. R.V. Comerford, Charles J. Kickham; a study in Irish nationalism and literature (Dublin 1979).
7. John Wilson Foster, Fictions of the Irish Literary Revival: A Changeling Art (Syracuse, 1987), pp.xi-xx.
8. John Wilson Foster, ibid, p.xvii.
9. Ibid. p.xiv.
10. Oliver MacDonagh. 'The Politics of Gaelic', States of Mind: a study of Anglo-Irish Conflict 1780-1980 (London, 1983), pp.104-126.
11. 'Marban', Leader 30 April 1904.
12. Fr Thomas Murphy, The Literary Crusade in Ireland (Limerick, 1912), pp.11-12.
13. Charles Gavan Duffy, The Revival of Irish Literature (London, 1894), p.17.
14. W.B. Yeats, 'The Irish Intellectual Capital: Where is it?' United Ireland 14 May 1892 p.12.
15. Fr. Joseph Guinan, 'The Silent Sermon of the Months' Irish Monthly XLV (Jan, Dec., 1917, pp.3-56; 49-53, republished in pamphlet form as Months and Days and The Mood and the Moral by the Catholic Truth Society of Ireland, (Dublin, n.d.).
16. Joseph Guinan, 'Priest and People in Ireland' Catholic Bulletin I (Feb., 1911), p.62.
17. L.P. Curtis, Apes and Angels: the Irishman in Victorian Caricature (London, 1971).
18. Joseph Guinan, Priest and People in Doon (Dublin, 1903), p.45, (hereafter Doon).
19. Fr Joseph Guinan, 'The Silent Sermon of the Months' Irish Monthly XLV (Jan., Dec., 1917, pp.3-56; 49-53.
20. G. O'Brien, 'The Fictional Irishman 1665-1850' Studies (Winter, 1977), p.328.
21. Daniel Corkery, The Hidden Ireland (Dublin, 1925), p.27.
22. Wayne E. Hall, Shadowy Heroes: Irish Literature of the 1890s (Syracuse, 1980), pp.10-11.
23. Irish Rosary (1), 1897.
24. Patrick J. Corish, The Catholic Truth Society Annual (Dublin, 1949: Special 50th anniversary issue), pp.1-11.
25. E.J. Cahill, S.J., Irish Ecclesiastical Record (hereafter IER) XXXVI (July-Dec., 1930).
26. Emmet Larkin, 'Church, State and Nation in Modern Ireland', The Dimensions of Irish Catholicism (New York, 1976), pp.122-3.

27. F.S.L. Lyons, *Ireland Since the Famine* (London, 1971), pp.87-93.

28. Mary Castleleyn, *A History of Literacy and Libraries: the long traced pedigree* (Hants. and Vermont, 1984), p.86.

29. 'Marban', *Leader* 30 April 1904.

30. Patrick J. Corish, op. cit, p.219.

31. Gerald O'Donovan, *Father Ralph*, (London, 1913), p.264.

32. J.A. Murphy, 'Priests and People in Modern Irish History' *Christus Rex* XXIII (Oct. 1969), pp.235-59.

33. Liam Kennedy, 'The Early Response of the Irish Catholic Clergy to the Co-operative Movement', *Irish Historical Studies* XXI (1977-8), pp.58-74.

34. Fr M. Kavanagh, *The Will and the Way* (Dublin, 1920), p.92.

35. R. Kane, *From Fetters to Freedom: Trials and Triumphs of Irish Faith* (London, 1915), p.vi.

36. Fr M. Phelan *The Will and the Way* (Dublin, 1920), p.84.

37. J.A. Murphy, op. cit, p.240.

38. George A. Birmingham, *Irishmen All* (London, 1913), p.32.

39. Francis Sheehy Skeffington, *Irish Review* (June, 1912), p.222.

40. Horace Plunkett, *Ireland in the New Century*, (London, 1904), p.11.

41. George Russell ('AE'), *Priest or Hero* (Dublin, 1910), p.5.

42. Paul Dubois, *Contemporary Ireland* (Dublin, 1908), p.560.

43. Walter MacDonald, *Reminiscences of a Maynooth Professor* (Dublin, 1925), p.55.

44. *Leader* 30 April 1904.

45. J.A. Murphy, op. cit, p.245.

46. *Leader* 30 April 1904.

47. Fr J. Fullerton, *The Will and the Way* (Dublin, 1920), p.19.

Chp 1: Canon Sheehan

1. P. O'Dargain, *Capuchin Annual* (1952), p.405.

2. Ibid., p.405.

3. H.J. Heuser *Canon Sheehan of Doneraile* (London, 1919), p.11.

4. Ibid, p.22.

5. P.A. Sheehan, 'The Moonlight of Memory', *The Literary Life and other Essays* (Dublin, 1921) ed. pp.170-3.

6. Ibid., pp.170-3.

7. Ibid., p.180.

8. Ibid., pp.114-20.

9. Ibid., p.185.

10. *The Literary Life,* p.61.

11. *Maynooth College Kalendarium*, (1870).

12. Ibid., (1871).

13. Sheehan, *The Literary Life and other Essays* p.119

14. *The Literary Life*, pp.114-20.

15. Fr Matthew Russell, 'Luke Delmege' *Irish Ecclesiastical Record* XI (Jan. 1902) p.212.

16. Linehan, op cit, p.33.

17. H.J. Heuser, *Canon Sheehan of Doneraile*, (London and New York, 1917), p.39.

18. T.W. Moody, *Davitt and the Irish Revolution* (1846-82), (Oxford, 1981), p.267.

19. Rev. Francis Boyle, *Canon Sheehan: A Sketch of his life and works*, (Dublin, 1927), p.25.

20. Sheehan, inaugural address to the Literary and Debating Society of Mallow, (Nov. 1880), c.f. Boyle, pp.28-9.

21. *IER* II (Sept. 1881), pp.521-31.

22. Sheehan, 'A Visit to a Dublin Art Gallery' *IER* II (Dec. 1881) pp.726-7.

23. Sheehan, 'The Effects of Emigration on the Irish Church' *IER* III (Oct. 1882), pp.602-15.

24. Emmet Larkin, 'Economic Growth, Capital Investment, and the Roman Catholic Church in Nineteenth Century Ireland, *The Historical Dimensions of Irish Catholicism* (Washington DC, 1984), pp.13-55.

25. Mrs William O'Brien, 'Canon Sheehan' *Studies* XIX (Sept. 1930), pp.492-8.

26. Ibid., p.492.

27. Heuser, op cit, p.14.

28. *My New Curate*, (1928 ed.), p.10.

29. Anon, 'Concerning the Author of Luke Delmege', *Irish Monthly*, p.661.

30. c.f. Fr. Tom Finlay, an active founder of magazines: *Lyceum* (1887); *New Ireland Review* (1894); *Irish Monthly* (1873), though he did later write pseudonymously as 'A. Whitelock', 'The Chances of War' first serialised in the *Irish Monthly* and then republished as *With the Army of the O'Neill* in 1930 under his own name, also Rev. Matthew Russell S.J. editor of the *Irish Monthly* 1873-1913.

31. Rev R. Fullerton, 'What is the Good of It?' (The Irish Language) in Irish Priests, *The Will and the Way* (Dublin n.d.), p.18.

32. *My New Curate*, p.187.

33. *The Blindness of Dr Gray* (Phoenix ed.), p.35.

34. Sheehan, 'The Irish Priesthood and Politics', *The Literary Life*, p.114.

35. Sheehan's commonplace book, McLysaght papers, N.L.I., MS 24,950.

36. *Luke Delmege*, (London, 1919 ed.) p.91.

37. Sheehan, *The Literary Life*, p.9.

38. Linehan, p.55.

39. Anon, (probably Fr M. Russell), 'Concerning the author of Luke Delmege', *Irish Monthly*, XXX (Dec, 1902), pp 661-9 cites an article entitled 'Books that influenced me' earlier in the *Weekly Register* to which Sheehan had contributed.

40. Sheehan 'Unpublished Preface' [to *The Triumph of Failure*], *The Literary Life*, p.64.

41. Ibid., p.64.

42. Ibid., p.64.

43. Ibid., p.65.

44. P.E.K., 'An Interview with Brother Mulhall' *Capuchin Annual*, (1952), p.386, (Br. Mulhall was superior of the Christian Brothers school in Doneraile and long-standing friend of Sheehan's).

45. Fr M. Gaffney, 'Herman J. Heuser and Canon Sheehan', *IER*, LIV (Oct. 1939), p.370.

46. 'Unpublished Preface', *The Literary Life,* p.60.

47. Ibid., p.61.

48. Russell to Sheehan, McLysaght papers, NLI, Ms 24,950.

49. *Literary Life,* p.63.

50. Boyle, p.67.

51. H.J. Heuser, op.cit, pp.132-33

52. Fr M.H. Gaffney, 'Dr. Herman J. Heuser and Canon Sheehan', *IER* LIV (Oct. 1939), pp.367-374,

cites a letter of Sheehan's to Heuser of 1899.

53. Sean O'Faolain, *The Irish*, (London, 1947), pp.108-10.

54. George Birmingham, *Irishmen All*, (London, 1913), p.49.

55. Fr Peter Connolly, 'The Priest in Modern Irish Fiction', *Furrow* IX (Dec. 1958).

67. Heuser, p.141.

68. *Luke Delmege*, p.15.

69. Ibid., p.19.

70. J.F. Hogan, op. cit, p.152.

71. Heuser, *Canon Sheehan of Doneraile* cites letter from Sheehan, 13 June, 1912, p.181.

72. Review of *Under the Cedars and the Stars*, (probably by Fr M. Russell), *Irish Monthly* XXI (March, 1903), p.702.

73. Heuser, p.237.

74. Mr. Barry was the uncle of M.P. Linehan, author of a biography of Canon Sheehan.

75. Heuser, p.191.

76. Preface to *Early Essays and Lectures*, (London, 1906).

77. *My New Curate*, pp.50-1.

78. *Lisheen, or the Test of Spirits*, (Phoenix ed., n.d.), p.6.

79. J.F. Hogan, *IER*, XXI (Feb. 1907), pp.640-2.

80. *Capuchin Annual*, (1952), p.231.

81. *The Intellectuals*, (London, 1921 ed.), p.371.

82. Fr M.H. Gaffney, 'Dr. Herman J. Heuser and Canon Sheehan', *IER*, LIV (Oct. 1939), p.371.

83. Fr S. Rigby, 'Jottings on Canon Sheehan', *IER*, LXXVIII (Nov. 1952), pp.321-9.

84. Heuser, p.189, cites a letter from Sheehan, 13 June 1904.

85. Fr Michael, 'Canon Sheehan's

Letters to Heuser and Russell', *Capuchin Annual*, (1942), p.276.

86. 'M.' *IER* I (Feb. 1913), pp.220-2.

87. *The Literary Life*, p.173.

88. Sheehan to Oliver Wendell Holmes, 25 February 1913, cited in David H. Burton, *The Letters of Justice Oliver Wendell Holmes and Canon Sheehan* (New York, 1976), p.61.

89. *The Graves at Kilmorna*, p.258.

90. 'How Character is Formed', CTSI pamphlet n.d.

91. *Cork Free Press*, Oct. 1913, p.19.

92. Interview by 'M.B.' with Fr. Sheehan, *St. Stephen's: a magazine of university life*. (1902), pp.64-5.

93. Fr M.J. Phelan, *IER*, IX (Jan. 1917), p.35.

94. Sir Francis C. Burnand, ed. *English Who's Who and Yearbook, 1912*.

95. Fr M.J. Phelan, *IER*, IX (Jan. 1917), p.35.

96. *The Triumph of Failure*, (London, 1899; Dublin, 1956 ed.), p.17.

97. D.C. Kelleher, 'Canon Sheehan, Philosopher and Friend' *Capuchin Annual* (1952), pp.350-352.

98. Kenneth McGowan, *Capuchin Annual*, (1952).

99. Ibid.

100. Ibid.

101. Fr M.J. Phelan, 'Canon Sheehan', *IER*, IX, (Jan. 1917), p.43.

102. Fr. M.H. Gaffney, op. cit. p.371.

103. Heuser, p.291.

104. P. O'Dargain, *Capuchin Annual*, (1952), p.406.

105. J.F. Horgan, *Irish Monthly*, XLII (Jan. 1914), p.12.

106. 'Panegyric by Bishop of

Cloyne', *Cork Free Press*, 9 Oct. 1913, pp.5-6.

107. 'B.M.' *Capuchin Annual* (1952), p.386.

108. *Cork Examiner*, 9 Oct. 1913; *Cork Free Press*, 9 Oct. 1913.

109. 'Panegyric by the Bishop of Cloyne', *Cork Free Press* p.6.

110. *Capuchin Annual*, (1952) p.127.

Chp 2: Canon Guinan

1. *Doon*, pp.5-6.

2. *The Soggarth Aroon* (Phoenix edn.), p.80.

3. J.J. MacNamee, *History of Ardagh*, pp.59-60.

4. *Journal of Ardagh and Clonmacnoise Antiquarian Society* I, no.3 (1932), pp.49-53.

5. Ibid., p.3.

6. *History of Ardagh,* pp.559-60.

7. *Journal of Ardagh,* p.3.

8. *History of Ardagh,* p.559.

9. Ibid., p.559.

10. *Doon*, p.69.

11. *History of Ardagh,* pp.568-70.

12. *Catholic Herald,* 6 Jan. 1932, p.10.

13. *Longford Leader,* 9 Jan. 1932, p.5. *Catholic Herald*, 6 Jan., 1932, p.10.

14. Ibid.

15. *Catholic Herald,* 6 Jan. 1932 and *Irish Catholic,* 6 Jan. 1932.

16. *Soggarth Aroon,* p.127.

17. Ibid., p.128.

18. Ibid., p.129.

19. Ibid., p.130.

20. *Soggarth Aroon,* p.134.

21. Ibid., p.132.

22. Ibid., p.218-220.

23. 'The Apostolate of the Press',

Irish Monthly, XXXVIII (June, 1910), pp.320-37.

24. Ibid., p.36.

25. *Soggarth Aroon*, pp.23-24.

26. Ibid., p.2.

27. Stephen Brown, *Ireland in Fiction*, (Dublin, 1969 edn.), p.124.

28. *The Moores of Glynn*, (London, 1928), pp.311-312.

29. *Doon*, p.6.

30. 'Priest and People in Ireland', *Catholic Bulletin*, I (Feb., 1911) p.63.

31. 'Wanted: Apostolate of the Press', *Catholic Bulletin*, I (Sept., 1911), pp.470-3.

32. *Doon*, pp.91-99.

33. 'Priest and People in Ireland', p.63.

34. 'Apostolate of the Press', *Irish Monthly* XXXVIII (June, 1910), pp. 320-7.

35. *Doon*, p.95.

36. 'Priest and People in Ireland', p.65.

37. 'The Silent Sermons of the Month', *Irish Monthly* XLV (Jan-Dec., 1917), p.752.

38. *Doon,* preface.

39. *Soggarth Aroon*, p.128.

40. *Annamore, or the Tenant at Will,* (Dublin, 1925), p.90; (hereafter *Annamore*).

41. 'The Famine Years', a lecture delivered at St. Joseph's Temperance Hall, Longford (12 Nov. 1907), published by CTSI as a pamphlet (Dublin, 1908).

42. *The Patriots* (New York, Cincinnati and Chicago, 1928), p.10.

41. Ibid, p.325.

Chp 3:O'Donovan

1. Maynooth College Calendar (1894).
2. 'Two Pioneer Convents', *IER* (Dec. 1898), pp.503-12; 'Irish Workhouse Reform', *IER* (Jan. 1899), pp.48-60); 'The Celtic Revival of To-Day', *IER* (Mar. 1899), pp.238-256.
3. 'In reply to 'The Celtic Revival of To-Day', *An Claidheamh Solais,* 18 March 1899, pp.10-11.
4. 'The Celtic Revival of To-Day', *IER* (Mar. 1899), p.252.
5. *Annual Report I.A.O.S. 1899* (Dublin, 1900), p.90.
6. *Irish Homestead* 20 Jan. 1900, pp.33-36.
7. Ibid., 3 Feb. 1900, p.73.
8. Ibid., 2 April 1904, p.273.
9. Horace Plunkett unpublished Diary (1 Feb., 1899), Plunkett Papers, Plunkett Reference Library, St. Giles, Oxford. See J.F. Ryan 'Gerald O'Donovan: Priest, Novelist, Intellectual: A forgotten leader of the Irish Revival' (unpublished M.A. Thesis, U.C.G., 1983).
10. Gerald O'Donovan, 'Priests and Industrial Development in Ireland', *Record of the Maynooth Union 1899-1900* (Dublin, 1901), pp.38-48.
11. *Irish Homestead* 'Is Ireland Doomed?', April 1899, p.68.
12. Ibid.
13. Ibid.
14. Ibid. 21 Oct., 1899, p.716.
15. In 1908 the Dept. did end its financial support for the IAOS after a letter of T.W. Rolleston to Irish American businessmen, 21 Dec. 1907 spoke of the gombeen- men as controlling the parliamentary representative of the country and who used their influence to weaken the co-op movement. It was accomplished in the *Freeman's Journal,* 20 Jan. 1908 with a defensive letter from John Redmond who challenged that the Rolleston letter was evidence of a conspiracy against the Irish Party, cited in Bolger, *History of Irish Cooperative Movement* (Dublin, 1977), pp.100-102.
16. *Western News*, 24 Feb. 1900.
17. J.F. Ryan, 'Gerald O'Donovan: Priest, Novelist and Intellectual: A forgotten leader of the Irish revival' (M.A. Thesis, UCG, 1983); 200 shares at 5d. subscribed and 30 shares owned by workers.
18. *Irish Weekly Independent and Nation* 19 Jan. 1901, p.5.
19. Jeremiah O'Donovan, 'An O'Growney Memorial Lecture', *Gaelic League Pamphlets*, No. 26 (Dublin, 1902).
20. *Record of the Maynooth Union,* (Dublin, 1905), p.12.
21. *Irish Homestead,* 16 March, 1901, p.167.
22. *Irish World and American Industrial Liberator* 3 Jan. 1903, cited in J.F. Ryan, op. cit. p.66).
23. Jeremiah O'Donovan, 'Toleration' *Leader,* 18 July 1903, p.344.
24. *Ireland in the New Century,* (popular ed. London, 1905), pp.118-9.
25. Plunkett Diary, 4 May 1904.
26. J.F. Ryan, op. cit. p.96.
27. Lecture at the Rotunda, 'Our Duty to the Language Movement', reported in *Western News*,

6 Nov. 1901, p.6.

28. 'An O'Growney Memorial Lecture', Gaelic League pamphlets, No. 26, (Dublin, 1902), pp.9-10.

29. *Duilleachan an Oireachtais* (11, 12 Aug. 1905), p.6.

30. 'Priests and Industrial Development in Ireland' *Record of Maynooth Union 1899-1900*, (Dublin, 1900), pp.38-48.

31. O'Donovan to John Redmond, undated, N.L.I. Ms 15,269.

32. 'Roman Catholic Church in Ireland 1898-1918', *Eire-Ireland*, no.3, 1968, p.75.

33. 'Priests and Industrial Development', p.44.

34. 'Priests as Nation Builders', *Record of the Maynooth Union 1900-1901*, (Dublin, 1901), pp.45-55.

35. Liam Kennedy, 'Roman Catholic Church and Economic Growth in the Nineteenth Century', *Economic and Social Review*, (Oct. 1978), p.59.

36. 'The Churches and the Child', *Independent Review* (Feb. 1905), pp.78-89; *Littles Living Age*, (1905); *Eclectic Magazine*, (May 1905).

37. Peter Costello, *The Heart Grown Brutal, The Irish Revolution in Literature from Parnell to Yeats 1891-1939*, (Dublin, 1977), p.61.

38. *Waiting*, p.40.

39. 28 Nov. 1901, George Moore letters to Colonel Maurice Moore, George Moore Letters, N.L.I., Ms 2646.

40. *Irish Homestead* 16 June 1906, p.495.

41. J.A.R. Pimlott, *Toynbee Hall: 50 Years of Social Progress 1884-1934*, (London, 1935).

42. 'An Irish Station', *Saturday Review*, 20 July 1912, pp.77-79.

43. 'An Irish Marriage', *Saturday Review*, 24 Aug. 1913, pp.234-35.

44. 'An Irish Peasant', *Saturday Review*, 4 Sept. 1912, pp.239-40.

45. Personal Communication of David Harper, Macmillan Accounts and Administration Ltd., 22 Jan. 1987.

46. 'Locusts Food', unpublished reminiscences of Beryl O'Donovan, O'Donovan papers, p.85.

47. Letter to Beryl, 2 Sept. 1914, O'Donovan papers, in possession of Ms. Brigid O'Donovan, New York.

48. Letter to Beryl, 10 Dec. 1914, O'Donovan papers.

49. S. Webb letter to Horace Plunkett, not dated, but probably early March 1913. Plunkett papers, Ms Webb 7.

50. Plunkett Diary, 8 Feb., 1928.

51. Letter to Beryl, 4 July, 1915.

52. J.F. Ryan, op. cit. p.186.

53. J.F. Ryan, p.198.

54. Letter to Beryl, 26 April, 1917.

55. Ibid.

56. Constance Babington-Smith, *Rose Macaulay: A Biography*, (London, 1972), pp.89-193.

57. Ibid. p.100.

58. *Conquest*, (London, 1920), p.35.

59. Letter to Beryl, 26 April, 1916.

60. *Boston Evening Transcript*, 17 Aug. 1921, p.6; and Norreys J. O'Conor, *Literary backgrounds of the Irish Free State 1889-1922*, (London, 1924), pp.199-204.

61. J. O'Donovan, 'Dishonouring Irish Saints', *Leader*, 10 Jan.

1901, p.333.

62. Plunkett Diary, 8 Feb. 1928.

63. O'Donovan letter to Hone, 17 July, 1935, Hone Papers, Texas, cited in John F. Ryan, p.23.

64. O'Donovan believed that Moore had no special interest in religion, and that the words 'speculative' and 'empirical' with regard to Moore conveyed little if anything. O'Donovan letter to Hone, 14 Oct. 1934, Hone Papers, Texas, in John F. Ryan, p.22.

65. Peter Costello, *Macmillan Dictionary of Irish Literature* ed. R. Hogan, (London, 1980), p.512.

66. Constance Babington-Smith, pp.159-60.

Chp 4: Sheehan's Ireland

1. Daniel Corkery, *Hidden Ireland* (Dublin, 1970 edn.) p.79.

2. George A. Birmingham, *An Irishman looks at his World* (London, 1950), p.80.

3. *The Graves at Kilmorna*, p.336.

4. *Literary Life*, p.65.

5. Ibid., p.72.

6. J.F. Hogan, 'Luke Delmege' *Irish Ecclesiastical Review* XI (Feb. 1902) p.150.

7. *Literary Life*, p.61.

8. J.F. Hogan, op. cit., pp.145-155.

9. Matthew Russell to Sheehan, n.d. Russell made this remark having read the somewhat affected *Intellectuals* (1911), Russell papers, 35 Lr. Leeson St., Dublin.

10. Matthew Russell S.J. Review of *Under the Cedars and the Stars, Irish Monthly* XXI (March 1903), p.702.

11. *My New Curate,* pp.79-80.

12. *Glenanaar*, p.155.

13. *A Spoiled Priest and other stories*, p.328.

14. *The Blindness of Dr. Gray*, p.328.

15. *The Intellectuals: an experiment in club life*, p.223.

16. Ibid., p.55.

17. *My New Curate*, p.254.

18. Ibid., p.254.

19. *The Graves at Kilmorna*, p.64.

20. *The Intellectuals*, p.358.

21. Ibid., p.358.

22. 'Our Personal and Social Responsibilities' *IER*, IX (Feb. 1899), p.15.

23. Sheehan to Matthew Russell S.J., 10 March n.d., Russell papers.

24. *The Graves at Kilmorna*, p.258.

25. *The Intellectuals,* p.104.

26. *The Graves at Kilmorna*, p.20.

27. Ibid., p.20.

28. Ibid., p.51.

29. *The Intellectuals*, p.358.

30. *The Blindness of Dr. Gray*, p.230.

31. Ibid., p.230.

32. *Glenanaar*, p.236, 254.

33. *The Blindness of Dr. Gray,* p.72.

34. Ibid., p.242.

35. Sheehan, *Cork Free Press,* 9 Oct. 1910.

36. Ibid.

37. Sheehan to Oliver Wendell Holmes, 26 Aug. 1910, in *Holmes - Sheehan Correspondence: the letters of Justice Oliver Wendell Holmes and Canon Sheehan*, ed. David H. Burton, (New York/London, 1976) pp.35-36.

38. *Literary Life*, p.189.

39. Mrs. William O'Brien, 'Canon Sheehan' *Studies*, XIX (Sept. 1930), pp.492-8.

40. Sheehan to Russell, 19 Mar. n.d., Russell papers.

41. Daniel Kelleher, cites a letter from Canon Sheehan in 'Canon Sheehan' *Capuchin Annual*, 1952, p.35.
42. Sheehan to Holmes, 25 Feb. 1915, cited in Burton, op. cit. p.61.
43. *The Graves at Kilmorna*, p.261.
44. *My New Curate*, p.95.
45. Ibid., p.96.
46. Ibid., p.97.
47. *Luke Delmege,* p.144.
48. *The Triumph of Failure*, p.155.
49. *Miriam Lucas,* p.248.
50. 'Our Personal and Social Responsibilities', *IER*, IX, (Feb. 1899), pp.69-80.
51. *Luke Delmege, The Blindness of Dr. Gray, Miriam Lucas.*
52. *The Intellectuals*, p.355.
53. *My New Curate,* p.101.
54. *The Blindness of Dr. Gray,* p.28.
55. *Geoffrey Austin, Student*, p.59.
56. *The Blindness of Dr. Gray,* p.71.
57. *Miriam Lucas*, p.153, also *Lisheen*, pp.134-5.
58. *Miriam Lucas*, pp.135-6.
59. *The Triumph of Failure,* p.155.
60. Ibid., p.162.
61. Ibid., p.160.
62. Ibid., p.160.
63. *Lisheen,* pp.129-30.
64. *The Intellectuals,* pp.278-80.
65. *The Blindness of Dr. Gray*, p.391, *The Intellectuals,* pp.25-26.
66. 'Our Personal and Social Responsibilities', *IER,* IX (Feb. 1899), p.15.
67. Ibid., p.17.
68. *Luke Delmege*, pp.417-20.
69. *My New Curate*, p.164.
70. Ibid., p.173.
71. Ibid., p.165.
72. Ibid., p.166.

73. Ibid., p.167.
74. Ibid., p.252.
75. *The Blindness of Dr. Gray*, p.192.
76. Ibid., p.169.
77. Ibid., p.307.
78. Ibid., p.197.
79. Ibid., p.192.
80. *Luke Delmege*, p.42.
81. *The Blindness of Dr. Gray*, p.219.
82. *My New Curate*, pp.306-7.
83. *The Triumph of Failure*, p.25.
84. *A Spoiled Priest and other stories*, pp.3-4.
85. *A Spoiled Priest*, p.1.
86. Ibid., p.3.
87. Ibid., p.82.
88. *Luke Delmege*, pp.475-6.
89. *The Blindness of Dr. Gray*, p.129, *The Graves at Kilmorna*, pp.76-77.
90. *The Blindness of Dr. Gray*, pp.4-6.
91. Ibid., p.4-5.
92. Ibid., p.73.
93. *The Blindness of Dr. Gray*, p.215 offers a good example.
94. Ibid., p.351.
95. *My New Curate*, p.58.
96. *Luke Delmege*, p.37.
97. c.f. 'The Monks of Trabolgan', *a Spoiled Priest*, pp.47-48; *My New Curate*, p.306; *Luke Delmege*, p.76.
98. *Luke Delmege*, p.37.
99. Ibid., p.87.
100. *The Intellectuals*, p.61.
101. *Luke Delmege*, p.344.
102. *Miriam Lucas*, p.135.
103. *Luke Delmege*, p.406.
104. *The Intellectuals*, p.319.
105. *My New Curate*, p.372.
106. Ibid., p.43.
107. Ibid., p.43.
108. Ibid., p.59.

109. *Lisheen*, p.257.
110. Ibid., p.50.
111. *Miriam Lucas*, p.362.
112. *Lisheen*, p.28.
113. Ibid., p.440.
114. *The Blindness of Dr. Gray*, p.228.
115. Ibid., p.229.
116. Ibid., p.313.
117. Ibid., p.235.
118. *The Intellectuals*, p.61.
119. *The Graves at Kilmorna*, p.153.
120. *Miriam Lucas*, p.43.
121. *The Blindness of Dr. Gray*, p.366.
122. *The Graves at Kilmorna*, pp.276-284.
123. Ibid., p.362.
124. *Glenanaar*, p.141; 317; 122.
125. *The Graves at Kilmorna*, p.359.
126. Ibid., p.272.
127. Ibid., p.274.
128. Ibid., p.281.
129. *Lisheen*, p.168.
130. *My New Curate*, p.52.
131. Ibid., pp.37-8.
132. *Glenanaar*, p.187.
133. *Lisheen*, p.230.
134. Sheehan interview with 'M.B.', *St. Stephen's: a Magazine of University Life*; (1902), pp.64-5.

Chp 5: Guinan's Ireland

1. *The Curate of Kilcloon*, (Dublin, 1912), p.176.
2. Ibid., p.202.
3. *The Graves at Kilmorna*, p.282.
4. *The Soggarth Aroon*, p.148.
5. Ibid., p.148.
6. *The Island Parish*, (Dublin, 1908), p.62.
7. *The Soggarth Aroon*, p.71.
8. Ibid., p.71.
9. *The Island Parish*, p.129, *Annamore*, p.113.
10. *Annamore*, p.116.
11. *The Curate of Kilcloon*, p.182.
12. Ibid., p.183.
13. Ibid., pp.173-3
14. *The Soggarth Aroon*, p.36.
15. Ibid., p.200.
16. *The Island Parish*, p.12.
17. *The Soggarth Aroon*, p.112.
18. *Annamore*, p.220.
19. Ibid., p.70.
20. Ibid., p.80.
21. *The Curate of Kilcloon*, p.101.
22. *The Island Parish*, pp.96-7.
23. *The Soggarth Aroon*, p.124.
24. *The Island Parish*, pp.96-7.
25. *The Soggarth Aroon*, p.257.
26. *An Island Parish*, p.143.
27. *Doon*, p.70.
28. *The Soggarth Aroon*, p.17.
29. *The Curate of Kilcloon*, p.70.
30. Ibid., p.71.
31. Ibid., pp.14-15.
32. Ibid., p.68.
33. Ibid., p.35.
34. *Annamore*, pp.11-14.
35. *The Soggarth Aroon*, p.66.
36. Ibid., p.66.
37. *The Soggarth Aroon*, p.119.
38. *The Curate of Kilcloon*, p.164.
39. Ibid., p.168.
40. *The Soggarth Aroon*, p.117.
41. Ibid., p.123.
42. Ibid., p.117.
43. *The Curate of Kilcloon*, p.215.
44. Ibid., p.215.
45. Ibid., p.77.
46. *An Island Parish*, p.71.
47. *An Island Parish*, p.248.
48. *The Soggarth Aroon*, pp.136-7.
49. *An Island Parish*, p.11.
50. Ibid., p.15.
51. Ibid., p.23.

52. Ibid., pp.278-80.
53. *The Curate of Kilcloon*, p.45.
54. Ibid., p.50.
55. *The Curate of Kilcloon*, p.269.
56. *An Island Parish*, p.189.
57. *Waiting*, p.119.
58. *An Island Parish*, p.98.
59. Ibid., p.75.
60. *Annamore*, p.79.
61. Ibid., p.79.
62. *Annamore*, p.80.
63. Ibid., p.129.
64. *The Soggarth Aroon*, p.143.
65. *Annamore*, p.31.
66. Ibid., p.41.
67. *The Curate of Kilcloon*, p.37.
68. *An Island Parish*, p.178.
69. *The Soggarth Aroon*, p.199.
70. *An Island Parish*, p.317.
71. *The Soggarth Aroon*, p.112.
72. Ibid., p.240.
73. Ibid., p.180.
74. *An Island Parish*, p.41.
75. *The Patriots*, p.81.
76. Ibid., p.83.
77. Ibid., p.330.
78. Ibid., p.10.
79. Ibid., p.297.
80. Ibid., p.300.
81. Ibid., p.290.
82. Ibid., p.291.
83. Ibid., p.290.
84. Ibid., p.253.
85. Ibid., p.290.
86. Ibid., p.279.
87. Ibid., p.267.
88. Ibid., p.148.
89. Ibid., p.142.
90. Ibid., p.150.
91. Ibid., p.162.
92. Ibid., p.235.

Chp 6:O'Donovan's Ireland

1. *Waiting* (London, 1914), p.54.
2. *Conquest* (London, 1920), p.160.
3. Ibid., p.284.
4. Ibid., p.160.
5. Ibid., p.77.
6. Ibid., p.7.
7. Ibid., p77.
8. Ibid., p.80.
9. Ibid., p.80.
10. Ibid., p.171.
11. Ibid., p.176.
12. Ibid., p.176.
13. Ibid., p.86.
14. *Father Ralph*, p.144.
15. Ibid., pp.318-9.
16. Ibid., p.332.
17. Ibid., p.342 also c.f. chapter 4.
18. *Waiting*, p.72.
19. *Father Ralph*, p.233.
20. *Waiting*, pp.91-2.
21. *Father Ralph*, p.395.
22. *Waiting*, p.46.
23. Ibid., p.372.
24. *Vocations*, (London, 1921), p.203.
25. Ibid., p.107.
26. Ibid., p.105.
27. Ibid., p.206.
28. Ibid., p.209.
29. Ibid., p.271.
30. Ibid., pp.270-2.
31. *Father Ralph*, pp.2-3.
32. Ibid., pp.17-18.
33. Ibid., p.250 and *Waiting*, p.23,27.
34. *Waiting*, p.77.
35. Ibid., p.72.
36. *Father Ralph*, pp.70-71.
37. Ibid., p.41.
38. Ibid., p.307.
39. Ibid., pp.281-2.
40. Ibid., p.315.
41. *Father Ralph*, p.264.

42. Ibid., p.377.
43. *Waiting*, p.298.
44. Ibid., pp.287-8.
45. Ibid., p.301.
46. *Conquest*, pp.110-11.
47. *Father Ralph*, p.94.
48. Ibid., p.323.
49. *Conquest*, p.114.
50. *Father Ralph*, p.20.
51. *Conquest*, p.20.
52. *Waiting*, pp.103-4.
53. *Father Ralph*, p.87.
54. *Waiting*, pp.103-4.
55. *Conquest*, p.137-8.
56. Ibid., p.99; *Waiting*, p.87.
57. *Conquest*, p.49.
58. *Waiting*, p.266.
59. *Conquest*, p.115.
60. *Conquest*, p.8.
61. *Father Ralph*, p.372.
62. *Conquest*, p.30.
63. *Vocations*, p.12.
64. *Father Ralph*, p.292.
65. Ibid., p.313.
66. *Waiting*, p.36.
67. *Vocations*, p.48.
68. Ibid., p.156.
69. *Father Ralph*, p.292.
70. Ibid., P.410.
71. *Waiting*, p.36.
72. Ibid., pp.62-3.

Chp 7: Sheehan — The Reception

1. M.H. Gaffney, 'Herman J. Heuser and Canon Sheehan', *IER* LIV (Oct., 1939), p.372.
2. Ibid., p.70.
3. Heuser, preface to *Tristram Lloyd*, (1928), p.xxx.
4. *Irish Monthly*, XVIII (Jan., 1900), p.87.
5. Gaffney, op. cit., p.4.
6. *Irish Monthly*, XVII (1899), p.670.
7. Heuser, *Canon Sheehan of Doneraile*, (N.Y., 1918), p.72.
8. 'Concerning the author of *Luke Delmege*', *Irish Monthly*, XXX (Dec., 1902), pp.666-7.
9. J.F. Hogan, 'My New Curate', *IER*, VII (Feb., 1900), pp.189-191.
10. Heuser, *Canon Sheehan of Doneraile* (N.Y., 1971), p.82.
11. Sheehan to Longmans, Longmans correspondence 30 Sept., 1901.
12. Ibid.
13. Agreement, Longman's archives, Oct., 3, 1901.
14. Contract on *L.D.*, Longman Archives Reading University.
15. Translation Agreement, Longman Archives, 27 May, 1902.
16. *Maria Laach* (Jan., 1904), cited in *Guide to Catholic Literature*, (Detroit, 1940).
17. *Catholic World*, Feb., 1902.
18. *Guide to Catholic Literature*, (Detroit, 1940).
19. J.F. Hogan, *IER*, XI, (Feb., 1902), pp.145-155.
20. Ibid, p.150.
21. *St. Stephen's*, I (1902), pp.63-73.
22. *Irish Monthly*, XXXII (1904), p.13-17.
23. Gaffney, op. cit., p.6.
24. Agreement on *Under the Cedars and the Stars*, Longmans Archives.
25. *Irish Monthly*, XXXIII (Feb., 1905), p.415.
26. W.H.G.F. *New Ireland Review*, XXIII (Aug., 1905), p.380.
27. Edward Nagle, 'Dr. Sheehan's latest work', *IER*, VIII (1908).
28. 'Some Aspects of Canon Shee-

han', *New Ireland Review*, XXVII (March, 1907), pp.15-27.

29. *IER*, XXII (March, 1907), pp.640-2.

30. Heuser preface to *Tristram Lloyd*, (Dublin, 1928), p.xxxvi.

31. Royalty divide ledger 5, 1907.

32. Spectator, cited in *Irish Book Lover*, (Feb., 1910), p.85.

33. Production ledger, 1909, Longman Archives.

34. J.F.H., 'The Blindness of Dr. Gray', *IER* XXVII, (Feb., 1910), pp.213-4.

35. *Irish Monthly*, XXXVII, pp.702-3.

36. Correspondence, 22 Aug., 1908.

37. Gaffney, op. cit., p.373.

38. Royalty divide 5, p.17 OST 20 13/10

Made 9 15 4, Longman Archives.

39. Correspondence of Sheehan to Longmans, 21 Aug., 1911, Longmans.

40. Correspondence of Sheehan to Longmans, 21 Sept., 1911.

41. 'Miriam Lucas', *Irish Monthly*, XL (Dec., 1912), p.693.

42. 'M', *IER* I (Feb., 1913), pp.220-2.

43. *Catholic Bulletin*, III (Nov., 1913), p.786.

44. *Irish Catholic*, 11 Oct., 1913.

45. *The Times*, 11 Oct., 1913.

46. *Morning Times*, 11 Oct., 1913.

47. *Westminster Gazette*, 11 Oct., 1913.

48. *Cork Free Press*, 6-12 Oct., 1913.

49. Ibid., 8 Oct., 1913.

50. Ibid., 6 Oct., 1913.

By 'the gifted Irish American priest Rev. J.B. Dollard ('Slievenamon')' The pride and priest of Doneraile

Athwart the shimmering seas we hail! Light may the years upon him fall Whose pen hath helped and cheered us all! ....

51. *Irish Book Lover*, VI (April, 1915), pp.148-19.

52. Con Houlihan, *Irish Times*, 20 May, 1971.

53. Heuser, preface to *Tristram Lloyd*, p.XL.

54. Rev. Michael J. Phelan S.J., 'Canon Sheehan' *IER* IX (Jan.-June, 1917), pp.28-39.

55. John D. Colclough, *Studies* I (June, 1917), pp.275-288.

56. Professor George O'Neill, S.J., M.A., 'A relic of Canon Sheehan', *Studies* VII II (1917), pp.358-397.

57. S. Brown, *Ireland in Fiction*, (Dublin, 1968).

58. Longmans letter to Dr. Brown, Bishop of Cloyne, 24 Nov., 1927.

59. Longmans London branch to New York branch, 4 Sept., 1927.

60. Longmans Receipt-Royalty divide 5.

61. Longmans letter to Bishop of Cloyne, 9 June, 1927.

62. Longmans letter to Bishop of Cloyne, 14 June, 1930.

63. D.J. Hickey, T.E. Doherty, *A Dictionary of Irish History since 1800*, (Dublin, 1980).

64. T.J.H., Review of *Tristram Lloyd, Dublin Magazine*, IV (April-June, 1929), pp.75-6.

65. Easons Monthly Bulletin, (Sept. 1928).

66. Ibid., (Nov., 1928).

67. 'A Library of Fiction by Irish Priests', *Catholic Bulletin* XVI (Nov., 1926), pp.1214-16.

68. Mrs. William O'Brien, 'Memo-

ries of Canon Sheehan', *Studies*, XIX (Sept. 1930), pp.492-8.

69. P. Ivers Rigney, 'Canon Sheehan as Teacher', *IER* XXXVI (July-Dec., 1930).

70. D.M., *IER*, XXX (July-Dec., 1927), p.671.

71. Dr. William Stockley, *Essays in Irish Biography*, (Cork, 1933), p.115.

72. Agreement with Minister of Education of Irish Free State, Longmans Archives, (27 Aug., 1937).

73. Seamus O Suilleabhain of government publications office supplied these figures to Fr. Michael, O.F.M., 'Twilight and Dawn', *Capuchin Annual* (1942), pp.263-287.

74. Neil Kevin, *I remember Maynooth*, (Dublin, 1945), first published in 1937 by 'Donn Boyne'.

75. M.H. Gaffney, 'Herman J. Heuser and Canon Sheehan', *IER* LIV (July-Dec., 1939), pp.367-374.

76. *Easons Book Notes*, (Nov., 1928), p.3.

77. Fr. Michael, 'Canon Sheehan', *Capuchin Annual* (1942).

78. Longmans Archives, Agreement, 4 Sept., 1946.

79. *New Easons Bulletin* I (March, 1946).

80. Declan Meehan, *Irish Bookman*, II (1947), p.49.

81. Special 50th Anniversary *Annual of The Catholic Truth Society of Ireland*, (1949), p.49.

82. M.P. Linehan, *Canon Sheehan of Doneraile*, (Dublin, 1952), p.67, 152.

83. Ibid., p.153.

84. Heuser, p.284.

85. Linehan, op. cit., pp.156-7.

86. Ibid., p.149.

87. Winefride Nolan, *Capuchin Annual*, (1952), p.322.

88. L.G. Wrenne, *Capuchin Annual*, (1952), p.319.

89. Liam Brophy, 'The inspiring voice', Canon Sheehan's Call to Catholic Action, *Capuchin Annual* (1952), pp.392-5.

90. Padraig O Dargain, *Capuchin Annual* (1952), pp.404-412.

91. B.M., 'Mother Ita O'Connell', *Capuchin Annual* (1952), pp.574-8.

92. Very Rev. John O'Buchanan, *Capuchin Annual* (1952), pp.396-401.

93. Mrs. William O'Brien, 'The most cherished of my friends', *Capuchin Annual* (1949), pp.388-9.

94. Gladys V. Towers, *Irish Monthly*, LXXX (Mar., 1952), p.114.

95. Rev. S. Rigby, 'Jottings on Canon Sheehan', *IER* LXXV (Nov., 1952), pp.321-9.

96. The Director to R.H. Lyon of Talbot, Longmans Correspondence, 14 Sept., 1953.

97. *Easons' Bulletin*, X, (Jan.-Mar., 1954).

98. Personal communication from Sally Mimnagh, Book Purchasing Manager (15 Dec., 1986).

99. Linehan, 27 Nov., 1968.

100. Ibid., 29 Nov., 1968.

101. Ibid., 27 Nov., 1968.

102. 'Friends of Canon Sheehan Society', McLysaght papers, N.L.I., Ms. 26, 780.

103. Ibid.

104. Sean O Broin, Drama section, Radio Centre, R.T.E. and Ar-

chives Dept. and Phoenix Stock Book Account, Talbot papers P.R.O.I., Ref. 10 48/33/2.

105. Information from Dr. Sean J. Whyte, Institute of Irish Studies Dublin, Michael Gill and Kevin Etchingham (formerly of Talbot Publishing Co.).

106. Con Houlihan, *Irish Times*, 20 May, 1971.

107. Longmans Correspondence with Folens, Dublin, 19 Sept., 1973.

108. Frank O'Connor, *Towards the Appreciation of Literature* (Dublin, 1945), p.173.

109. Francis MacManus, *Bell* XV (Nov. 1917), pp.35-40 cites William O'Brien letter to Sheehan (source unknown).

110. Benedict Kiely, *Modern Irish Fiction, A Critique*, (Dublin, 1950), p.viii.

111. Benedict Kiely, 'Canon Sheehan: The Reluctant Novelist' *Irish Writing*, XXXVII (Autumn, 1957), pp.35-45.

112. Benedict Kiely, 'A Triumph and a Tragedy', (18 Aug., 1970), (cutting with McLysaght papers, Ms. 24,950, N.L.I.).

113. Sean O' Faolain, *The Irish*, (London, 1949, second edn., 1972), p.109.

114. Fr. Peter R. Connolly, 'The Priest in Modern Irish Fiction, *Furrow* IX (Dec., 1958), p.793.

115. Jeremiah Lovett, 'Vision and Technique in the novels of P.A. Canon Sheehan', (M.A. Thesis, Maynooth, 1974).

116. Anthony Coleman, 'Canon Sheehan: The Dilemma of Priest as Artist', Studies LVIII (Spring,

1969), pp.30-40.

117. Oliver MacDonagh, *The Nineteenth Century Novel and Irish Social History: Some Aspects*, (O'Donnell lecture UCC 1970), p.12.

118. Kenneth H. Connell, 'Catholicism and Marriage in the century after the Famine' in *Irish Peasant Society*, (Oxford, 1968).

119. Padraic O'Farrell, *Ireland's English Question: Ireland and England since 1800*, (London, 1975), p.232.

120. Tom Garvin, 'Priest and Patriots; Irish Separatism and fear of the Modern, 1890-1914', *IHS* XXV (May, 1986), pp.67-81.

The lecture in question 'The Dawn of the Century' *The Literary Life and Other Essays* (Dublin, 1921), pp.121-151.

121. J. Lovett, op. cit., pp.146-7.

122. Tom Garvin, op. cit., p.80.

123. J.F. Hogan, 'Luke Delmege', *IER* XI (Feb., 1902), pp.145-57.

124. *Intellectuals*, p.216.

Chp 8: Guinan — The Reception.

1. Notices in *Island Parish*, (Dublin, 1912).

2. Personal communication with Michael Gill 20 Jan., 1987.

3. Benziger records were not available from Benziger.

4. Some press notices in *Island Parish*.

5. Ibid.

6. *Irish Times* 4 Sept., 1903.

7. *Freeman's Journal* 9 Sept., 1903.

8. *Westmeath Independent* 30 Aug., 1903.

9. *Cork Sun* 4 Sept., 1903.
10. *Leader* 7 Sept., 1903.
11. *Irish Independent* 7 Sept., 1903.
12. *Ave Maria*, in Island Parish.
13. Fr. Hudson, letter to Fuinan editor *Ave Maria*, *Island Parish* notices.
14. *Southern Cross* in *Island Parish*, Parish notices.
15. *Tablet* ibid.
16. *Catholic Watchman* ibid.
17. *Southern Cross* ibid.
18. Editor *Ave Maria* ibid.
19. *Boston Pilot* ibid.
20. *Pall Mall Gazette* ibid.
21. *Glasgow Herald* ibid.
22. *Liverpool Daily Post and Mercury* ibid.
23. *The Manchester Guardian* 15 Sept., 1912.
24. Rosa Mulholland, *Irish Monthly* XXXVIII (Feb., 1912), p.66.
25. Ibid.
26. *Irish Independent* 9 May, 1907.
28. *Irish News* 7 May, 1907.
29. *IER* III (Mar., 1907), p.1251.
30. *Ave Maria* in Island Parish.
31. *Irish Rosary* 8 July, 1907.
32. *Freeman's Journal* 4 July, 1907.
33. *Tablet* 17 July, 1907.
34. *Southern Cross* Island Parish notices.
35. *Catholic Herald of India* ibid.
36. *Bombay Examiner* ibid.
37. *Irish Independent* 22 Mar., 1908.
38. *Catholic Weekly* 27 Mar., 1908.
39. *Irish Monthly* (Feb., 1908), p.124.
40. *Freeman's Journal* 29 Jan., 1908.
41. *IER* VIII (Feb., 1912), p.315.
42. *Freeman's Journal* 26 Apr., 1912.
43. *Canadian Messenger Curate of Kilcloon* notices.
44. Stephen Brown, *Ireland in Fiction*.
45. *The Soggarth Aroon* (Dublin, 1925 edn.).
46. *Easons' Newsletter* (Nov., 1925).
47. *Catholic Bulletin* (Nov., 1926).
48. Ibid.
49. Katherine Hearne Kelley, 'Confessions of a Literary Snob', *The Magnificat 1913, Curate of Kilcloon* notices.
50. *Guide to Catholic Literature 1888-1940: An Author-Subject-Title index* (Detroit, 1940).
51. Will probate (53) P.R.O.I.
52. *D.N.B.*
53. J.S. Crone, *Dictionary of Irish Biography*, (Dublin, 1923).
54. D.J. Hickey and J.E. Doherty, *Dictionary of Irish History since 1800*, (Dublin, 1980).
55. J. Hogan ed., *Dictionary of Irish Literature*, (London, 1980).
56. B. Cleeve, *Dictionary of Irish Writers*, (Dublin, 1966).

Chp 9: O'Donovan — The Reception

1. Personal communication from David Harper, Macmillan accounts, 22 Jan., 1987.
2. *Pall Mall Gazette* (18 June, 1913).
3. *Irish Times* 18 June 1913, p.3.
4. *Church of Ireland Gazette* 6 June 1913, p.489.
5. *Northern Whig* 17 May, 1913, p.10.
6. *New Statesman* 14 June, 1913, pp.315-6.
7. *Irish Book Lover* IV (May, 1913), p.188.
8. *Times Literary Supplement* 8 May, 1913, p.197.

9. *Truth* 21 May, 1913, p.1291.
10. *Nation* 12 July, 1913, p.579.
11. *Spectator* 24 May, 1913, pp.887-8.
12. *Daily Chronicle* 20 May, 1913, p.21.
13. *Tablet* 31 May, 1913, p.846.
14. *The Catholic Times and Catholic Opinion* 13 June, 1913, p.3.
15. *Catholic Herald* 5 July, 1913, p.9.
16. *Manchester Guardian* 24 May, 1913, p.10.
17. *The Church Times* 9 May, 1913, p.648.
18. *Freeman's Journal* 23 April, 1914.
19. *Sunday Observer* 23 April, 1914.
20. J.B. Pinker letter to O'Donovan 8 April, 1914. O'Donovan papers cited in John F. Ryan 'Gerald O'Donovan'. According to Desmond Bowen, Carleton University, Ottawa personal communication to John F. Ryan 12 Dec., 1982 the bibliography in R.S. Pennefather *Documents in the history of the Orange Order Ontario and West 1890-1940* cites three pro-Orange newspapers *The Farmer's Sun*, *The Sons of England Record*, *The Sentinel and Orange Protestant Advocate* (Toronto). Professor Bowen suggests that the paper most likely to have contacted Pinker was the latter, 'but the book was not serialized during 1914-15, if at all'.
21. Letter to Quinn, O'Donovan papers, (13 Jan., 1914).
22. Ibid., 11 Aug., 1913.
23. Letter to O'Donovan, Quinn papers, 13 Nov., 1913.
24. Ibid., 28 Nov., 1913.

25. *Catholic* July 1914, p.86.
26. Ibid., Aug., 1914, p.98.
27. George Birmingham, *Irishmen all*, (1919), pp.180-4.
28. Authors Accounts, Macmillan (22 Jan., 1987).
29. *Irish Times*, 13 June, 1914, p.12.
30. *Times Literary Supplement*, 30 April, 1914.
31. *Irish Book Lover* (May, 1914), p.199.
32. *Daily Mail* (22 May, 1914), p.3.
Saturday Review, 6 June, 1914, p.742.
Dublin Daily Express, 30 April, 1914, p.7.
33. *Observer* 2 May, 1914, p.7.
Spectator 9 May, 1913, pp.793-4.
Nation 20 June, 1913, pp.464-6.
34. 'A.N.M.', *Manchester Guardian*, 29 April, 1914.
35. Catholic World, Oct., 1915, p.116.
36. Stephen Brown, *Ireland in Fiction*.
37. 'F.R.', *Manchester Guardian*, 19 Nov., 1920.
38. *Times Literary Supplement* 25 Nov., 1920.
39. *Irish Book Lover* XII Jan., 1922, p.107, and *Times Literary Supplement*, 17 Nov., 1921, p.750.
40. *Truth* Dec., 1920, pp.1010-12.
41. Cablegram from N.Y. to Constable London, unsigned but dated 29th Dec. 1920. Personal communication from Constable 25 Feb., 1987.
42. Norreys Jephson O'Conor, *Changing Ireland: Literary Backgrounds of the Irish Free State 1889-1922*, (Mass., 1924), pp.199-204.
43. *Observer* 30 Oct., 1921, p.17.

44. *Irish Book Lover* XIII (Dec., 1921), p.91.
45. 'Some Irish Novelists',*Irish Book Lover* VXIII (Jan, 1922), p. 107 and *Times Literary Supplement* 17 Nov. 1921, p. 750.
46. C.C. Martindale, S.J., *Dublin Review* (1922), pp. 139-41
47 *The Times* 20 Oct., 1921, p.8.
48. *New Statesman* 7 Sept., 1921, p.650.
49. *Times Literary Supplement* 22 Sept., 1921.
50. *The Times* 20 Oct., 1921, p.8.
Westminster Gazette 24 Sept., 1921, p.9.
Spectator 14 Jan., 1921, p.35.
Time and Tide 30 Sept., 1921, p.935.
Daily Herald 28 Sept., 1921, p.7.
Sunday Times 20 Oct., 1921, p.7.
51. *Observer* 16 Oct., 1921, p.4.
52. *Freeman* (N.Y.), 2 Aug., 1922, p.497.
53. *Boston Evening Transcript* 27 May, 1922, p.4.
54. Louis M. Freedman, *New York Times Book Review and Magazine* 7 May 1922, p.14.
55. *Nation* (N.Y.), 14 May, 1922, p.19.
56. *Times Literary Supplement* 15 Aug., 1942, p.3.
57. Hugh Alexander Law, *Anglo-Irish Literature*, (Dublin & Cork, 1926), p.297.
58. J.F. Ryan, 'Gerald O'Donovan', 11 June 1976, p.213.
59. Benedict Kiely, *Modern Irish Fiction A Critique* (Dublin, 1950), p.145.
60. Frank O'Connor, *The Backward Look*, London, 1967, p.195.
61. Cited in *Irish Book Lover* XV (March, 1925), p.16.
62. 'Catholicism and Marriage after the Famine' *Irish Peasant Society* (Oxford, 1968), pp.124-53.
63. Tom Garvin, *I.H.S.* XXV (May, 1986), pp.67-81.
64. A. Norman Jeffares, *Anglo-Irish Literature*, (Dublin, 1982), p.203.
65. Peter A. Costello, *The Heart Grown Brutal: The Irish Revolution in Literature from Parnell to Yeats* (Dublin, Ottawa, N.Y., 1978).
66. J.F. Ryan, p.321.

Closing Comments

1. *The Graves at Kilmorna*, p.282.
2. The *Ave Maria* included religious, philosophical and fictional material, edited by Daniel Eldred Hudson, Holy Cross Father, Notre Dame, South Bend, Indiana from its inception in 1865 to 1929. A survey of American Catholic journalism of this type is to be found in Sr M. Avelina Dawson, C.S.C. *A Survey of Catholic Americana and Catholic Book Publishing in the United States, 1881-1900* (Catholic University Press, Washington D.C., 1951).
3. See *The Blindness of Doctor Gray*, and *My New Curate*.
4. R.V. Comerford, *Charles Kickham: A Study in Literature and Nationalism* (Dublin, 1979).
5. Archbishop D'Alton, *Furrow* I, no.i (1950), p.2.

Sources

The task of tracing the paths of these novels once they left the writers' hands required exploration in some areas generally untrodden by historians.

While the bigger publishing houses which survive were eager to help, many of the smaller ones had simply disappeared. The larger ones, for the most part, mainly kept records of production and contracts. The first are of little or no use to the cultural historian and the second differ little from book to book or indeed from novelist to novelist. However, some companies such as Longmans have taken care to store their archives for research purposes. The correspondence of the writer, or of his literary executor(s), with the publishing company provided a great insight into how the writer assessed himself and his audience, while those from the publishing company provided a reasonably objective and realistic perspective on sales potential. However, material such as this was scarce. The records of most publishers, if they had kept any to begin with, had long since been destroyed — a sad case in point is the 1972 fire in Gill's Dublin premises.

Besides agreements and correspondence, the royalty ledgers occasionally provided some record of sales. The main source of information in the published records, however, were generally the impression ledgers and stock books, which recorded the dates and amounts of copies printed. This, of course does not mean that they were promptly sold, or even bound but the implications of frequent printings are obvious. The means of distribution and circulation of the novels is an area which would reward some detailed study. The bookshop was not a prominent feature of Irish life at the turn of the century, so that the sales of works throughout the country hardly constituted more than a sketchy side-line business for the newsagent/general merchandise shop.

Easons from 1928 published a most informative monthly bulletin for distribution to booksellers. Their alert reminders and warnings about the anticipated demand for certain 'types' of books, to prepare for coming public events (e.g. the Eucharistic Congress of 1929) seasonal festivities etc., shows how the taste of the Irish reading public was at once whimsical and predictable. Invaluable, too, are their running commentaries on the popularity of certain books, and their classification of novels into certain types.

A study of the Irish publishing houses and book trade would make an invaluable contribution to Irish history. The recent deaths of Owen O'Keefe of Duffy's publishing company and Liam Miller of Dolmen underlines the urgency of the need for such a study, as much of the colour, episodes and live history of Irish publication has remained, with lots of other vital information, outside the ledgers, in the heads of mere mortals. A comprehensive bibliographical study of the works of Canon Sheehan, Joseph Guinan and on those of all the other scores of writers of Irish popular literature would be a most worthwhile exercise.

WORKS OF REFERENCE

Boylan, Henry A., *A Dictionary of Irish Biography* (Dublin, 1978).
Brown, Stephen J., S.J., *Ireland in Fiction* (Dublin, 1968) reprint of 1919 edition.
CLE: Directory of the Irish Book Trade (Dublin, 1983).
Cleeve, B., *A Dictionary of Irish Writers* (Dublin, 1966).
Crone, J.S., *A Dictionary of Irish Biography* (Dublin, 1928).
A Guide to Catholic Literature: An Author-Subject-Title Index (Detroit, 1940).
Hogan, R., *A Dictionary of Irish Literature* (London, 1980).
Hickey, D.J.; Doherty, J.E., *A Dictionary of Irish History since 1800* (Dublin 1980).
Irish Catholic Directory Kernowski, F.; and Spinks, C.W., *A Bibliography of Modern Irish and Anglo-Irish Literature* (Texas, 1976).
Maynooth College Kalendarium, (1860-1900).
Pocock, K. Livingstone, *Directory of Book Publishers and Wholesalers with their terms, and agents for overseas Publishers* (London, 1982).
Thom's Irish Who's Who (Dublin, 1923).

PRIMARY SOURCES
The Fiction Examined

CANON SHEEHAN
Geoffrey Austin, Student (Dublin and Belfast: Phoenix edn., nd).
The Triumph of Failure (Dublin: Clonmore and Reynolds, 1956).
My New Curate (Dublin: Talbot, 1958).
Luke Delmege (London: Longmans, 1919).
Glenanaar (Dublin and Belfast: Phoenix edn., nd).
A Spoiled Priest and Other Stories (Dublin and Belfast: Phoenix edn., nd).
Lisheen (Dublin and Belfast: Phoenix edn., nd).
The Blindness of Dr. Gray (Dublin and Belfast: Phoenix edn., nd).
The Intellectuals (London: Longmans, 1921).
Miriam Lucas (Dublin and Belfast: Phoenix edn., nd).
The Graves at Kilmorna (Dublin and Belfast: Phoenix edn., nd).

JOSEPH GUINAN

Scenes and Sketches in an Irish Parish or Priest and People in Doon (Dublin and New York: Gill and Benziger, 1903).
The Soggarth Aroon (Dublin and Belfast: The Phoenix Edition, nd).
The Island Parish (Dublin: Gill, 1908).
The Moores of Glynn (Burns, Oates and Washbourne: London, 1928).
The Curate of Kilcloon (Dublin: Gill, 1912 1st ed).
Donal Kenny (Burns, Oates and Washbourne, 1910 1st ed).
Annamore, or a Tenant-at-Will (London: Burns Oates and Washbourne 1922).
The Patriots (New York, Cincinnati, Chicago, 1928).

GERALD O'DONOVAN

Father Ralph (London: Macmillan, 1913).
Waiting (London: Macmillan, 1914).
Conquest (London: Constable, 1920).
Vocations (London: Martin Secker, 1921).

OTHER WRITINGS OF THE AUTHORS' USED:
CANON SHEEHAN

The Literary Life and other Essays (Dublin, 1921).
'Religious Education in Intermediate Schools', *IER* II (Sept., 1881), pp.521.
'In a Dublin Art Gallery', *IER* II (Dec. 1881), pp.726-743.
'The Effects of Emigration on the Irish Church', *IER* IV (Mar., 1883), pp. 137-152
'The German Universities',. *IER* VII (June, 1886), pp.496-511, (July, 1886) pp.617-631, (Aug., 1886), pp.685-698.
'Recent Augustinian Literature' *Dublin Review* XX (July, 1888), pp.87-107.
'Our Personal and Social Responsibilities', *IER* IX (Feb., 1899), pp. 69-89.
'Certain Elements of Character' *St. Stephen's: A Magazine of University Life* I (June, 1902), pp.135-141.
'Non-dogmatic Religion' *New Ireland Review* XXIII (Aug., 1905), pp.321-33.

JOSEPH GUINAN

'The Apostolate of the Press', *Irish Monthly* XXXVIII (June, 1910), pp.320-7.
'Priest and People in Ireland', *Catholic Bulletin* I (Feb., 1911), pp.62-5.
'Wanted: Apostles of the Press', *Catholic Bulletin* I (Sept., 1911), pp.420-23.
'The Silent Sermons of the Month', *Irish Monthly* XLV (Jan.-Dec., 1917), pp.3-5, pp.749-53.
The Famine Years C.T.S.I. pamphlet (Dublin, 1908).

GERALD O'DONOVAN

'The Celtic Revival of Today' *IER* IX (March, 1899) pp.238-50.
'Village Libraries', *Irish Homestead* 20 Jan., 1900, pp.34-36.

'Irish Art Revival' *Leader* 12 Jan., 1901.

'Dishonouring Irish Saints' *Leader* 19 Jan., 1901, pp.333-4.

'Practical Schools for Girls' *Leader* 9 Feb., 1901, pp.385-86.

'Toleration' *Leader* 18 Mar., 1902, pp.249-50.

'Priest and Industrial Development in Ireland' *Record of the Maynooth Union 1899-1900* Dublin 1900, pp.34-48.

'Our Duty to the Language Movement' *Freeman's Journal* 8 Nov. 1901.

OTHER CONTEMPORARY WORKS

Arnold, Sidney, *Irish Literature and Its Influence* (Dublin, 1953).

— Birmingham, G. (pseud. Canon James Owen Hannay), *An Irishman Looks at his World* (London, 1919).

Irishmen All (Edinburgh and London, 1913).

Bulfin, W., *Rambles in Eirinn* (Dublin, 1907).

Carton, R.P. *Novels and Novel Readers: a lecture delivered to the members of the Catholic Association* (Dublin, 1872).

Connolly, James, *Labour, Nationality and Religion* (Dublin, 1920).

Corkery, D., *The Hidden Ireland*, (Dublin, 1925).

— *Synge and Anglo-Irish Literature* (Cork, 1931).

Chesterton, G.K., *Heretics* (London, 1905).

Dubois, Paul, *Contemporary Ireland* (Dublin, 1908).

Duffy, Charles Gavan, *The Revival of Irish Literature* (London, 1894).

Healy, J., *Maynooth College: Its Centenary History* (Dublin, 1895).

Hogan, (Cardinal), *The Catholic Truth Society: Its Origin and Purpose* (Dublin, 1900).

Irish Catholic Association Handbook (Dublin, 1903).

Irish Priests, *The Will and the Way* (Dublin, 1921).

Kane, R., S.J., *From Fetters to Freedom: Trials and Triumphs of Irish Faith* (London, 1915).

Krans, H., *Irish Life in Irish Fiction* (New York, 1903).

Lady Gregory, *Literary Ideals in Ireland* (Dublin 1989).

McCarthy, M., *Five Years in Ireland* (London, 1901).

— *Priests and People in Ireland* (Dublin, 1902).

— *Rome in Ireland* (London, 1904).

— *Gallowglass, or Life in the Land of the Priests* (London, 1904).

— *Irish Land and Irish Liberty: A Study of the New Lords of the Irish Soil*, (London, 1911).

MacDonald, W., *Reminiscences of a Maynooth Professor* (London, 1925).

Moran, P.F., (Cardinal) *The Priests and People of Ireland in the Nineteenth Century* (Dublin, 1905).

Murphy, Thomas A. (Rev.), *The Literary Crusade in Ireland* (Limerick, 1912).

O'Donnell, F.H., *Paraguay on Shannon: The Price of a Political Priesthood* (Dublin, 1908).

O'Riordan, M., *Catholicity and Progress in Ireland* (London, 1908).

Plunkett, H., *Ireland in the New Century* (London, 1904).

Russell, G. ('A.E.'), *Ideals in Ireland: Priest or Hero* (Dublin, 1910).

— *Twenty-five Years of Irish Nationality* (New York, 1929).

— *The National Being* (Dublin, 1913).

— *Nationality and Cosmopolitanism in Art* (Dublin, 1906).

Ryan, W.P., *The Plough and The Cross* (Dublin, 1910).

— *The Pope's Green Island* (London, 1912).

— *Society for the Protection of Protestant Interests Reply to the Catholic Association and its allies the Leader and the Irish Rosary* (Dublin, 1903).

Wells, W.B., *Irish Indiscretions* (London, 1922).

Wheeler, R.M., *Ireland Today: a Political Pilgrimage* (London, n.d.).

Young, F., *Ireland at the Cross Roads: an essay in explanation* (London, 1907).

NEWSPAPERS AND REVIEWS:

*Catholic Bulletin, Catholic Herald, Cork Constitution, Cork Examiner, Cork Free
Press, Dublin Magazine (New Series), Dublin Review, Eason's News Letter,
Eason's Monthly Bulletin, Eire — Ireland, Freeman's Journal, Irish Catholic,
Irish Book Lover, Irish Book Man, Irish Ecclesiastical Record, Irish Inde-
pendent, Irish Rosary, Irish Writing, Irish Monthly, Irish Review, Irish Times,
Leader, London Mercury, Manchester Guardian, New Ireland Review, New
Statesman, Pall Mall Gazette, St. Stephen's A Magazine of Student Life, The
Times, Times Literary Supplement, United Ireland*

MANUSCRIPT SOURCES:
NATIONAL LIBRARY OF IRELAND

Letters of Matthew Russell, S.J. to P.A. Sheehan c.1904-1907 Ms. 24, 950.

Mc Lysaght Papers: Letters of Sheehan and Commonplace Book (microfilm) Ms.
24, 950.

National Literary Society Minute Book Ms. 646.

JESUIT ARCHIVES

Letters of P.A. Sheehan to Matthew Russell S.J., Jesuit Archives, 35 Lr. Leeson
St., Dublin.

UNIVERSITY OF READING ARCHIVES

Longman Archives: Royalty; Divide; Miscellaneous Expenses and Impression
Ledgers; Agreements; Contracts and Correspondence between Canon Sheehan
and Longmans; Bishop of Cloyne and Longmans; New York and London
branches of Longmans.

PUBLIC RECORD OFFICE, IRELAND

Talbot Papers Ref 1048/23/2.

Probate of Wills of Joseph Guinan (53).

CONSTABLE PUBLISHERS 10 ORANGE ST., LONDON.

Constable accounts, agreements, contracts and sales records of *Conquest* (on Photocopy).

ORAL INTERVIEWS

Canon John Corkery, P.P. Aughnacliffe, Co. Longford. Formerly Librarian of St. Patrick's College, Maynooth.

Kevin Etchingham, (Formerly of Talbot Press)

Michael Gill, Gill and MacMillan Ltd., Goldenbridge, Inchicore, Dublin 8.

Michael Guinan, Millbrook, Cloghan, Co. Offaly, (Nephew of Joseph Guinan).

The Irish People - A cross section of these were asked if they had heard of, read, or knew people who read the work of the four writers, and if so, why they read them and what they thought of them.

PERSONAL COMMUNICATION

Longman Copyright Dept. D.S. Lea, 21 Jan., 1987.

Heinemann, Roger Smith, 10 Upper Grosvener St., 20 Feb., 1987.

Hodder and Stoughton, Mill Road, Dunton Greens, Kent, Mar., 1987.

Hodges and Figgis, 56 Dawson St., Dublin 2. 15 Jan., 1987.

George Allen and Unwin, 40 Museum St., London. 22 Jan., 1987.

SECONDARY SOURCES:

BOOKS

Allen, W., *The English novel: A Short Cultural History* (London, 1968).

Babington Smith, C., *Rose Macaulay* (London, 1972).

Barry, M., *By Pen and Pulpit: The Life and Times of the Author Canon Sheehan* (Fermoy, 1990).

Bew, P., *Conflict and Conciliation in Ireland 1890-1910: Parnellites and Radical Agrarians* (Oxford, 1987).

Bolger, P., *History of Irish Co-operative Movement* (Dublin, 1977).

Boyd, E.A., *Ireland's Literary Renaissance* (Dublin, 1922 edn.).

Boyle, F., *Canon Sheehan: A sketch of his life and works* (Dublin, 1927).

Bradbury, H., *The Social Context of Modern English Literature* (Oxford, 1971).

Braybrooke, P., *Some Catholic Novelists: Their Art and Outlook* (London, 1931).

Brown, M., *Politics of Irish Literature: From Thomas Davis to W.B. Yeats* (London, 1972).

Burton, David H., (ed). *The Letters of Justice Oliver Wendell Holmes and Canon Sheehan* (New York, 1976).

Cahalan, J.M., *Great Hatred, Little Room: The Irish Historical Novel* (Dublin, 1983).

Casey, D.J., and Rhodes R.E., *Views of the Irish Peasantary (1800-1916)* (Hamden, CT, 1977).

Castleleyn, M., *A History of Literacy and Libraries in Ireland* (Hants and Vermont, 1984).

Catholic Truth Society Annual: The First Fifty Years (Dublin, 1949) special anniversary issue.

Cave, R., (ed.), *Hail and Farewell* (Buckinghamshire, 1976).

Cendrowska-Werner, B., *The National Tradition in the Anglo-Irish Novel* (London, 1977).

Chapman, R., *The Victorian Debate: English Literature and Society 1832-1909* (London, 1970).

Clarke, I.F., *Voices Prophesying War 1763-1884* (Oxford, 1966).

Cockburn, Claude, *Bestseller: the Books that Everyone Read 1900-1939* (London, 1972).

Comerford, R.V., *Charles Kickham: A Study in Literature and Nationalism* (Dublin, 1979).

Connell, K.H., *Irish Peasant Society* (Oxford, 1968).

Connolly, P., (ed.), *Literature and The Changing Ireland* (N.Y., 1982).

Corish, P.J., *The Irish Catholic Experience: A Historical Survey* (Dublin, 1985).

Costello, P., *The Heart Grown Brutal: The Irish Revolution in Literature from Parnell to the Death of Yeats 1891-1939* (Dublin, 1977).

Cross, K.G.W.,; and Jeffares N.A., *In excited Reverie: a tribute to W.B. Yeats 1865-1939* (N.Y., 1965).

Crotty, *Irish Agricultural Production* (Cork, 1966).

Curtis, L.P., *Apes and Angels: The Irish Man in Victorian Caricature* (London, 1971).

Dawson, M. Avelina, *A Survey of Catholic Book Publishing in the United States 1881-1900* (Washington D.C. 1951-8).

Deane, S., *Irish Writers 1886-1986* (Dublin, 1986).

De Laura, D., *Victorian Prose - A Guide to Research* (N.Y., 1973).

Denson, A., *John Hughes: Sculptor* (Westmorland, 1969).

Dunne, Tom, The Writer as Witness: literature as historical evidence: papers read before the Irish conference of historians 1985, (Cork, 1987).

Drudy, P.J., *Irish Studies I* (Cambridge, 1980).

Eglington, J., *Irish Literary Portraits* (London, 1935).

Elliot, R., *Art and Ireland* (Dublin, 1902).

Fallis, R., *The Irish Renaissance: An Introduction to Anglo-Irish Literature* (Dublin, 1977).

Fennell, D., *The Changing Face of Catholic Ireland* (London, 1968).

Finneran, R.J., *Anglo-Irish Literature: A Review of Research* (N.Y., 1983).

— *Anglo-Irish Writers: A Supplement to Anglo-Irish Literature A Review of Research* (N.Y., 1983).

Foster, J.W., *Forces and Themes in Ulster Fiction* (Dublin, 1974).

— *Fictions of the Anglo-Irish Literary Revival: A changeling Art* (Syracuse, 1988).

Foster, R.F. *Modern Ireland 1600-1972* (London, 1988).

Garvin, T., *The Evolution of Irish Nationalist Politics* (Dublin, 1981).

Goldring, M., *Faith of our Fathers: The formation of Irish Nationalist Idealogy 1890-1920* (Paris, 1975).

Gross, H., *History and Fatality in Modern Literature* (N.Y., 1971).

Guide to Catholic Literature 1880-1940: An Author-Subject-Title Index (Detroit, 1940).

Gwynn, S., *Irish Books and Irish People* (Dublin, 1919).

Hall, W.E., *Shadowy Heroes: Irish Literature of the 1890's* (Syracuse, 1980).

Harmon, *Select Bibliography for the study of Anglo-Irish Literature and its Background* (Dublin, 1977).

— *Modern Irish Literature 1800-1867 A Reader's Guide* (Dublin, 1967).

— *Image and Illusion: Anglo-Irish Literature and its Contexts* (Dublin, 1979).

Harmon, M., *The Irish Writer and the City* (Dublin, 1984).

Heuser, H.J., *Canon Sheehan of Doneraile* (Dublin, 1918).

Howarth, H., *Irish Writers 1880-1940: Literature under Parnell's Star* (London, 1985).

Houghton, W., *The Victorian Frame of Mind: 1830-1870* (New Haven, C.T., 1951).

Hutchinson, J., *The Dynamics of Cultural Nationalism: The Gaelic Revival and the Creation of the Irish Nation State* (London, 1987).

Kee, R., *The Green Flag: A History of Irish Nationalism* (London, 1972).

Keenan, D.J. *The Catholic Church in Nineteenth Century Ireland: A sociological study* (Dublin, 1983).

Kenny, H.A., *Literary Dublin* (Dublin & N.Y., 1974).

Kevin, N., *I Remember Maynooth* (new edn. 1945).

Kiely, B., *Modern Irish Fiction - A Critique* (Dublin, 1950).

Larkin, E., *The Historical Dimensions of Irish Catholicism* (Washington D.C., 1976).

Law, H.A. *Anglo-Irish Literature* (Dublin and Cork, 1926).

Leavis, Q.D., *Fiction and the Reading Public* (London, 1978).

Lowenthal, L., *Literature, popular culture and society* (New York, 1961).

Linehan, M.P., *Canon Sheehan of Doneraile: Priest, Novelist, Man of Letters* (Dublin, 1952).

Loftus, R.J., *Nationalism in Modern Ireland* (Wisconsin, 1964).

Lyons, F.S.L., *Ireland Since the Famine* (London, 1973).

Lyons, F.S.L., *Culture and Anarchy in Ireland 1890-1939* (Oxford, 1979).

McCaffrey, L.J. (ed.) *Irish Nationalism and the American Contribution* (N.Y., 1976).

McCormack, W.J., *Ascendancy and Tradition in Anglo-Irish Literary History from 1789 to 1939* (Oxford, 1985).

MacDonagh, O., *The Nineteenth Century Novel in Irish Social History: Some Aspects* (Dublin, 1970).

— *States of Mind: A study of Anglo-Irish conflict 1780-1980* (London, 1983).

MacDonagh, O.; and Mandle, W.F.; and Travers, P., *Irish Culture and Nationalism 1750-1950* (London, 1983).

MacGowan, K., *Canon Sheehan of Doneraile* (Dublin, 1963).

MacManus, F., *Imaginative Literature and the Revolution* (Dublin, 1966).

MacNamee, J.J., *History of the Diocese of Ardagh* (Dublin, 1954).

Manseragh, N., *The Irish Question 1840-1921* (London, 1975).

Marcus, P.L., *Yeats and the Beginning of the Irish Renaissance* (Dublin, 1970).

Miller, D.W., *Church, State and Nation in Ireland 1798-1921* (Dublin, 1974).

Morrissey, T., S.J. *Towards a national University: William Delaney and an era of initiative in Irish Education* (Dublin, 1985).

Nowlan, K.B., *The Making of 1916: Studies in the History of the Rising* (Dublin, 1969).

O'Brien, C.C., *The Shaping of Modern Ireland* (London, 1960).

O'Brien, J.V., *William O'Brien and the Course of Irish Politics 1881-1918* (California, 1976).

O'Brien, W., *Irish Fireside Hours* (Dublin, 1927).

O'Conor, N., *Changing Ireland: Literary Backgrounds of the Irish Free State 1889-1922* (Mass., 1924).

O'Driscoll, R., *Theatre and Nationalism in twentieth century Ireland* (London, 1971).

— *The Celtic Consciousness* (Dublin, 1981).

O'Faolain, S., *The Irish* (London, 1947).

O'Farrell, P., *Seán Mac Eoin: The Blacksmith of Ballinalea* (Mullingar, 1993).

O'Farrell, P.J., *Ireland's English Question: England and Ireland since 1800* (London, 1975).

Rafroidi, P.; and Brown, T., *The Irish Short Story* (Buckinghamshire, 1979).

Reardon, B., *Roman Catholic Modernism* (London, 1970).

Ronsley, M., *Myth and Reality in Irish Literature* (Ontario, 1977).

Solow, B.L., *The Land Question and the Irish Economy 1870-1903* (Cambridge Mass., 1971).

Stockley, W.F.P., *Essays in Irish Bibliograph* (Cork, 1933).

Summerfield, H., *That Myriad-Minded Man: a biography of George William Russell 'A.E.' 1867-1935* (Gerards Cross, Buckinghamshire, 1975).

Thompson, W.I., *The Imagination of an Insurrection* (Dublin, 1966).

Tudor, N., *Political Myth* (London, 1972).

Turner, J.E. *A Theory of Direct Realism and the Relation of Realism to Idealism* (London, 1925).

Ussher, A., *Face and Mind of Ireland* (London, 1949).

Watson, G.J., *Irish Identity and the Literary Revival: Synge, Yeats, Joyce and O'Casey* (London and N.Y., 1979).

Welch, R., *The Way Back: George Moore's The Untilled Field and The Lake* (Dublin, 1982).

Williams, R., *A Vocabulary of Culture and Society* (London, 1976).

— *Culture and Society 1780-1950* (London, 1963).

Yeats, W.B.; and Kinsella, T., *Tradition and the Irish Writer: Davis, Mangan Ferguson?* — The Tower Series of Anglo-Irish Studies II (Dublin, 1970).

ARTICLES

Brown, Terence, 'Yeats, Joyce and the Current Irish Critical Debate' in Michael Kenneally (ed.) *Cultural Contexts and Literary Idioms in Contemporary Irish Literature* (Gerrard's Cross, 1988).

— 'Canon Sheehan and the Catholic Intellectual' *Ireland's Literature: Selected Essays* (Mullingar Press, 1988), pp.65-75.

Buckley, Mary, 'Attitudes to Nationality in four Nineteenth century Novelists' *Journal of the Cork Historical and Archaeological Society* LXXVII (1973), pp.27-35, 109-117, LXXIX (1974), pp.129-36, LXXXI (1975), pp.91-95.

Coleman, Anthony, 'Canon Sheehan: The dilemma of priest as artist' *Studies* (Spring, 1969), pp.215-245.

Connolly, Peter R., 'The Priest in Modern Irish Fiction' *Furrow* IX (Dec. 1958), (A paper delivered at the Maynooth Summer School, 1957), pp.782-797.

Cullen, Louis, M., 'The Hidden Ireland: a reassessment of a concept' *Studia Hibernica* IX (1969), pp.7-47.

Deane, Seamus, 'Irish National Character 1790-1900' in Tom Dunne (ed.) *The Writer as Witness: literature as historical evidence* (Cork, 1987), pp.90-113.

Foster, R., 'Anglo-Irish Literature, Gaelic Nationalism and Irish Politics in the 1890s in J.M.W. Bean (ed.) *The Political culture of Modern Britain: Studies in the Memory of Stephen Ross* (London, 1987).

Garvin, Tom, Priests and Patriots: Irish separatism and fear of the modern, 1890-1914' *Irish Historical Studies* XXV (May, 1986), pp.67-81.

James, Edward, 'The Anglo-Irish Disagreement: past Irish Futures' *Linenhall Review* III (Winter, 1986), pp.9-10.

Kennedy, Brian, 'Twentyfive Years of Studies' *Studies*, (Winter, 1986), pp.361-73.

Kennedy, L., 'The early response of the Irish Catholic clergy to the co-operative movement' *Irish Historical Studies* XXL (1977-8), pp.58-74.

— 'The Roman Catholic Church and Economic Growth in nineteenth century Ireland: *Economic and Social Review* X (Oct. 1978), pp. 45-60.

Kiberd, Declan, 'The Fall of the Stage Irishman' in R. Schleifer (ed.) *The Genres of the Literary Revival* (Dublin and Oklahoma, 1980), pp.39-60.

Kiely, Benedict, 'Canon Sheehan: the reluctant novelist' *Irish Writing* XXXVII (1957), pp.35-45.

Larkin, Emmet 'Socialism and Catholicism in Ireland' *Studies*, LXXIV (Spring, 1985), pp.66-92.

McHugh, R., 'The Famine in Irish Oral Tradition' in R.D. Edwards (ed.) *The Great Famine: studies in Irish History 1845-52* (Dublin, 1956).

McMahon, Eileen, 'The Irish American Press' *The Ethnic Press in the United States* ed. Sally M. Miller (Westport, Connecticut: 1987).

McMahon, Joseph N., 'The Catholic Clergy and the Social Question in Ireland, 1891-1910' *Studies* LXX (Winter, 1981), pp.263-288.

MacManus, Francis, 'The Fate of Canon Sheehan' *Bell* XV (1947), pp.16-27.

Murphy, Brian, 'The Canon of Irish Cultural History: Some Questions' *Studies*, (Spring, 1988), pp. 68-83.

Murphy, John A., 'Priests and People in Modern Irish History' *Christus Rex* XXIII (Oct. 1969), pp. 235-59.

O'Ferrall, Fergus, 'The only Lever ...?' The Catholic Priest in Irish Politics 1823-39' *Studies* LXX (Winter, 1981), pp.308-325.

Silke, J.J. 'The Roman Catholic Church in Ireland 1800-1922: a survey of recent historiography', *Studia Hibernica*, 1975, pp.61-104.

Williams, M., 'Ancient Mythology and Revolutionary Ideology in Ireland, 1878-1916' XXVI (1983) *Historical Journal* pp.23-42.

UNPUBLISHED THESES

Lovett, Jeremiah, 'Vision and Technique in the novels of P.A. Canon Sheehan' (M.A. thesis, Maynooth, 1974).

O'Callaghan, Margaret, 'Language and Religion: The Quest for Identity in the Irish Free State, 1922-27' (M.A. thesis, University College Dublin, 1981).

Ryan, John F., 'Gerald O'Donovan, Priest, Novelist and Intellectual: A Forgotten Leader of the Irish Revival' (M.A. thesis, University College Galway, 1983).

BELIEVING IN GOD
Reason and Religious Belief

P J McGrath

Is it reasonable to believe in God even though there is no satisfactory argument for God's existence? Is it possible to reconcile the suffering that human beings and animals experience with the existence of a loving creator? Do miracles happen? These are some of the issues that are discussed in *Believing in God*. Throughout this book the author subjects the claims of religious faith to the scrutiny of reason. The result is a contribution to the philosophy of religion that is designed not only for the scholar, but for everyone who takes religious belief seriously.

PB £12.99; 224pp
ISBN 0 86327 510 9

LITERARY TOUR OF IRELAND
Elizabeth Healy

'A passionate, intimate and often illuminating book.'
Irish Times
Elizabeth Healy's route-by-route guide reveals a land which has for centuries inspired poets and storytellers.
Your guides are, among others, Yeats, Lady Gregory, Synge, O'Flaherty, O'Connor, the ancient Táin, Seamus Heaney, Goldsmith, O'Casey, Shaw, Swift, Joyce and Beckett.
Elizabeth Healy is a former editor of Bord Fáilte's
Ireland of the Welcomes.
HB £24.99; 272pp
ISBN 0 86327 446 3

THE IRISH CIVIL WAR
An Illustrated History

Helen Litton

The Irish Civil War continued to inspire passion, hatred and idealism long after the Free State Army took control in 1923. In this concise history Helen Litton recounts the events leading up to the signing of the Treaty and the outbreak of hostilities. Here are the personalities – the pragmatism of Arthur Griffith, the charisma of Michael Collins, the resounding rhetoric of de Valera, the military tactics of Liam Lynch.

Using newspaper reports, speeches, eyewitness accounts, and a mass of illustrative material, Helen Litton describes the mixture of confusion, inexperience and sometimes misguided vision that characterised both the Provisional Government and those commanding the Irregulars.

From a maelstrom of divided families and divided neighbours a new Ireland had to emerge. *The Irish Civil War: An Illustrated History* tells the complete story of its emergence, a story with the power to captivate both those who believe they know the period well and those who may want to understand it for the first time.

PB £6.99; 144pp
Colour & B/W photos, maps & drawings
ISBN 0 86327 480 3

Also published by Wolfhound Press

THE IRISH FAMINE
An Illustrated History

Helen Litton

This is an account of one of the most significant — and tragic — events in Irish history. The author, Helen Litton, deals with the emotive subject of the Great Famine clearly and succinctly, documenting the causes and their effects. With quotes from first-hand accounts, and relying on the most up-to-date studies, she describes the mixture of ignorance, confusion, inexperience and vested interests that lay behind the 'good *v* evil' image of popular perception.

Here are the people who tried to influence events — politicians like Peel, public servants like Trevelyan, Quaker relief workers, local committees, clergy and landlords — who wrestled with desperate need, and sometimes gave up in despair. Why did millions of starving people seem to accept their fate without rebelling? Why starvation on the very shores of seas and rivers plentifully stocked with fish?

This is a story of individuals such as Denis McKennedy — dying in Cork in 1846 because his Board of Works wages were two weeks late — and of a society in crisis. It should be read by anyone who seeks a fuller understanding of the Irish past.

Helen Litton took her Master of Arts degree in History at University College Dublin. She is a leading Irish reseracher, editor and indexer.

PB £6.99; 144pp
ISBN 0-86327-427-7